MEN OF THE BIBLE

God's Word *for the* Biblically-Inept™ SERIES

D. Larry Miller

CARTOONS BY

Reverend Fun
(Dennis "Max" Hengeveld)
Dennis is a graphic de-
signer for Gospel Films and
the author of *Has
Anybody Seen My Locust?*
His cartoons can
be seen worldwide at
www.reverendfun.com.

STARBURST PUBLISHERS®

P. O. Box 4123, Lancaster, Pennsylvania 17604

To schedule author appearances, write:
Author Appearances
Starburst Publishers
P.O. Box 4123
Lancaster, Pennsylvania 17604
(717) 293-0939

www.starburstpublishers.com

CREDITS:
Cover design by Dave Marty Design
Text design and composition by John Reinhardt Book Design
Illustrations by Melissa A. Burkhart and Bruce Burkhart
Cartoons by Dennis "Max" Hengeveld

Unless otherwise noted, or paraphrased by the author, all Scripture quotations are from the New International Version of The Holy Bible.

GOD'S WORD FOR THE BIBLICALLY-INEPT™
www.biblicallyinept.com

First Printing, November 1999

ISBN: 1-892016-07-9
Library of Congress Number 98-83170

Printed in the United States of America

READ THESE PAGES BEFORE YOU READ THIS BOOK...

Welcome to the *God's Word for the Biblically-Inept*™ series. If you find reading the Bible overwhelming, baffling, and frustrating, then this Revolutionary Commentary™ is for you!

Each page of the series is organized for easy reading with icons, sidebars, and bullets to make the Bible's message easy to understand. *God's Word for the Biblically-Inept*™ series includes opinions and insights from Bible experts of all kinds, so you get various opinions on Bible teachings—not just one!

There are more *God's Word for the Biblically-Inept*™ titles on the way. The following is a partial list of upcoming books. We have assigned each title an abbreviated **title code**. This code along with page numbers is incorporated in the text *throughout the series*, allowing easy reference from one title to another.

Men of the Bible—God's Word for the Biblically-Inept™
D. Larry Miller   TITLE CODE: GWMB

Benefit from the life experiences of the powerful men of the Bible! Learn how the inspirational struggles of men such as Moses, Daniel, Paul, and David parallel the struggles of men today. It will inspire and build Christian character in your walk with the Lord.

(trade paper) ISBN 1892016079 $16.95   AVAILABLE NOW

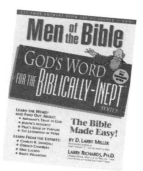

Women of the Bible—God's Word for the Biblically-Inept™
Kathy Collard Miller   TITLE CODE: GWWB

Finally, a Bible perspective just for women! Gain valuable insight from the successes and struggles of such women as Eve, Esther, Mary, Sarah, and Rebekah. Interesting icons like "Get Close to God," "Build Your Spirit," and "Grow Your Marriage" will make it easy to incorporate God's Word into your daily life.

(trade paper) ISBN 0914984063 $16.95   AVAILABLE NOW

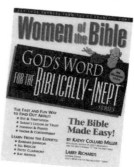

The Bible—God's Word for the Biblically-Inept™
Larry Richards   TITLE CODE: GWBI

Get serious about learning the Bible from cover to cover! Here is an overview of the Bible written by Larry (Lawrence O.) Richards, one of today's leading Bible writers. Each chapter contains select verses from books of the Bible along with illustrations, definitions, and references to related Bible passages.

(trade paper) ISBN 0914984551 $16.95   AVAILABLE NOW

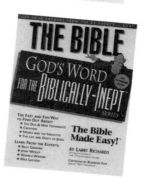

Revelation—God's Word for the Biblically-Inept™

Daymond R. Duck   TITLE CODE: GWRV

Revelation—God's Word for the Biblically-Inept™ includes every verse of the book of Revelation along with quotes from leading experts, icons, sidebars, and bullets. Learn and enjoy as end-time prophecy expert Daymond R. Duck leads us through one of the Bible's most confusing books.

(trade paper) ISBN 0914984985 $16.95   AVAILABLE NOW

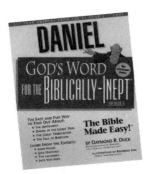

Daniel—God's Word for the Biblically-Inept™

Daymond R. Duck   TITLE CODE: GWDN

Daniel is a book of prophecy and the key to understanding the mysteries of the Tribulation and end-time events. This verse-by-verse commentary combines humor and scholarship to get at the essentials of Scripture. Perfect for those who want to know the truth about the Antichrist.

(trade paper) ISBN 0914984489 $16.95   AVAILABLE NOW

Health & Nutrition—God's Word for the Biblically-Inept™

Kathleen O'Bannon Baldinger   TITLE CODE: GWHN

The Bible is full of God's rules for good health! Kathleen O'Bannon Baldinger reveals scientific evidence that proves that the diet and health principles outlined in the Bible are the best for total health. Experts include Pamela Smith, Julian Whitaker, Kenneth Cooper, and T. D. Jakes.

(trade paper) ISBN 0914984055 $16.95   AVAILABLE NOW

Genesis—God's Word for the Biblically-Inept™

Joyce L. Gibson   TITLE CODE: GWGN

Joyce L. Gibson breaks the Bible down into bite-sized pieces making it easy to understand and incorporate into your life. Readers will learn about Creation, Adam and Eve, the Flood, Abraham and Isaac, and more. Includes chapter summaries, bullet points, definitions, and study questions.

(trade paper) ISBN 1892016125 $16.95   AVAILABLE NOW

Prophecies of the Bible—God's Word for the Biblically-Inept™

Daymond R. Duck **TITLE CODE: GWPB**

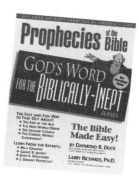

God has a plan for this crazy planet, and now, understanding it is easier than ever! Best-selling author and end-time prophecy expert Daymond R. Duck explains the complicated prophecies of the Bible in plain English. Read with wonder as Duck shows you all there is to know about the End of the Age, the New World Order, the Second Coming, and the Coming World Government. Includes useful commentary, expert quotes, icons, sidebars, chapter summaries, and study questions! Find out what prophecies have already been fulfilled and what's in store for the future!

(trade paper) ISBN 1892016222 $16.95 **AVAILABLE FEBRUARY 2000**

Life of Christ—God's Word for the Biblically-Inept™

Robert C. Girard **TITLE CODE: GWLC**

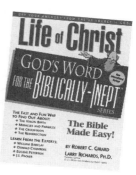

Girard takes the reader on an easy-to-understand journey through the gospels of Matthew, Mark, Luke, and John, tracing the story of Jesus' life on earth. Icons, illustrations, chapter overviews, study questions, and more make learning about the Virgin Birth, Jesus' miracles and parables, the Crucifixion, and the Resurrection easier than ever!

(trade paper) ISBN 1892016230 $16.95 **AVAILABLE MARCH 2000**

Purchasing Information

www.starburstpublishers.com

Books are available from your favorite bookstore, either from current stock or special order. To assist bookstores in locating your selection, be sure to give title, author, and ISBN. If unable to purchase from a bookstore, you may order direct from STARBURST PUBLISHERS. When ordering please enclose full payment plus shipping and handling as follows:

Post Office (4th class)
$3.00 with a purchase of up to $20.00
$4.00 ($20.01–$50.00)
8% of purchase price for purchases of $50.01 and up

Canada
$5.00 (up to $35.00)
%15 ($35.01 and up)

United Parcel Service (UPS)
$4.50 (up to $20.00)
$6.00 ($20.01–$50.00)
12% ($50.01 and up)

Overseas
$5.00 (up to $25.00)
20% ($25.01 and up)

Payment in U.S. funds only. Please allow two to three weeks minimum (longer overseas) for delivery. Make checks payable to and mail to:

Starburst Publishers® • P.O. Box 4123 • Lancaster, PA 17604

Credit card orders may be placed by calling 1-800-441-1456, Mon.–Fri., 8:30 A.M. to 5:30 P.M. Eastern Standard Time. Prices are subject to change without notice. Catalogs are available for a 9 x 12 self-addressed envelope with four first-class stamps.

What Readers Tell Us . . .

"Congratulations on an outstanding piece of work! I look forward to seeing the entire *Biblically-Inept*™ series. I absolutely love it!"

—Ken Abraham, *best-selling author*

"Fantastic! What a fascinating approach to presenting the book of Revelation. It makes studying Bible prophecy easy, exciting, and interesting for everybody. Good content, great quotes, dynamic graphics. This book has more 'bells and whistles' than anything I've ever seen. It's user-friendly to the max!"

—Dr. Ed Hindson, *Assistant Pastor,*
Rehoboth Baptist Church, and best-selling author

"I am currently involved in studying the book of Revelation and find your study guide very informative, concise, and helpful. It makes reading and understanding the book of Revelation easier . . ."

—Jeffrey, *Bloomington, Indiana*

"The Revelation book arrived this morning. I spent a few minutes glancing through it and am confident that you have a winner. The layout—the artwork—the interaction are marvelous. . . . I AM IMPRESSED!"

—Dan Penwell, *Manager, Trade Products,*
Hendrickson Publishers

"I am writing to voice my approval of Starburst Publishers' *God's Word for the Biblically-Inept*™ series. I have three books in the series: THE BIBLE, DANIEL, and REVELATION. . . . I hope Starburst Publishers continues to add to the *God's Word for the Biblically-Inept*™ series. Ideally, I would like the series to include 67 books—one for each book of the Bible, plus your already published [books] . . . May I compliment you for this new, interesting, and easy-to-understand series."

—Wayne, *Burr Oak, Kansas*

CHAPTERS AT A GLANCE

Part One: Men of the Old Testament

Part Two: Men of the New Testament

ILLUSTRATIONS

INTRODUCTION

Welcome to **Men of the Bible—God's Word for the Biblically-Inept™**. This book is part of a series designed to bring God's encouraging and loving message to you in an easy-to-understand and relevant style. You are about to discover a REVOLUTIONARY COMMENTARY™ that will change your outlook on the Bible forever. You *will* Learn the Word™.

To Gain Your Confidence

You will also gain confidence, as you skip the complicated stuff and zero in on the truth of God's Word. If you want clear information, **Men of the Bible—God's Word for the Biblically-Inept™** is for you! I wrote this book using the *New International Version* (NIV) of the Bible. The NIV is a scholarly translation of the Bible's original Hebrew, Aramaic, and Greek that remains faithful to the thoughts of the people who wrote the Bible.

What Is The Bible?

The Bible is like no other book. Written over a span of 1,500 years, it is a collection of 66 books written by at least 40 different authors but with one message to tell: God loves you and wants the best for you!

The Bible is divided into two main sections: an **"Old" Testament** and a **"New" Testament** (for a listing of all the Biblical books, see Appendix B). The Old Testament was written between 1400 and 400 B.C. ("Before Christ"). The New Testament was written in about 60 years, between 40 and 100 A.D. ("Anno Domini," which is Latin for "in the year of our Lord") The Old Testament deals with "the old covenant" that God had with his chosen people (the Hebrews) before the birth of Jesus Christ, while the New Testament is about "the new covenant"—Jesus' birth, life, resurrection, and the spread of the early **Church** by Jesus' followers.

CHAPTER HIGHLIGHTS

(Chapter Highlights)

Let's Get Started
(Let's Get Started)

Genesis 1:1 In the beginning God created the heavens

(Verse of Scripture)

THE BIG PICTURE

Genesis 1:1–2:3
The Bible begins, "In the beginning..."

(The Big Picture)

Old Testament: *a collection of the first 39 books of the Bible, the oldest section of the Bible*

New Testament: *a collection of the last 27 books of the Bible, all written in the 60 years following Jesus' death*

Church: *the followers of Jesus Christ, as opposed to the building where people meet to worship*

☞ **GO TO:**

Matthew 9:14-15
(fasting)

(Go To)

KEY POINT

When we acknowledge our guilt and trust Jesus as Savior, God forgives our sins freely and completely.

(Key Point)

disciples: the 12 original followers of Jesus Christ

Holy Spirit: one of the three ways God reveals himself, the third person of the Trinity

Trinity: God, the father; Jesus, the son; and the Holy Ghost

Hebrew: most of the Old Testament, the oldest section of the Bible, was written in Hebrew, an ancient language commonly spoken until about 500 years before Christ

Aramaic: Hebrew was replaced by Aramaic, the international language of the Persian Empire, until about 200 years before Christ

Greek: the New Testament was written in Greek, which became the language of the people the century before Christ, and remained the most widely spoken language for about 500 years

Centuries later, experts divided the books of the Bible into chapters and verses. Thus Genesis 12:3 refers to the twelfth chapter and the third verse in the book of Genesis. If you know the name of the book and its chapter and verse number, you can locate specific Bible verses, stories, and teachings.

Who Wrote The Bible?

At least 40 different people wrote the Bible, but all of them believed they were writing the Word of God. Some were educated; some were not. Some were mighty kings, and others were lowly shepherds. Moses, for example, was a prisoner and a slave before freeing the Hebrews with God's help. He is credited with writing the first five books of the Old Testament: Genesis, Exodus, Leviticus, Numbers, and Deuteronomy. King David, on the other hand, was Israel's greatest king and wrote many worship songs and poems in the book of Psalms. Four of Jesus' **disciples**, all from different backgrounds, wrote what are known as the New Testament "gospels," which are titled by the names of those disciples: Matthew, Mark, Luke, and John.

The disciple John also wrote the book of Revelation under the guidance of its true author—the **Holy Spirit**, the third person of the **Trinity**. The word "trinity" is not found in the Bible, but we use the term to describe the three ways God reveals himself: God the Father, his Son Jesus Christ, and the Holy Spirit. Think of the Trinity as three different expressions of God just as you express yourself in actions, spoken words, and written words.

The Languages Of The Bible

The first books of the Bible and most of the Old Testament were written in **Hebrew**. Parts of the books of Daniel and Ezra, however, were written in **Aramaic**, a related language spoken by most Near Eastern peoples from about 600 B.C. onward. The people of Jesus' day also spoke Aramaic in everyday situations but studied the Bible in their ancient tongue, Hebrew. About 100 years before Christ, the Old Testament was translated into **Greek**, because most people throughout the Roman Empire spoke Greek.

The New Testament was written in the Greek spoken by ordinary people. This meant that the New Testament was easy for all people throughout the Roman Empire to understand so the message of Jesus spread quickly.

Because the Old and New Testament books were recognized as holy, first by Jews and then by Christians, they were copied accurately and carefully preserved.

Why Study The Bible?

BECAUSE . . . For over 2000 years, millions of people have improved their lives by following its wisdom. The Bible tells us repeatedly that when we study the Bible we will receive valuable blessings.

BECAUSE . . . Many people believe that God communicates with us through the Bible. Within its pages God tells us he wants us to know him and to follow his guidelines for how to live. Romans 15:4 tells us, *For everything that was written in the past was written to teach us, so that through endurance and the encouragement of the Scriptures we might have hope.*

BECAUSE . . . All of us want to respond to life's challenges in a godly way. Even though the Bible was written many years ago in a totally different place and culture than ours, the Bible offers answers to the troublesome situations and the difficult questions we all face today.

Why Learn About Men Of The Bible?

The men of the Bible can show us how to live, what choices to make, and why. These men faced failure and success just as we experience them. No matter where we are in our lives, we can gain courage and wisdom from these men. They struggled through difficulties, yet most endured and built their faith. Moses led the Israelites from Egypt but struggled with fear and uncertainty. David led a kingdom but succumbed to temptation; he is remembered as a *"man after God's own heart."* We can learn to lead our families and lives with purpose and confidence by examining these examples in the Bible.

God had a purpose for each man in the Bible, from Caleb's faithful and courageous walk to Saul's utter collapse. God also has a purpose for each one of us. By studying the lives of the men of the Bible, we can know God, bring him into every area of our lives, and build our faith and character.

Many men failed and then rallied to success. Some men compromised and demonstrated their faithlessness. When we examine each life, principles for success are showcased and the consequences of disobedience are painfully driven home. (For a time line of the men of the Bible covered in this book, see Appendix A.)

KEY Outline:

Elijah's Ministry
the power of God

Elisha's Ministry
God's grace and willingness to support his people

(Key Outline)

What Others are Saying:

(What Others Are Saying)

ACT OF GOD

creation of Adam (man) and Eve (woman)

(Act of God)

Something to Ponder

(Something to Ponder)

Remember This . . .

(Remember This)

Matriarchs: *important women, in this case, the most important women of the Bible*

(Warning!)

(Build Your Spirit)

(Overcoming Struggles)

(Leadership principle)

How To Use *Men Of The Bible— God's Word for The Biblically-Inept™*

As you read this book, keep in mind its main sections:

- Part One, "Men of the Old Testament" (Chapters 1–12), discusses major men of the Old Testament—Adam, Abraham, Isaac, Jacob, Joseph, Moses, and David—as well as some others whose stories you will find enlightening.
- Part Two, "Men of the New Testament" (Chapters 12–15), presents the stories of Paul, Peter, and other men who were influenced by Jesus.

The Features

This book contains a number of features that will help you learn. They're illustrated in the sidebar of this introduction. Here is a list of descriptions for each of them.

Sections and Icons	What's It For?
CHAPTER HIGHLIGHTS	the most prominent points of the chapter
Let's Get Started	a chapter warm-up
Verse of Scripture	what you came for—the Bible
THE BIG PICTURE	summarizes passages and shows where they fit in the Bible
Commentary	my thoughts on what the verses mean
GO TO:	other Bible verses to help you better understand (underlined in text)
What?	the meaning of word (bold in text)
KEY POINT	major point of the chapter
KEY Outline	minioutline of information
What Others are Saying:	if you don't believe me, listen to the experts
Illustrations	a picture is worth a thousand words
Time Lines	shows how events fit into history
ACT OF GOD	indicates God's personal intervention in history or people's lives
Something to Ponder	interesting points to get you thinking
Remember This . . .	don't forget this
Warning	red lights to keep you from danger
BUILD YOUR SPIRIT	inspiration to strengthen your faith
Overcoming Struggles	ways to cope with trouble
LEADERSHIP PRINCIPLE	principles for godly leadership
Grow Your Family	getting closer without bumping into each other
Study Questions	questions to get you discussing, studying, and digging deeper
CHAPTER WRAP-UP	the most prominent points revisited

Dates

Unlike any other book, the Bible was written over a span of 1,500 years! Because of this long period of time, Biblical experts sometimes differ in the dates they give for various events. Thanks to archeologists and their discoveries, however, the accuracy of these dates has improved. We can now accurately date many of the events in the Bible. See Appendix A for time lines that show when in history the men of the Bible lived.

A Word About Words

As you read *Men of the Bible—God's Word for the Biblically-Inept™*, you'll notice some interchangeable words: Scripture, Scriptures, Word, Word of God, God's Word, etc. All of these terms mean the same thing and come under the broad heading of "the Bible."

In most cases the phrase *"the Scriptures"* in the New Testament refers to the Old Testament. Peter indicated that the early writings of the Apostle Paul were quickly accepted in the early church as equal to *"the other Scriptures"* (2 Peter 3:16). Both Testaments consistently demonstrate the belief that is expressed in 2 Timothy 3:16, *"all Scripture is God-breathed."*

One Final Tip

God gave us these stories of the men of the Bible so we could learn from them. With God's help, you can use what you learn from this book to improve and bless your life. Open your heart. Ask God to speak his Word to you.

Grow Your Family

(Grow Your Family)

Study Questions

(Study Questions)

CHAPTER WRAP-UP

(Chapter Summary)

Bible Quote: This is where you'll read a quote from the Bible.

James 1:5 If any of you lacks wisdom, he should ask God, who gives generously to all without finding fault, and it will be given to him.

Decisions, Decisions: In Or Out?

James, the brother of Jesus, is writing to the new believers who were scattered about the Roman world (see GWBI, pages 213–214) when they fled from persecution. James knows that godly wisdom is a great gift. He gives a simple plan to get it: if you want wisdom, ask for it. God will give it to us.

Up 'til now we've concentrated on finding the wind for the sails of your drifting marriage and overcoming marital problems. But you may be the reader who is shaking her head, thinking that I just don't understand what you're going through. You can't take the abuse any longer; you've forgiven the **infidelity** time after time; and in order for you and your children to survive, you see no alternative but divorce.

So let me say that your husband a... ... your get out a... ... ...nues, abuse sec... ... ...eep the ing to you; they are also harmful to your children's physical and emotional state.

When you feel you've depleted all of your options, continue to ask God for wisdom in order to have the knowledge to make the right decisions. Wise women seek God. God is the source of wisdom and wisdom is found in Christ and the Word.

Commentary: This is where you'll read commentary about the biblical quote.

"What?": When you see a word in bold, go to the sidebar for a definition.

infidelity: sexual unfaithfulness of a spouse

Go To: When you see a word or phrase that's underlined, go to the sidebar for a biblical cross-reference.

☞ **GO TO:**

Psalm 111:10 (source)

Remember This . . .

Gary Chapman, Ph.D.: Is there hope for women who suffer physical abuse from their husbands? Does reality living offer any genuine hope? I believe the answer to those questions is yes.[6]

Give It Away

You don't have to be a farmer to understand what the Apostle Paul wrote to the Corinthian church (see illustration, page 143). A picture is worth a thousand words, and Paul is painting a masterpiece. He reminds us of what any smart farmer knows: in order to produce a bountiful harvest, he has to plan for it.

What Others are Saying:

What Others Are Saying: This is where you'll read what an expert has to say about the subject at hand.

Feature with icon in the sidebar: Throughout the book you will see sections of text with corresponding icons in the sidebar. See the chart on pages xv–xvi for a description of all the features in this book.

Part One

MEN OF THE OLD TESTAMENT

REVEREND FUN

"I think you have some serious faith issues."

1 ADAM: MAN OF DUST AND DESTINY

CHAPTER HIGHLIGHTS

- Creation of Man
- Creation of Woman
- The Fall
- Blaming Others
- Consequences of the Fall

Let's Get Started

Imagine waking up and being the only person alive. Of course, for Adam, it didn't seem strange at all because he didn't know anything different. For us, the idea of being utterly alone on the planet is incomprehensible. God saw right away that it wasn't good for Adam to be without a companion and so he created woman.

God designed Adam and Eve for fellowship with himself. He asked only one thing: they could not eat of the Tree of the Knowledge of Good and Evil. It seems such a simple request, but they couldn't obey it. The consequence of their disobedience serves as a powerful motivator for us to do what God says!

> **Genesis 2:7–9** The Lord God formed the man from the dust of the ground and breathed into his nostrils the breath of life, and the man became a living being. Now the Lord God had planted a garden in the east, in Eden [see illustration, page 4]; and there he put the man he had formed. And the Lord God made all kinds of trees grow out of the ground—trees that were pleasing to the eye and good for food. In the middle of the garden were the tree of life and the *Tree of the Knowledge of Good and Evil.*

Let's Create A Man

On the sixth day of <u>Creation</u> God, who desired fellowship, made Adam from the dust of the ground by breathing life into him. Adam was created a fully-grown man and had everything he needed to survive. Adam did not evolve.

☞ **GO TO:**

Psalm 8:5 (Creation)

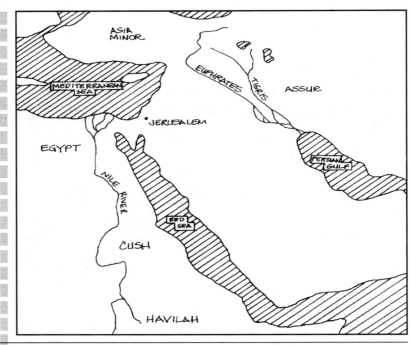

What Others are Saying:

Something to Ponder

Allen P. Ross: God's breathing the breath of life into man transformed his form into a living being (lt., "a living soul"). This made man a spiritual being, with a capacity for serving and fellowshiping with God.[1]

God could have formed this first human creation of anything he desired in any way he desired. This new creation could have had six eyes or three legs or any number of other appendages or parts, but everything created within man's body had a purpose and a reason. Then God provided for man by placing him in a garden, giving him all the food and supplies he needed.

Nothing God created was happenstance or by mistake. During Creation, God never said, "Oops!" There was a reason behind everything he did in creation and in the way he created Adam. The word in the Hebrews for "formed" refers to the work of an artist. Adam was the masterpiece!

BUILD YOUR SPIRIT: God wants every one of us to feel special, for he created each one of us for a specific purpose. Psalm 139:13, 14 says, *"For you created my inmost being; you knit me together in my mother's womb. I praise you because I* *am fearfully and wonderfully made; your works are wonderful, I know that full well."*

> **Genesis 2:15–17** The Lord God took the man and put him in the Garden of Eden to work it and take care of it. And the Lord God commanded the man, "You are free to eat from any tree in the garden; but you must not eat from the **Tree of the Knowledge of Good and Evil**, for when you eat of it you will surely die."

Let's Give This "Man" Something To Do

Right from the beginning, man had work to do. But Adam's work was purposeful and meaningful. Drudgery and trouble would enter the picture only after the **Fall**.

But the plot thickens: there was also a possible **temptation** in a tree that contained the knowledge of good and evil, with a consequence for disobedience.

If Adam hadn't been presented with a choice to obey God, he would have been a robot. But with this commandment, God made it possible for Adam to prove his love and devotion to his Creator.

Charles R. Swindoll: Americans did not invent the idea of freedom. . . . It began with God, way back in the Garden of Eden when he made Adam and Eve. God made them—and he has made you and me—to enjoy the pleasures and responsibilities of freedom. How?

- God made us with a mind . . . that we might think freely.
- God made us with a heart . . . that we might love freely.
- God made us with a will . . . that we might obey freely. [2]

BUILD YOUR SPIRIT: God never tempts you to do evil, but he does give you occasions to prove your love for him. His commandments are not some helter-skelter mistake to trap you in **sin**. They are rules intended for your best and to <u>test</u> your love and **devotion** for your Creator. God created you to have a relationship with him.

Just as God clearly defined the rules and the consequences for disobedience, fathers must clearly communicate the rules of their households to their children. They must express the advantages of obeying, and they must make clear the consequences for disobedience.

Tree of the Knowledge of Good and Evil: *signified the ability to know right from wrong by personal experience*

☞ **GO TO:**

Matthew 26:41 (temptation)

Fall: the first sin of Adam and Eve

temptation: wanting what God doesn't want

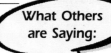

What Others are Saying:

KEY POINT

Love without a choice is not love at all.

sin: disobedience to God

devotion: commitment

☞ **GO TO:**

James 1:13 (test)

Grow Your Family

> **Genesis 2:18–20** The Lord God said, "It is not good for the man to be alone. I will make a helper suitable for him." Now the Lord God had formed out of the ground all the beasts of the field and all the birds of the air. He brought them to the man to see what he would name them; and whatever the man called each living creature, that was its name. So the man gave names to all the livestock, the birds of the air and all the beasts of the field. But for Adam no suitable helper was found.

The Name Game

☞ **GO TO:**

Genesis 1:4, 10, 12, 18, 21, 25 (good)

God created Adam as a thinking, reasoning human with a need to be creative—like himself. Naming the animals gave Adam purpose. However, it wasn't satisfying.

Man was all by himself and God, the Creator who wanted his creation to be perfectly happy, recognized that this wasn't good. Everything else God had created was immediately labeled "<u>good</u>," but it wasn't good that Adam was alone.

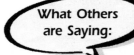

What Others are Saying:

Raymond C. Ortlund, Jr.: Surprisingly . . . God did not immediately create this helper. Instead God paraded the animals before the man for him to name them. Why? Because the man did not yet see the problem of his aloneness. . . . In serving God man encountered his own need. [3]

> **Genesis 2:21–25** The Lord God caused the man to fall into a deep sleep; and while he was sleeping, he took one of the man's ribs and closed up the place with flesh. Then the Lord God made a woman from the rib he had taken out of the man, and he brought her to the man. The man said, "This is now bone of my bones and flesh of my flesh; she shall be called 'woman,' for she was taken out of man." For this reason a man will leave his father and mother and be united to his wife, and they will become one flesh. The man and his wife were both naked, and they felt no shame.

Wow! She's Just Like Me!

God created a woman from Adam's rib (see GWWB, pages 3–26). Now Adam had a suitable complement for the new task of running Eden. She could walk like him, talk like him, and reason like him. She was just like him! What a relief after dealing with all those animals who couldn't talk. In fact, she likely gave Adam an earful! The first marriage was complete and even though they were not yet parents, God predicted the future of new couples: they should be independent from their parents. But the best thing about this new couple was that they were unashamed of their naked bodies. They had complete acceptance and total love for each other. Ahh . . . Paradise!

Raymond C. Ortlund, Jr.: These are the first recorded human words, and they are poetry. What do they express? The joy of the first man in receiving the gift of the first woman. . . . The man perceived the woman not as his rival but as his partner, not as a threat because of her equality with himself, but as the only one capable of fulfilling his longing within.[4]

What Others are Saying:

Some writers have said about this passage that Adam gave the first "wolf whistle" when he saw Eve. She must have been a perfect beauty—because God would have wanted him to be attracted to her. God knew what would please Adam and made sure she fulfilled his expectations, even though he hadn't yet formed any. She was perfectly suited just for him.

Something to Ponder

*God had said that he would make a **helper** suitable for Adam. When Scripture uses the word "<u>helper</u>" in reference to a woman, it isn't meant to be demeaning. God himself is called "<u>Helper</u>." The word "suitable" can also be expressed as "a help opposite him" or "corresponding to him." God intended to provide for Adam exactly according to Adam's needs. That's how God wants men to view their wives: as someone valuable who completes what we lack (see WBFW, page 90). In fact, God asks men to love their wives so much they should be willing to <u>give</u> their lives up for them. Now that is a valuable asset.*

helper: assistant

Grow Your Family

THE BIG PICTURE

Genesis 3:1–7 Satan appeared in the Garden of Eden as a serpent [see illustration, page 8] and tempted the woman into eating from the forbidden "*Tree of the Knowledge of Good and Evil.*" Then she gave some of the fruit to Adam and he ate too. It didn't take long for them to realize they had disobeyed, for they became conscious of their nakedness. Ashamed, they tried to make their own clothing from fig leaves.

☞ **GO TO:**

Genesis 2:18 (helper)

John 14:16, 17 (Helper)

Ephesians 5:25 (give)

Satan: the devil

Uh-oh, There's Trouble In Paradise

Just imagine the front-page headlines that could have been after the <u>Fall</u>:

- Why Wasn't Adam Watching the Store?
- First Man Fails; Everyone Else Pays with Their Lives.
- Warning Signs Improperly Posted at the Tree of Knowledge. Liability Questioned.
- Eve Says, "Adam Never Told Me."

From the Biblical account we don't know if Adam was there when Satan tempted Eve, or whether he appeared after she had taken her first bite. Regardless, they both knew that something was wrong. They had never looked at each other before and felt vulnerable. Now clothing seemed like something they could hide behind. Even though Satan had promised something good to Eve, neither she nor Adam saw the promised results.

What Others are Saying:

soul: the immortal, spiritual part of a person

Something to Ponder

Herschel H. Hobbs: The devil opened their eyes, but not to becoming as God, but rather to shame. Their physical nakedness suggests their greater nakedness of **soul**. Theirs was the self-consciousness of guilty hearts. [5]

Do you wonder how Adam could have blown it so big? He had it made. He had perfect health, a perfect domain, the perfect job, and the perfect wife. He talked daily with his Creator. He was placed in the Garden to take care of it. It was his service to God, and it was marked by ease and pleasure. Yet it wasn't enough. He thought the forbidden fruit would bring additional satisfaction.

Ever since the sin of our first parents, man has hurt himself, his relationship with others, and his relationship with God. Like dominos, the consequences of sin have tumbled into the present. Marriages and families suffer from selfishness. Society is self-indulgent and our culture is rotting as sin's poison spreads. The arts, sciences, disciplines, and structures of our world are an apple with a worm in it. And the worm is hungry! What was originally meant to reflect the glory of God became a support mechanism for sin.

BUILD YOUR SPIRIT: We are not to *"love the world or the things that are in the world or the love of the Father is not in us"* (1 John 2:15). We are not to be insulated nor isolated from the things of the world. We are to live in the world without being of the world.

> **Genesis 3:8–13** Then the man and his wife heard the sound of the Lord God as he was walking in the garden in the cool of the day, and they hid from the Lord God among the trees of the garden. But the Lord God called to the man, "Where are you?" He answered, "I heard you in the garden, and I was afraid because I was naked; so I hid." And he said, "Who told you that you were naked? Have you eaten from the tree that I commanded you not to eat from?" The man said, "The woman you put here with me—she gave me some fruit from the tree, and I ate it." Then the Lord God said to the woman, "What is this you have done?" The woman said, "The serpent deceived me, and I ate."

It's Her Fault!

God knew what Adam and Eve had done, yet he patiently questioned them. This is the first recorded incident where God demonstrates his willingness to have an open relationship with us in spite of our disobedience.

Adam and Eve responded to God's appearance by hiding and then blaming each other and Satan. God tried to reach out to them, but their guilt prevented them from feeling his love. Distance, separation, and fear took their first sneaky steps into the hearts of men. No one wanted to take responsibility. Instead, they pointed fingers, trying to transfer the blame and shame. This is the first buck that was passed—and it'll continue passing for the rest of humanity's existence.

What Others are Saying:

providence: divine guidance

Something to Ponder

☞ **GO TO:**

Exodus 3:11 (Moses)

KEY POINT

Don't hide your sin— 'fess up!

Alan Redpath: So often the **providence** of God seems to run completely counter to his promises, only that he may test our faith, only that he may ultimately accomplish his purpose for our lives in a way that he could never do if the path were always smooth.[6]

Adam told God he was fearful. Even though his hiding didn't help the situation, at least he expressed his fear, showing he still had an open relationship with God. Moses was another biblical leader who once was filled with enough courage to kill an Egyptian. Yet forty years later when facing God at the burning bush, he fearfully told God he couldn't deliver the Hebrews. Each man struggled with fear in his daily life but both candidly expressed their feelings to God.

Men today often hide their feelings, but the first man didn't have any trouble describing his emotions. Neither should you.

THE BIG PICTURE 🔍

Genesis 3:14–4:2 God responded to the sin in the Garden by disciplining the serpent, Eve, and Adam with different consequences for each. Then God provided clothes from animal skins for Adam and his wife. Adam gave the woman her name, "Eve," because it means "living" or "life." She would become the mother of all the living. They were finally banished from the Garden.

God referred to his provision of a Savior in the future when he told Satan, *"I will put enmity between you and the woman, and between your offspring and hers; he will crush your head, and you will strike his heel"* (Genesis 3:15).

Consequences For Adam

Adam and Eve thought they would experience the freedom of becoming god-like. Instead, they got painful consequences that reminded them even more of their humanness. God rebuked Adam for not being a leader. He should have refused Eve's encouragement to eat the fruit: *"Because you listened to your wife and ate from the tree about which I commanded you, 'You must not eat of it,'* *"Cursed is the ground because of you; through painful toil you will* eat of it all the days of your life. It will produce thorns and thistles for you, and you will eat the plants of the field. By the sweat of your brow you will eat your food until you return to the ground, since from it you were taken; for dust you are and to dust you will return" (Genesis 3:17–19). To Adam's credit, he didn't try to change God's mind, argue, or blame his wife again. He accepted his correction—like a man.

Results of the First Sin

Verse .... Person	Consequences
3:15 ...... Satan	Serpent will crawl on belly. Satan will be defeated by Jesus Christ.
3:16 ...... Eve	Pain in childbirth. Desire to please husband and be mastered by him.
3:17 ...... Adam	Work and toil to survive. Physical death and return to dust.

Herschel H. Hobbs: The Bible does not say it specifically, but the **spiritual tenor** is that Adam and Eve believed this promise and were saved, looking forward in faith to him who would be the seed of the woman.[7]

Adam and Eve tried to have their needs met by disobeying God, but it only brought greater pain. Sin is anything we do when we try to meet our own needs in a way that God doesn't want for us.

If we will remember that God only wants the best for us, we'll be more motivated to try to meet our needs in the way he has laid out. God never plans to withhold something good from us. He is the <u>giver</u> of all good gifts and promises to <u>meet</u> all our true needs. If we'll trust his love for us, we'll sin less often.

Study Questions

1. What instructions did God give Adam about the trees in the Garden? Why were these instructions necessary?
2. What did God call "not good"?
3. What did God create that did not adequately "help" Adam?

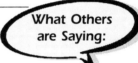

What Others are Saying:

spiritual tenor: underlying belief

Overcoming Struggles

☞ **GO TO:**

James 1:17 (giver)

Philippians 4:19 (meet)

4. What consequences did God give Adam, Eve, and Satan?

5. Who named Eve and why was that name chosen?

CHAPTER WRAP-UP

- God created a man in his own image to rule over the world and because he wanted fellowship with him. He created a perfect world for Adam to rule over. This world involved work, but it wasn't troublesome work; that would come later. (Genesis 1:26–2:7)

- Because animals didn't completely satisfy Adam's need for companionship, God created Eve from Adam's rib. This companionship would be intimate and blessed by God. (Genesis 2:18–25)

- God gave the couple only one thing to avoid: *"the Tree of the Knowledge of Good and Evil."* Adam and Eve disobeyed God by eating of its fruit. (Genesis 3:1–7)

- After sinning no one wanted to accept responsibility. Finger pointing and rationalization rocked Eden. Adam blamed his wife for his sin and Eve blamed the serpent. (Genesis 3:12–13)

- For Adam, the consequences of sin were that he would have a difficult time working the ground. Work would never be easy again. For Eve, she would experience pain in childbirth and would desire to serve her husband. For the serpent, he would crawl on the ground and be defeated by Jesus Christ on the cross. (Genesis 3:17–19)

2 ABRAHAM: THE FATHER OF PROMISE

Let's Get Started

Life was never easy for the **patriarch** Abraham. He was tested in many ways. Some tests he passed with flying colors and others he just barely passed. With a few, he failed completely.

Yet, in spite of Abraham's occasional faithlessness, God proved himself always faithful. Over and over again, God kept his promises. Abraham didn't always understand God's timing, but, in the end, Abraham reviewed God's work in his life and saw how God had strengthened his trust and faith.

God wants us to learn, like Abraham did, that trials draw us closer to him. Then we'll have a joy and contentment like Abraham had when he saw Isaac, his son of promise, born.

THE BIG PICTURE

> **Genesis 11:27–12:9** Abram's **genealogy** revealed his family background. His ancestors lived in Ur of the Chaldeans. People of that area worshiped many gods, but **Jehovah** appeared to Abram and gave him instructions to leave his father's country. He was to head out without knowing exactly where he was going or where he would settle.

A Big Step

When the one true God, Jehovah, appeared to Abram and told him to leave the land of his ancestors, he was faced with a big decision. Why did he respond to the God of heaven (as opposed to all the pagan gods of his culture [see illustration, page 14])? In the stories

patriarch: the head or founder of a family

genealogy: tracing family history

Jehovah: self-existent one

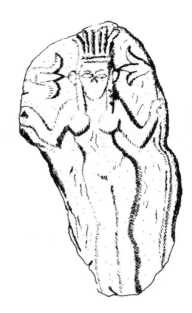

☞ **GO TO:**

Genesis 28:13 (Jacob)

Exodus 3:4 (Moses)

of <u>Jacob</u> and <u>Moses</u> we are allowed to see the glory of the meeting, but we have no idea how God revealed himself to Abram. We do know, however, that the experience ignited Abram's faith and trust such that he chose to leave the familiar and walk toward an unknown future (see illustration, page 15).

What Others are Saying:

Charles R. Swindoll: Abraham demonstrated faith by moving into an uncharted course with one guarantee—that God was with him. Think about this: Christianity is not complicated. The neglect of your walk is complicated. And the secret is to distill this walk through the filter of simplicity so that you come back to the basics, which is faith. Visit Abraham regarding faith. Learn from him.[1]

Something to Ponder

We can't fully appreciate the step Abram took without understanding the fact that his culture trusted in many gods because each one had its own function or area of expertise. Each god also had its own designated geographical area, and therefore to go outside a particular boundary meant leaving the protection of a particular god. Rejecting all of this, Abram chose to believe in the one God, Jehovah. In light of the culture surrounding him, Abram took a tremendous step in believing this "new" God was one who transcended boundary lines and ruled the whole earth. He had to believe that Jehovah could be <u>everywhere</u> Abram traveled.

☞ **GO TO:**

Proverbs 15:3 (everywhere)

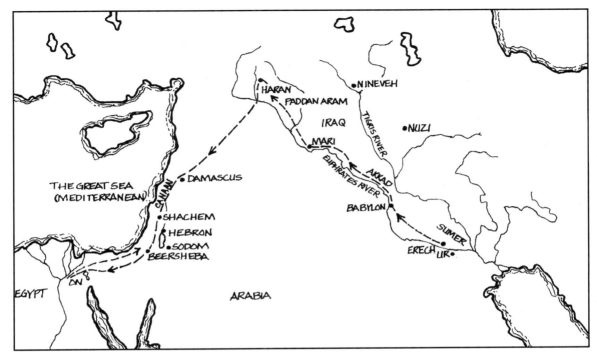

Abraham's Travels

Abram and his wife, Sarai, traveled from Ur of the Chaldeans, through Haran and Egypt, to Canaan.

BUILD YOUR SPIRIT: God only said he would show Abram the land. He didn't promise to give him the land at this point. Sometimes all we have to go on is God's promise to <u>guide</u> and <u>strengthen</u> us without knowing all the details. Yet, we can depend on the very smallest of his promises.

Incredible Appearance

As far as the text tells us, this was the first time God had appeared to Abram. It would not be the last. In total, Scripture says God personally appeared to Abram seven times. In Bible language, such an appearance is called a **theophany**.

Harold Ockenga: One of the means used by God in revealing his will unto men in the early stage of divine revelation was by means of a theophany.[2]

☞ **GO TO:**

Psalm 25:5 (guide)

1 Thessalonians 3:13 (strengthen)

theophany: *when God appears in human, visible form*

What Others are Saying:

God's Appearances to Abram

Bible Passage	Circumstances	Promises or Challenge
Genesis 12:1–3	God's call for Abram to leave his area	Abram will be made a great nation. He will have blessings. God will make his name great. He will be a blessing to others. Those who bless him will be blessed and those who curse him will be cursed. All the families of the earth will be blessed through him.
Genesis 12:7	Abram arrives in land of Canaanites	*"To your offspring I will give this land."*
Genesis 13:14	After Lot separates from Abram	God promises land to Abram.
Genesis 15:1	After Abram refuses reward from Melchizedek	God promises a child who will be a blood heir. God promises descendants as numerous as stars in the sky.
Genesis 17:1	When Abram is 99 years old	God establishes his covenant with Abram, and promises to multiply his family into many nations. God changes his name from Abram to Abraham.
Genesis 18:1	At oaks of Mamre	Three men promise that Sarah will give birth to a child a year from then. Abraham also is given an opportunity to pray for any righteous people at Sodom.
Genesis 22:1	Testing of Abraham's dedication	God asks Abraham to sacrifice his son, Isaac. Then, when Abraham is about to do it, an angel stops him.

THE BIG PICTURE 🔍

Genesis 12:10–20 Famine hit Canaan and drove Abram to Egypt. Abram feared for his life when he considered how beautiful his wife, Sarai, was and how the Egyptian king might want to kill him in order to take her as his wife. He told Sarai to lie and say they were brother and sister. The Egyptian took Sarai into his harem, but before he could consummate the relationship, God used a plague to warn Pharaoh and bring riches to Abram.

The Big Lie

Abram went to Egypt where there was food. He had proved his faithfulness in his initial move from Ur, but his faith in God's provision and protection collapsed when he suspected someone might kill him to get his beautiful wife (see GWWB, pages 32–33). Abram was asking Sarai to give a half truth since Sarai was a relative of

Abram's before she became his wife. Some Bible experts believe she was his <u>half-sister</u> (the daughter of Abram's father <u>Terah</u>, but not his mother), whereas some believe she may have been his niece (the daughter of <u>Haran</u>—Abram's brother). Even though Sarai was taken into the king's home, God intervened by giving Pharaoh the sense to see the connection between a plague and Sarai (we don't know how). He returned Sarai to Abram and **chastised** Abram for lying. How embarrassing for a man of God.

☞ **GO TO:**

Genesis 20:12 (half-sister)

Genesis 11:24 (Terah)

Genesis 11:26 (Haran)

Gene A. Getz: Abraham's fears were not without reason. History records that Egyptian men were very impressed with **Semitic** women. Furthermore, it was rather standard procedure in those days for men to secure women as their wives by murdering their husbands and previous possessors.[3]

What Others are Saying:

chastised: *corrected*

Semitic: *Jewish*

Something to Ponder

If a superstar of the faith can fail so badly, then we must be alert to the possibility that we could also be one step away from surrendering to fear. We will be constantly <u>tested</u> but with God's help, we can be faithful. We haven't seen God in person like Abram did, but we have the <u>Bible</u> and the example of other Christians to encourage us and help us know the right thing to do.

☞ **GO TO:**

1 Peter 1:6–7 (tested)

Colossians 3:16 (Bible)

Jude 1:4 (license)

1 John 1:9 (confess)

BUILD YOUR SPIRIT: Just as Abram was not counted as unfaithful because of his temporary lack of faith, God doesn't give up on us when we make mistakes or even sin. All our sin was in the future at the time of the cross, and it was nailed there. Of course, that doesn't give us a <u>license</u> to sin, but it can give us hope to turn back to God over and over again. All we have to do is <u>confess</u> sin and receive God's forgiveness.

THE BIG PICTURE 🔍

Genesis 13:1–18 After the famine Abram returned to Canaan a wealthy man. His nephew Lot returned with him. Their shepherds were fighting because there wasn't enough land to support all of the herds. Abram graciously offered first pick of the land to his nephew. Lot chose the best part. After this, God again spoke to Abram and promised him many descendants.

Lot Walks By Sight, Abram By Faith

Abram wisely separated from Lot. Both of them were wealthy but conflict was something Abram did not want. Abram was the head of the family and could have dictated the terms of living together or a separation. Instead, he graciously offered Lot first choice. Lot headed for the city of Sodom. Abram met God again and was now promised all the land he could see. God marvelously promised to bless him with countless generations.

Jamie Buckingham: When Lot said there was not room enough for the two of them, Abram chose again to obey God. Jealous for the integrity of his tribe and its testimony before the corrupt society that was so closely observing him, he determined he should not dishonor God by causing disunity and conflict within his family—a family that had professed a loyalty to God, making them different.[4]

Remember
This . . .

☞ **GO TO:**

Romans 4:9 (faith)

God's promise to Abram was not fulfilled in his lifetime. He didn't own the land and he only had one descendant, Isaac, when he died. Yet, that's why Abram was counted by God as such a man of <u>faith</u>. He trusted that what God said would come to pass, even if he didn't experience it. And it did. *"All these people were still living by faith when they died. They did not receive the things promised; they only saw them and welcomed them from a distance. And they admitted that they were aliens and strangers on earth"* (Hebrews 11:13).

THE BIG PICTURE 🔍

marauding: robbing

> **Genesis 14:1–24** Lot settled in Sodom but was captured by Chedorlaomer, a king and his army. When Abram heard about it, he quickly pursued the **marauding** armies and rescued his nephew. The king of Sodom wanted to reward Abram for his courage, but Abram refused. However, he did receive a blessing and some provisions from Melchizedek, the king of Salem.

KEY POINT

Faith means we believe even if we don't see the results immediately.

Abram's Courage And Humility

The easygoing Abram reacted decisively and formed a rescue party to recover Lot from an invading army. He marched 140 miles north to engage in a night battle. He then chased the enemy for another 100 miles, ensuring victory. Lot and all of the possessions taken from Sodom were returned.

Charles R. Swindoll: Abraham was willing to sacrifice himself for the sake of others. . . . When Abram heard that Lot was in trouble, he could have reacted with indifference: "So what? I've got my own problems to deal with here." He could have been critical: "Well, he finally got what he had coming." Instead Abram chose to lead the charge to rescue his nephew.[5]

What Others are Saying:

Abram acted quickly because he <u>planned</u> for trouble and had faith in God's ability to give victory. Abram was also ready because he had 318 men trained for trouble. His faith gave him confidence because God had promised him earlier, *"I will bless those who bless you, and whoever curses you I will curse"* (Genesis 12:3).

Something to Ponder

When the evil king of Sodom wanted to reward Abram, Abram refused. He didn't want others thinking that anyone or anything had made him rich, except God. His faith went beyond any riches the king of Sodom could provide. Abram passed this test of faith. God promised to bless him and that was enough.

☞ **GO TO:**

Proverbs 14:22 (planned)

LEADERSHIP PRINCIPLE—As leaders we can trust that the Lord has prepared us for our tasks. He promises to be there and guide us, but we'd better make sure those people depending upon our leadership have been properly trained. We owe them a duty to prepare, plan, and position them for success.

Remember This . . .

THE BIG PICTURE

> **Genesis 15:1–21** God again appeared to Abram and repeated his promise that Abram would have many children, even though Sarai hadn't yet been able to conceive a child. God **solidified** his promise by making a **covenant** with Abram.

solidified: *hardened*

covenant: *agreement, like a treaty*

Waiting For A Son

God met Abram again and told him not to be afraid because he would be a shield to him. Because so much time had gone by without the promise of a child being fulfilled, Abram wondered aloud whether his faithful servant Eliezer, the current heir of his estate, would actually take over. But God confirmed that a son would indeed be born to Abram—a child from his own body. Then God pointed out the stars in the sky and said Abram's descen-

☞ **GO TO:**

Exodus 1–40 (history)

dants would be as numerous as them. By faith Abram believed God and *"he credited it to him as righteousness"* (Genesis 15:6). To affirm his promise, God conducted a ceremony called a covenant and gave Abram some other details of his future nation's <u>history</u>:

Abram's descendants would be
strangers in a foreign land. .... Exodus 1:1–7
They would be enslaved for 400 years. .... Exodus 1:11–14
God would judge the nation
they served. .... Exodus 11:1
They would leave with abundant
material goods. .... Exodus 11:2
Abram would die after a long life. .... Genesis 25:8
After the fourth generation, Abram's
descendants would return to the land
of the Amorites. .... Joshua 4:1
That land was determined as the land
from the river of Egypt (Wadi el-Arish)
as far as the river Euphrates. .... Genesis 15:18

What Others are Saying:

Remember This . . .

Smith Wigglesworth: Faith is an inward operation of that divine power which dwells in the contrite heart, and which has the power to lay hold of things not seen.[6]

A covenant is a solemn transaction between a person and God or between people and God. In it each person promises to fulfill certain things and is promised certain advantages. In God's covenant with Abraham, God promised everything and didn't receive anything. This demonstrates his unconditional love and grace. The **breach** of a covenant was and still is a serious offense.

☞ **GO TO:**

Ezekiel 17:12–20 (breach)

2 Corinthians 1:3–4 (help)

Overcoming Struggles

breach: breaking

If it seems like God is slow in supplying you with the help you need to overcome some sin or correct a weakness, just know that he has the power and a plan. Only he knows the right timing. In the meantime, you'll learn something that you can use to <u>help</u> others in the future. If you were to have an instantaneous deliverance, you wouldn't learn those things.

Genesis 16:1–16 Sarai still couldn't conceive a child so she suggested to Abram that he have the child through her maid, Hagar. When that happened and Hagar became pregnant, Hagar despised Sarai. That made Sarai so mad she mistreated Hagar and Hagar ran away. But an angel of God found Hagar in the wilderness and told her that her son would become a great nation. He also gave her the ultimate challenge: Hagar should return to Sarai and submit to her authority. She did, and in time her son Ishmael was born.

KEY POINT

God always has a reason for his delays.

A Human Plan Gone Awry

Cultural solutions to carry out God's plans don't work! Sarai suggested a solution that was considered appropriate by the surrounding culture (see GWGN, pages 135–137), but Abram and Sarai were supposed to be part of God's culture. Unfortunately, their poor choice would have unpleasant consequences.

Gene A. Getz: But Ishmael's birth began a new chapter in world history that has not yet ended. From Hagar's son have come the great Arab nations who have in recent years plagued the children of Israel, the promised seed of Abraham. They are still suffering from Abraham's mistakes—mistakes born out of a right motive on Abraham's part, but from a wrong method.[7]

What Others are Saying:

LEADERSHIP PRINCIPLE—Abram showed us again his willingness to avoid conflict when he refused to become involved in Sarai and Hagar's hostility. God had to intervene and provide temporary leadership for the family by meeting Hagar in the desert. Abram might be faithful, but when faced with his wife's suggestion, he seemed to want peace at any cost.

The trouble could have been avoided if Abram and Sarai had asked God to guide them. When we jump at a solution to our problem without praying about it, we are asking for trouble. Nothing is too small or large for us to ask for God's help and viewpoint. The Bible says for us to pray about <u>everything</u>.

Overcoming Struggles

☞ **GO TO:**

Philippians 4:6–7 (everything)

Grow Your Family

As fathers, we need to remember the poor choices Abram made. As head of the family he had the responsibility of making a righteous choice. As we learn from Abram, our inaction with family problems weakens the impact we have on our children. It makes us distant and disengaged from them. It also weakens the respect and confidence our wives have in us. Wives often say that watching their husbands giving attention to the children strengthens their love for their husbands. That should be a strong motivator for getting involved.

THE BIG PICTURE

Genesis 17:1–27 God appeared to Abram again and repeated his promise to Abram that he would be the father of a multitude of nations. But this time, God did something new; he renamed the patriarch. Abram became Abraham and Sarai became Sarah. Not only that, he gave Abraham something new to do that would show that he and the male members of his household were unique and connected to God. God commanded all the males to be **circumcised**. Though it was painful, Abraham obeyed God's commands.

circumcised: to cut off the foreskin of a male

A New Name And A Unique Pain

It was thirteen years before God spoke again to Abram. At that time God gave himself a new name, El Shaddai, which refers to the one who actually causes nature to do the opposite. Abram was ninety years old at this time and God revealed a new name for Abram as well, Abraham. This signified God was giving him a great honor. He then asked Abraham to undergo circumcision to demonstrate the covenant between them. Talk about faith in action!

What Others are Saying:

KEY POINT

Obeying God might be painful sometimes but it always brings blessings.

Life Application Bible Notes: Why did God require circumcision? (1) As a sign of obedience to him in all matters. (2) As a sign of belonging to his covenant people. Once circumcised, there was no turning back. The man would be identified as a Jew forever. (3) As a symbol of "cutting off" the old life of sin, purifying one's heart, and dedicating oneself to God. (4) Possibly as a health measure.[8]

Genesis 18:1–15 God visited Abraham again, this time in the form of a man. With him are two angels disguised as men. These men tell Abraham that in a year, Abraham and Sarah will have a child. Now God was really getting specific. Sarah had been listening nearby and laughed when she heard such an impossible prediction. She was too old for childbearing. When one of the angels pointed out her lack of belief, she denied laughing.

A Big Laugh

God didn't withdraw his promise of a son for this old couple even though Sarah's faith was weak (see GWWB, pages 40–41). If we have the view of God as an ogre looking for something to get upset about, we would expect him to become offended by Sarah's doubt and take away the promised blessing. But he didn't do that because he's a loving God. Besides, a <u>promise</u> is a promise.

Sarah is nearly ninety years old, and Abraham is no spring chicken at one hundred. Is it any wonder they doubted? Perhaps the Lord delayed this promise because of their disobedience with Hagar. Or perhaps waiting this long would clearly focus appropriate glory on the Lord's provision.

GO TO:

Numbers 23:19 (promise)

Herschel H. Hobbs: One may wonder why the Lord delayed the event so long, twenty-five years after the first veiled promise was given. In a sense it was a test of Abraham's faith. Furthermore, when the promise was fulfilled, there must be no question that it was God's doing alone.[9]

What Others are Saying:

BUILD YOUR SPIRIT: God is <u>patient</u> with us. He knows we aren't perfect and don't have perfect faith. *"As a father has compassion on his children, so the Lord has compassion on those who fear him; for he knows how we are formed, he remembers that we are dust"* (Psalm 103:13, 14). God understands that our earthly perspective can diminish our ability to really believe he can do anything he wants.

GO TO:

2 Peter 3:9 (patient)

> **Genesis 18:16–19:38** Not only did the angels tell Abraham and Sarah about their future child, they also told of how God was going to destroy Sodom and Gomorrah. Abraham's nephew, Lot, lived in Sodom, so Abraham pleaded for mercy on the city. God graciously saved Lot and his family, but the sin of Sodom and Gomorrah was too great and the cities were destroyed.

When Pleading Won't Work

The prayer of a righteous man is <u>effective</u>, but God is <u>just</u>. The situation in these two cities was an **abomination** to the Lord. Although Abraham asked for mercy for the cities, God and the angels left without giving Abraham an indication of whether they would spare anyone for sure. But God, in his generosity, caused his angels to physically pull Lot and his family out of the city (see GWRV, page 76). Lot's wife was killed because she disobeyed the order to not look back at the destruction.

Abraham started out his prayer by asking whether God would destroy the righteous with the wicked. We don't know whether Abraham thought he knew of a certain number of righteous people, but maybe because he couldn't think of too many, he mentioned fifty righteous and then forty-five, then thirty, then twenty, and finally ten. Each time, God said he wouldn't destroy the city if that particular number were found. We don't know why Abraham stopped at ten. Maybe he sensed that God must destroy the city because of its great wickedness.

THE BIG PICTURE 🔍

> **Genesis 21:1–21** When Abraham was one hundred and Sarah was ninety, God fulfilled his promise. Sarah gave birth to Isaac. Their joy was boundless at first. But soon fourteen-year-old Ishmael, who had made fun of Isaac at his weaning party, spoiled it. Sarah was so angry that she insisted Abraham throw Hagar and Ishmael out of their home. God commanded Abraham to do that very thing and though it grieved him, he did so. As Hagar sat helpless in the wilderness, God again appeared to her and promised to provide for her and her son.

☞ **GO TO:**

James 5:16 (effective)

Job 4:17 (just)

abomination: *something loathed*

Something to Ponder

KEY POINT

Find out what God's will is and then ask for that in prayer.

Laughter Finally In The House!

The promise was finally fulfilled. Sarah and Abraham couldn't believe their joy. A baby—born to Sarah, the barren one. Isaac's name meant "laughter," and laugh they did, with joy. Whereas Sarah had previously laughed in doubt, she now laughed from faith. Abraham must have been doubly thrilled to see the son of promise in the flesh and to see the joy on his beloved wife's face.

But another kind of laughter occurred several years later at the party celebrating the weaning of Isaac: mocking laughter. Ishmael, Abraham and Hagar's son—the result of disobedience to God— must have felt intense jealousy because of all the attention being given the promised heir. Maybe he had secretly carried the thought he would somehow be the heir after all. Isaac's birth had spoiled that. He didn't laugh out of joy, but out of ridicule.

His mocking made Sarah so angry that she demanded Abraham throw Hagar and Ishmael out of the house. Abraham, loyal even to the son who wasn't the true heir, hated the idea, but God told him to do it. God then promised that he would take care of Ishmael by making a nation of him also. Most likely that comforted Abraham some. He obeyed God.

Patience and faith had paid off for Abraham and Sarah. God delivered just as he promised, even though they'd had imperfect faith, and at times, even disobeyed God's directions. That is just like God's faithfulness! Although he may have to discipline us at times for disobedience, he will still keep his promises.

Something to Ponder

THE BIG PICTURE 🔍

Genesis 22:1–24 God commanded Abraham to sacrifice his beloved son, Isaac, on an altar of his own making in the nearby mountains. In full obedience, Abraham made plans to kill his son, but God stopped him right before he did it. God affirmed Abraham's dependence on him and again confirmed his promise that Abraham would be the father of a multitude of people. When Abraham returned home, he learned that his brother, Nahor, was now the father of many children.

The Ultimate Challenge

Abraham and Isaac traveled fifty miles to reach Mt. Moriah. As they approached their destination, Abraham must have been deeply troubled. God had asked him to sacrifice his son! Abraham knew child sacrifice was practiced in the region, but God detested the practice. Pangs of love must have rocked Abraham's heart as every step brought them closer to Moriah and the ultimate surrender. God had given him this child; it didn't make sense that he would want him killed. Abraham no doubt remembered previous tests, but this one was the most painful.

When they arrived at the mountain, he instructed his servants, *"Stay here with the donkey while I and the boy go over there. We will worship and then we will come back to you"* (Genesis 22:5). As Abraham's hand brought the knife toward Isaac's bound body, God stopped him and provided a ram for the sacrifice.

What Others are Saying:

Oswald Chambers: Faith never knows where it is being led, but it loves and knows the One Who is leading.[10]

BUILD YOUR SPIRIT: What do you love most? Your children, job, possessions, or reputation? Do you hold onto your future waiting for one more life experience before really surrendering your heart to God? Abraham had to demonstrate his willingness to sacrifice his greatest love. When someone makes his or her first parachute jump, climbing out of the door signals willingness, but letting go proves the commitment. God needed to know Abraham was totally focused upon serve him. Abraham chose to place God before his son when he immediately readied the donkey and left for the mountain. Each step toward Mt. Moriah marked his willingness to obey El Shaddai through faith. When Abraham raised the knife, he let go. We must be as faithful.

THE BIG PICTURE

Genesis 23:1–20; 24:1–9, 67; 25:1–10 Sarah died at 127 years of age and Abraham bought a nearby field from the Hittites to bury his beloved wife.

Abraham did not want Isaac to marry one of the local women who didn't believe in Jehovah so he sent his servant to their distant relatives to find a wife. The servant was successful in bringing home a wife for Isaac.

> Abraham married another wife in his old age and had children through her. He died at the age of 175.

A Long Life Of Love And Challenge

Abraham's long life was a visual aid demonstrating the reality of God. Through Abraham, we are given these truths:

- God honors our faith but will test it through trials.
- Trials prove our faith is real and <u>prepare</u> us for service.
- God will be glorified through our obedience.
- God is faithful even when we are faithless.

☞ **GO TO:**

James 1:2–4 (prepare)

Charles R. Swindoll: God is pleased when we walk by faith. From cover to cover the Bible testifies to that fact. Nothing pleases the Lord more than when we walk by faith.[11]

Something to Ponder

Abraham consistently reviewed God's faithfulness in the past so that he could better deal with his current difficulty. We can do this by reviewing God's faithfulness as recorded in the Scriptures. *"For everything that was written in the past was written to teach us, so that through endurance and the encouragement of the Scriptures we might have hope"* (Romans 15:4).

Study Questions

1. What did God promise to Abram when he called him to leave his own country?
2. Since Abram and Sarai were childless, who did Abram initially think would be his heir?
3. How did Sarai encourage Abram to fulfill God's promise for an heir? What happened?
4. What new names did God give to Abram and Sarai?
5. What motivated Abimelech to want to make a treaty with Abraham?
6. What ultimate test did God give to Abraham?

CHAPTER WRAP-UP

- God told Abram to leave his present country and go to a land that God would show him. God promised to bless Abram greatly if he obeyed. By faith Abram left to follow God.

(Genesis 12:1–3)

- God promised Abram that he would have many descendants—so many that they couldn't be numbered. (Genesis 13:16)

- Since God delayed Sarai's ability to become pregnant, she tried to help God's plan by causing Abram to have a son through Sarai's maid, Hagar. That son was named Ishmael. (Genesis 16:1–16)

- To show Abram that he had a unique relationship with God, God changed Abram's name to Abraham and commanded Abraham and his male household to become circumcised. (Genesis 17:5–12)

- In spite of old age and many delays, the son of promise was finally born. He was named Isaac, which means "laughter." (Genesis 21:1–7)

- God tested Abraham by telling him to sacrifice Isaac on an altar in the mountains of Moriah. Abraham was willing to do it but was stopped by God's intervention. (Genesis 22:1–13)

3 ISAAC: A MAN OF PATIENCE AND SUBMISSION

Let's Get Started

His name meant "laughter," and that's what he brought into his family when he was born. As the son of Abraham and Sarah, Isaac learned of the great God Jehovah who had appeared to his father, Abraham. In some ways, Isaac was like his father. He avoided confrontation. Unlike Abraham, who rose to the occasion when pressed, Isaac was more interested in peace at any cost.

As a result, Rebekah, the wife found for him by his father's servant, became the powerhouse of the family. Rebekah came into the family as a stranger but quickly stole Isaac's heart and ruled the roost. That didn't bother Isaac. His favored son Esau was a skilled hunter, and Isaac just wanted to enjoy the game Esau brought to him.

Regardless of Isaac's weaknesses, it was God's plan for Isaac to be a great Hebrew patriarch. We can learn much from him because he represents many of us who would rather give in than fight.

THE BIG PICTURE

> **Genesis 21:1–7** God had promised for many years that Abraham and Sarah would have a child. Now the son he had promised was born. Abraham was a hundred years old and Sarah was ninety.

Laughter Is In The Family

Isaac inherited a rich heritage: a home of faith, filled with promise. No child of the Bible, except Jesus Christ, was surrounded by

What Others
are Saying:

Remember
This . . .

GO TO:

John 3:3 (born again)

2 Corinthians 5:17
(new creature)

Ephesians 1:18
(inheritance)

spiritual birth: *occurs at acceptance and faith in Jesus Christ*

repents: *turns away from sin*

born again: *receiving Jesus Christ as savior*

so much promise, expectation, and waiting. Time and again Sarah's <u>inability</u> to conceive seemed to place this longed-for promise in jeopardy. The wait seemed never-ending. Finally, Isaac was born and, appropriately, his name means "he laughs."

Charles R. Swindoll: The home is God's built-in training facility. The home is a laboratory where experiments are tried out. It is a place where life makes up its mind. It is a place where biblical truth permeates everyday life and where children are taught to seek and to follow the way of the Lord.[1]

In a spiritual kind of way, there is just as much anticipation in heaven as the angels wait to celebrate over the **spiritual birth** of each of God's newborn children. *"In the same way, I tell you, there is rejoicing in the presence of the angels of God over one sinner who **repents**"* (Luke 15:10).

BUILD YOUR SPIRIT: The Bible says we each must be "**born again**." That act of spiritual life makes us into a <u>new creature</u> in Christ. As a result, we have a spiritual <u>inheritance</u> just like Isaac. He inherited his father's possession and was raised with the knowledge of his spiritual ancestry.

THE BIG PICTURE

Genesis 22:1–19 God spoke to Abraham and told him to sacrifice Isaac. Isaac allowed his father to tie him down on an altar and watched as his father raised the knife. But God told Abraham to stop, and saved Isaac's life.

What Are You Doing, Dad?

Scholars believe Isaac was between seventeen and twenty-five when his father tied him to that altar. Imagine yourself in Isaac's place. What compelled him to stay put? Surely, it was a powerful act of his will and faith in God, who he knew was working—even if he didn't understand. When his father actually raised the knife, what thoughts flashed through his mind? His willingness to suffer death proved he trusted his father beyond a shadow of a doubt. It also meant Isaac was committed to serving the God of his father. And at that moment, if it hadn't already happened, his father's God became his own God.

Herschel H. Hobbs: Was this question asked out of a child's curiosity, or was the grim reality of the occasion beginning to dawn upon him? Perhaps he had noted the painful ordeal reflected in his father's face, hardly one to be experienced in anticipated worship. Was he himself to be the sacrifice? Isaac must have been familiar with the practice among the **Canaanites**.[2]

As Isaac and his father walked toward the place of sacrifice, he asked, *"Father?" "Yes, my son?" Abraham replied. "The fire and wood are here,"* Isaac said, *"but where is the lamb for the burnt offering?"* (Genesis 22:7). The tenderness in Abraham's voice must have comforted Isaac. He knew he was loved. He knew his father would never allow anything bad to happen to him. Isaac trusted his father when Abraham replied that God would provide the lamb.

Not only was Abraham commanded to kill Isaac, but he would then have to burn Isaac's body in order for Isaac to become the burnt offering God required. What a horrible thought. Even though the **heathen** of the surrounding area did such despicable things, Abraham knew that such a practice was <u>forbidden</u> by God. Isaac might have believed that his life wasn't actually in danger—until the knife was raised.

THE BIG PICTURE 🔍

> **Genesis 23:1, 2; 24:61–67** Isaac's mother, Sarah, died. Isaac, as her only son and long-awaited heir, must have felt close to her. Abraham sent a faithful servant back to his home country to find a wife for Isaac from their relatives. The servant brought back Rebekah, Isaac's cousin. When his mother died, Rebekah must have comforted him. Isaac fell in love with Rebekah.

Momma Is Gone, I Want A Wife

When Isaac was thirty-six, his mother died. He grieved deeply over the loss. Four years later, through his father Abraham's arrangements, Isaac met Rebekah, his wife. When she first arrived, Isaac was found praying and meditating. Isaac may have been seeking God's comfort from the loneliness he felt after the death of his mother. Or he may have been praying for the success of the servant's search for a wife. We don't know, but he most likely considered Rebekah an answer to prayer since she was beautiful and complemented his personality (see GWWB, pages 45–66).

Canaanites: people living in the land promised to Israel

Something to Ponder

Remember This . . .

heathen: unbeliever in Jehovah God

☞ **GO TO:**

Isaiah 57:4–5 (forbidden)

KEY POINT

Without knowing it, we often marry the opposite temperament to bring balance into our lives.

What Others are Saying:

Remember This . . .

☞ **GO TO:**

Genesis 24:15 (found)

Genesis 24:19 (water)

Genesis 24:58 (leave)

J. Vernon Magee: Notice that Isaac loved her. He was comforted after his mother's death. Christ loved the church and gave himself for her. This reveals to us that Christ gains a great deal in our salvation. He wants us. He longs for us.[3]

Isaac was the only patriarch to take solely one wife. Where Isaac was compliant and patient, Rebekah was strong-willed and energetic. When Abraham's servant had originally <u>found</u> Rebekah, she brought water from the well to <u>water</u> all his camels—an incredible feat (see illustration, this page). Then she was willing to <u>leave</u> her family and travel many miles with a stranger. She was a risk-taker. Isaac was the exact opposite.

BUILD YOUR SPIRIT: Isaac's example of praying and meditating is an encouragement to us. It was important to Isaac and it should be important to us. Without it, we cannot know God and we can't grow closer to him. Through prayer, we:

- Gain courage (2 Samuel 7:27)
- Know God has answered us (1 Kings 8:28)
- Know we are heard and cared about (2 Kings 2:20)
- Confess our sins (Nehemiah 1:6)
- Ask for success (Nehemiah 1:11)

- Express our faith in God (Matthew 21:22)
- Ask for God's miracles (Mark 9:29)
- Ask for others to be saved (Romans 10:1)
- Overcome anxiety and worry (Philippians 4:6)
- See people healed (James 5:15)

THE BIG PICTURE

> **Genesis 25:8, 19–34** Isaac's father, Abraham, died, and left everything to him. But for awhile, it seemed that Isaac would not be able to pass along his inheritance because Rebekah was barren. After much prayer, Rebekah conceived and then gave birth to twins, Esau and Jacob. Isaac favored Esau, and Rebekah favored Jacob. The sons lived out God's prediction that Jacob would be master over Esau when Esau exchanged his birthright for some food.

Favoritism Rules The Roost

Rebekah was initially barren like Isaac's mother, Sarah, but eventually bore twins, Esau and Jacob. Isaac avoided the conflict between the brothers, but both he and Rebekah contributed to it by each having his or her own favorite.

Isaac favored Esau because he loved the game that this son brought in from the fields. Esau was a skillful hunter, but he didn't value the spiritual life. Even though he must have seen his father's prayer life and heard of the spiritual journey of his ancestors, Esau was not interested in spiritual things. As a result, he sold his birthright to his brother Jacob for some food.

Rebekah favored Jacob because Jacob stayed more in the tents. Since he fixed a tasty meal that tempted his brother, Jacob must have been a good cook, no doubt trained by his mother. Mother and son were very close.

William Hendriksen suggests there are at least six ways a father can embitter his children:

1. Over-protection
2. Favoritism
3. Discouragement
4. Forgetting a child has ideas of his own and need not be an exact copy of his father
5. Neglect
6. Bitter words and physical cruelty [4]

ACT OF GOD

birth of Esau and Jacob

Something to Ponder

How interesting that Jacob was identified as *"a quiet man, staying among the tents"* (Genesis 25:27). That characteristic also described Isaac. Rebekah valued this quality in her son, Jacob, because it was the opposite of hers. Isaac valued Esau's aggression as a hunter—something he lacked. Both in marriage and in our children, we tend to value in others that which we need. (To read more about personality types, see WBFW, pages 106–108.)

Grow Your Family

*Showing favoritism will cause the **slighted** child to feel angry. "Fathers, do not exasperate your children; instead, bring them up in the training and instruction of the Lord" (Ephesians 6:4). When we train them, we must show God's kind of love that loves everyone equally.*

slighted: ignored

THE BIG PICTURE

> **Genesis 26:1–17** God appeared to Isaac and promised to give him the Canaanite land—a confirmation of the <u>promise</u> given to Isaac's father Abraham. As Isaac resided there, like his father's <u>reaction</u> years earlier, he was afraid Rebekah's beauty would cause his death. As a result, he told Rebekah to say they were sister and brother. The king of that area, Abimelech, saw them caressing and confronted Isaac. Isaac then told the truth. Isaac continued to live there and God greatly prospered him.

☞ **GO TO:**

Genesis 13:14 (promise)

Genesis 12:11–13 (reaction)

Genesis 26:4 (promised)

Genesis 26:7 (sacrificed)

Not Another Lie

God had <u>promised</u> a future for Isaac's family in their own land. Without a doubt, Isaac completely embraced his father's God. His life was marked by dedication to God and he proved himself faithful. In spite of this, when threatened by fear of possible death, he <u>sacrificed</u> truth. He lied about his relationship to his wife.

WARNING

Throughout the Bible, many men of faith struggled with telling the truth. These included:

- *The Israelites when Achan kept some of the plunder for Jericho (Joshua 7:11).*
- *Samson when he teased Delilah with the source of his strength (Judges 16:10).*
- *House of Judah and Israel when they said God would do nothing to them (Jeremiah 5:10).*
- *Ananias and Sapphira when they claimed they had given all to God (Acts 5:3–4).*

BUILD YOUR SPIRIT: Just as heart disease is prevented or reversed through diet and exercise, we need a remedy to reverse the disease that lying can inflict upon our spiritual lives. *"The Lord detests lying lips, but he delights in men who are truthful"* (Proverbs 12:22). Prayer and studying the Word are the cure. Honestly, earnestly, and humbly seeking God through a knowledge of the Bible is the best medicine for this spiritual heart problem.

THE BIG PICTURE

> **Genesis 27:1–29** As Isaac grew older, he grew blind. Since he anticipated his own death, he told his son Esau to prepare one of his favorite **venison** dishes so that he could give his son the blessing. When Rebekah heard of it, she manipulated Jacob into deceiving Isaac so that Jacob would get the blessing.
>
> In order to deceive Isaac, Rebekah dressed Jacob in Esau's clothing, put animal skins on his hands and arms to resemble Esau's hairiness, and then fixed a meal of goat meat to taste wild. When Jacob brought the meal to his father, Isaac believed Jacob was Esau and gave Jacob the blessing.

The Wrong Son

Isaac was trying to play God, for God said the <u>older would serve the younger</u>, but Isaac wanted nothing of God's plan. He wanted his favored son, Esau, to get the blessing. Isaac was not only physically blind, but he was spiritually blind. Even though he knew God's promises, he made preparations to give the blessing to Esau. He was suspicious because Jacob's voice didn't sound like Esau's, but he still gave the blessing because the meat tasted good. (For more about this special meat, see GWHN, pages 16–17.) Blinded by the desire of his heart, he sought disobedience; blinded by the hunger in his belly, he unwittingly helped in the final act of a **deception**.

Charles R. Swindoll: If you are in a position of authority, no matter how small or how large, the temptation to manipulate will never go away. You may have the authority to claim certain honors . . . to call attention to your right to be listened to. Don't yield. Resist at all costs![5]

KEY POINT

Just as there are early warning signs for heart disease, lying is an early warning sign for spiritual heart disease.

venison: *deer meat*

☞ **GO TO:**

Genesis 25:23 (older would serve the younger)

deception: *trickery*

What Others are Saying:

GO TO:

Ephesians 5:23 (head)

KEY POINT

Don't let your lower
desires rule your heart
and mind.

GO TO:

2 Kings 8:20 (serving)

Grow Your Family

Even though everyone in the family was at fault, Isaac was
supposed to be the spiritual <u>head</u> of them all. He wanted
peace at any cost. He didn't even ask a few simple questions
when he suspected an impostor.

THE BIG PICTURE 🔍

> **Genesis 27:30–28:5; 35:23–29** As soon as Jacob left
> Isaac's presence, Esau arrived and learned that Jacob
> had already received the blessing. Isaac was shaken to
> realize what had happened. The only "blessing left-
> overs" he could give was a disappointing prediction of
> Esau's future. Esau vowed to kill his brother. Knowing
> that, Rebekah convinced Jacob to go away to her fam-
> ily to find a wife.
>   Many years later, Jacob returned to show his wives
> and twelve children to Isaac before he died. Isaac died
> at age 180. Esau and Jacob, who had patched up their
> differences just a short time earlier, buried him.

A Disappointing Ending

Isaac physically trembled when he realized what had happened.
From his perspective, the wrong son had been given the blessing.
The blessing he would have for his favored son was a disappointment, for it included living in a more difficult terrain and Esau
<u>serving</u> his younger brother's relatives. It must have broken Isaac's
heart to know his favored son wouldn't receive great blessings.

*Men today can also give a blessing to their children, even if it doesn't
include a prediction of their child's future. Such a blessing should be a
positive reflection of the qualities God has put within the child and an
affirmation of the unconditional love the father has for his child.*

Study Questions

1. What does Isaac's name mean? What is its significance?
2. What was Isaac doing when Rebekah arrived as his wife? What
   does that say about his character?
3. Why did Isaac favor Esau? What were the consequences of the
   favoritism?
4. Why did Isaac lie about calling Rebekah his sister?
5. How could Rebekah and Jacob have deceived Isaac in giving
   Jacob the blessing?

- Isaac was born after his parents had waited for many years. He was the promised child who would be the beginning of the huge family that God had promised his father, Abraham. (Genesis 21:1–7)

- Isaac demonstrated his faith in God and Abraham when he was offered as a sacrifice. (Genesis 22:1–19)

- Abraham sent his servant away to their relatives to find a wife for Isaac and the servant returned with Rebekah. When she came into the camp, Isaac was meditating on the Lord. (Genesis 24:67)

- Twins were born to Isaac and Rebekah. Isaac favored his son Esau, and Rebekah favored the other twin, Jacob. Such favoritism brought great conflict and sadness into their family. (Genesis 25:27–28)

- Like his father Abraham, Isaac feared that the same king would kill him to steal his wife so he told Rebekah to lie and say she was his sister. (Genesis 26:9)

- When Isaac knew he would die soon, he told Esau to prepare a meal so that he could bless him. But that was not God's will. Rebekah and Jacob tricked Isaac into giving the blessing to Jacob. That made Esau revengeful. (Genesis 27)

4 JACOB: A DECEIVER WHO LEARNED DEPENDENCE ON GOD

CHAPTER HIGHLIGHTS

- Twins Are Born
- Jacob Cheats His Brother and Runs Away
- Jacob Works for His New Wife
- Jacob Meets God and His Brother
- Jacob Retires

Let's Get Started

Jacob can best be compared to the main character in Robert Louis Stevenson's *Dr. Jekyll and Mr. Hyde*. We see a side of Jacob that is **conniving** and manipulating. Next we see a man planning, praying, and wrestling with his God.

Jacob's name, which means figuratively "he deceives," is appropriate. He grabbed his brother Esau's heel at birth, and by the time he fled from home, he had also grabbed his brother's **birthright** and blessing. Throughout his life he continues to deceive others. God disciplines him for this behavior by allowing him to be deceived by others.

conniving: *deceptive*

birthright: *a special honor given to the firstborn son*

Jacob's Family

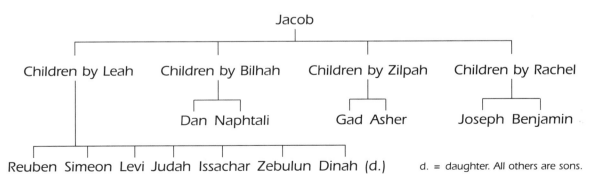

Jacob

Children by Leah	Children by Bilhah	Children by Zilpah	Children by Rachel
	Dan Naphtali	Gad Asher	Joseph Benjamin

Reuben Simeon Levi Judah Issachar Zebulun Dinah (d.)

d. = daughter. All others are sons.

But as Jacob grows and matures, God forms him into one of the patriarchs of the Jewish nation and the Old Testament. We have much to gain from studying his life.

THE BIG PICTURE 🔍

> **Genesis 25:19–34** After Isaac prayed for his wife, who was having a difficult time conceiving, she became pregnant, but it was a difficult pregnancy. God told her that two future nations were warring within her. The two "nations" were born and named Esau and Jacob.

Early Beginnings Show The Heart

Rebekah (see GWWB, pages 45–65) birthed twins who had made her pregnancy so uncomfortable that she prayed and asked God why. He told her, *"Two nations are in your womb, and two peoples from within you will be separated; one people will be stronger than the other, and the older will serve the younger"* (Genesis 25:23).

In that culture, it was very unusual for the older child to serve the younger, but God was already setting up the future of the Jewish people. Esau's descendants would live in the land of Edom, which was located at the southeast border of Palestine.

The Edomites would become one of the Jews' <u>enemies.</u>

When Esau and Jacob were born, Jacob followed Esau from the womb, grasping Esau's heel—as if to say, "I'm going to get you." The second twin was named Jacob because it means "one who takes by the heel," or **supplants**. Jacob grew up to fulfill the meaning of his birth name.

From the very beginning of Jacob's life, favoritism created strife and disunity. Jacob was favored by his mother, Rebekah, because he *"was a quiet man, staying among the tents"* (Genesis 25:27). His father, on the other hand, favored Esau. He was *"a skillful hunter, a man of the open country"* (Genesis 25:27). Isaac loved the taste of wild game, so he favored the son who could provide for his own lusts.

Many years later, when Esau returned from hunting, he asked Jacob for some food. Jacob knew his brother's weakness and used it for his own advantage. He offered to feed him in exchange for his birthright. Esau was so hungry that he rationalized, saying his birthright would be no good if he were dead. He promised the birthright to Jacob and then enjoyed his bowl of stew. (To learn more about this stew, see GWHN, page 44.) Even the finest, most expensive restaurant in the world doesn't offer a course that costs as much as this one did.

☞ **GO TO:**

Numbers 20:14–21 (enemies)

supplants: *takes the place of another, by treachery*

Herschel H. Hobbs: According to custom, the firstborn was to receive two-thirds of his father's estate, the younger getting only one-third. Furthermore, the older became the head of the family at the father's death. This involved not only family authority but also spiritual responsibility.[1]

Jacob wanted everything out of life he could get. Two rules guided his actions:

Rule One: Avoid work by scheming.
Rule Two: If conflicts arise, refer to rule one.

Our character and integrity never grow until we are deprived of what we want or we are required to work hard for what we have. If we cheerfully accept God's will when something is withdrawn from us that we want, we will develop true contentment. If we choose to <u>work hard</u>, we will develop a godly character that reveals our dignity. In contrast, when we take advantage of others, like Jacob did, the Mr. Hyde side of our lives shows others our ugliness and selfishness. Jacob would soon discover that <u>deceit</u> brings disunity and problems.

It may seem unjust for God to determine the future of these twins. Since God knows everything, he may have only been predicting what he knew the boys would choose to do. Regardless, God is sovereign and in control of everything that happens; yet he also allows humans to have free will, and he works with whatever happens. This paradox is something that theologians have trouble explaining to this day.

The birthright was the right of the firstborn male to be head of the clan. In Esau and Jacob's case, it also included being in the family line of Christ as God had promised their grandfather, Abraham, *"All peoples on earth will be blessed through you and your offspring"* (Genesis 28:14). Obviously, this birthright had great spiritual importance. When Esau treated it cheaply, it showed the awful condition of his heart. We should be careful lest something temporal take away our desire for spiritual blessings.

What Others are Saying:

Something to Ponder

Overcoming Struggles

☞ **GO TO:**

Proverbs 10:4 (work hard)

Proverbs 6:14 (deceit)

Remember This . . .

WARNING

KEY POINT

No matter how important a temporal need seems, it's never important enough to sacrifice a spiritual blessing.

The favoritism of Rebekah and Isaac brought great pain into their family. If we favor one child over another, we'll also experience great pain. We won't love equally and our children will notice. They will pit the parents against each other, and their feeling of not being loved could create low self-esteem. Although we may naturally prefer the personality of one of our children, we must take steps to love each one with equal attention.

THE BIG PICTURE

Genesis 27:1–29 When Isaac planned to give Esau the blessing, Rebekah intervened and convinced Jacob to trick his father by pretending to be Esau. It took several props to pull it off (dressing up in Esau's clothing, putting an animal's hairy hide on his hands, and serving a cooked goat made to taste like venison), but Isaac was deceived and gave Jacob the **patriarchal blessing**.

patriarchal blessing: the divine approval of a father

A Hairy Conspiracy

Like mother, like son. Jacob's mother hatched a conspiracy to ensure he received the birthright. Even though God had promised this blessing to Jacob, she intervened and made it happen herself. Her willingness to deceive gives us a clue as to how Jacob sharpened his slick-tongued skills. What was Jacob's reaction to Mom's scheme? He only worried about getting caught. The immorality did not trouble him. The fact he would be lying to his father and the Lord did not concern him.

Here's the blessing Jacob received from Isaac:

- He would receive the dew of heaven, the fatness of the earth, and an abundance of grain and new wine.
- People would serve him.
- Nations would bow down to him.
- He would be the master of his brothers.
- His mother's sons would bow down to him.
- Those who cursed him would be cursed.
- Those who blessed him would be blessed.

Fear of getting caught has always been a motivation for keeping our behavior moral. We need to let this fear be a warning. Doing right and living in honesty have small price tags compared to the consequences of lying. Jacob got the blessing and the riches it brought, but paid a huge price for carry-

Something to Ponder

ing out this dishonest plan. And he got caught: he had to flee from his own family.

THE BIG PICTURE

> **Genesis 27:30–28:9** After Esau discovered what had happened, he vowed to kill his brother. When Rebekah heard about this, she manipulated Isaac to send Jacob away to her own family to find a wife.

A Cheating Heart Runs Away

The price of Jacob's deceit was high. He fled from his own family and never saw his mother again. Imagine the fear of being "mama's boy" and knowing your brother, the Super Hunter, has vowed to kill you.

Rebekah told Jacob to go to her brother's home and "*stay with him for a while until your brother's fury subsides. When your brother is no longer angry with you and forgets what you did to him, I'll send word for you to come back from there. Why should I lose both of you in one day?*" (Genesis 27:44, 45). Both of them thought the separation would be temporary and easy. They had no clue they would never see each other again.

Something to Ponder

We may think the consequences of our dishonesty will be insignificant, and therefore what we'll gain through our deceit will be worth it. But God is not <u>mocked</u>. If we sow dishonesty, we'll reap the consequences.

WARNING

THE BIG PICTURE

> **Genesis 28:10–22** Jacob left his home and set out for Haran, his mother's original country. One night, Jacob had a dream that changed his life. Because of it he vowed to remain loyal to God.

☞ **GO TO:**

Galatians 6:7 (mocked)

Jacob Encounters God's Heavenly Ladder

Esau took God for granted. Esau easily traded away the truly important things in life. But God could see Jacob was a man ready to <u>know</u> him. As a result, God unveiled his majesty (see GWRV, page 224) to Jacob in a dream. He showed him a ladder that reached between the earth and heaven. Angels went up and down on it. God was revealing the spiritual realm that he wanted Jacob to experience.

☞ **GO TO:**

Philippians 3:10 (know)

Bruce H. Wilkinson and Larry Libby: Through the ladder, God is showing Jacob that there is no gulf between heaven and earth for the one who knows him. The ladder and the angels symbolize free access from the believer on earth to the Lord in heaven. The ladder is there; God is there. But the ladder must be used; God must be approached.[2]

**Something
to Ponder**

Jacob's early life lacked faith, goodness, and grace. Many have wondered how he could be the one to receive promises and blessing. Throughout the Bible, God uses broken, imperfect, and selfish people and in spite of Jacob's past, God awakened a personal knowledge of himself within this deceiver. We, too, can walk away from our past because God can awaken a spirit of <u>hope</u> for our future. As we climb our own ladder of life, God can help us lean it against the right wall!

☞ **GO TO:**

Jeremiah 29:11 (hope)

**Remember
This . . .**

Jacob had been raised on stories of how his grandfather Abraham was delivered by God from difficult circumstances. He also heard about the personal relationship his father had with God. Until this point there was no evidence such a spiritual awareness existed for Jacob. But in this encounter with God, Jacob made his own commitment. God is not in a <u>hurry</u> to work in someone's life, and he <u>never gives up</u> trying to do that.

Grow Your Family

Jacob's spiritual heritage eventually paid off. As parents, we should share our own spiritual stories with our children because sharing will bear fruit. Any time, no matter what we're doing, we can make a spiritual application and <u>draw</u> our children's attention to God.

THE BIG PICTURE 🔍

☞ **GO TO:**

Isaiah 5:19 (hurry)

Philippians 1:6 (never
gives up)

Deuteronomy 6:7
(draw)

> **Genesis 29:1–35** Jacob arrived in his mother's home country and quickly met a beautiful shepherdess named Rachel. It turned out she was the daughter of his mother's brother, Laban. He immediately fell in love with her and agreed to work seven years for Laban in order to earn the right to marry Rachel. But on their wedding night, Laban hoodwinked Jacob by substituting Rachel's less attractive sister, Leah, as the bride. Even though Jacob was angry about it, he agreed to serve another seven years in order to be the husband of Rachel. This was only the beginning of family troubles, because Leah could bear children but Rachel couldn't.

It's Love At First Sight

Jacob was a changed man. The desert experience with God had given him a new perspective on life. He walked into his uncle's territory with nothing but a fist full of promises—but that was all right. Within minutes of arriving at a well, he met his beautiful cousin, Rachel. Jacob was smitten by the love bug (see GWGN, pages 226–228). The problem? He couldn't pay the customary **dowry** and no scheme or trick would work to win his new bride. Laban negotiated the dowry to be seven years of Jacob's labor. Jacob agreed and 2,555 days later had earned the right to marry Rachel. But Laban didn't tell Jacob it was the custom for the older daughter to marry first.

Laban slipped Leah, Rachel's sister, into the wedding tent. He tricked Jacob into another seven years of hard work. Jacob, the deceiver, received a taste of his own bitter medicine. God says that will happen to us if we "invest" in unrighteousness or crafty schemes. The "interest" paid on our investment will be unpleasant <u>consequences</u>.

Herschel H. Hobbs: How this was done is not stated. Jacob must have been very drunk from the wedding feast. The bridal feast was literally a drinking feast.[3]

Just as God gives consequences for disobedience, parents should give consequences to their children for disobedience. Although it may be unpleasant and even inconvenient to discipline them, following through pays off with a better behaved child and someone who grows up to appreciate our efforts and consistency. The Bible says, "No discipline seems pleasant at the time, but painful. Later on, however, it produces a harvest of righteousness and peace for those who have been trained by it" (Hebrews 12:11).

THE BIG PICTURE

> **Genesis 30:1–43 Envy** filled Rachel's heart because of her sister's **prolific** childbearing ability. In order to cope with being **barren**, Rachel chose an ungodly but culturally acceptable way to **compensate**. Rachel offered her maid to Jacob to bear children and it worked. But Leah did the same thing and as a result, Jacob began to have the many descendants God had predicted he would have. But it brought great family conflict. Jacob made plans to leave the area and be on his own—without Laban benefiting from the blessings that God had given Jacob.

KEY POINT

It's never too late to turn to God or believe that God can work in a loved one's life.

☞ **GO TO:**

Genesis 34:12; Exodus 22:16 (dowry)

Ezekiel 44:12 (consequences)

dowry: bride price

What Others are Saying:

Grow Your Family

KEY POINT

God will allow unpleasant consequences for wrong choices.

envy: sad about another's good

prolific: productive

barren: unable to conceive

compensate: make up for

Lots Of Children And Lots Of Trouble

Although the situation is slightly different from his grandfather Abraham's situation, Jacob should have thought of the conflict that resulted when Sarah used the same technique to have a baby. Jacob most likely heard the stories from his father, Isaac, about how Isaac's brother, Ishmael, was conceived through using Sarah's maid and how it brought great trouble to the family.

Jacob's twelve sons were the ancestors of the twelve tribes of Israel. The entire nation of Israel came from these men.

Something to Ponder

THE BIG PICTURE

> **Genesis 31:1–55** Jacob ran away with all his wives and many children, along with the large flock he had amassed. When his father-in-law, Laban, heard about it, Laban chased him. Laban, the deceiver, then accused Jacob, another deceiver, of deceiving him. They eventually worked through their differences and Jacob left in peace.

KEY POINT

God is in charge of who is successful financially and materially.

From Deceiving To Working

The deceiver was now a worker. With God's blessings, he became wealthy even though Laban continually tried to siphon off wealth dishonestly. But Jacob went the extra mile to benefit his uncle. When his flocks were attacked, he took the losses rather than splitting them with Laban. He continued to work even after ten separate pay cuts. But God blessed him and his flocks began to multiply.

LEADERSHIP PRINCIPLE—A life marked by doing more than expected, or going the extra mile, pays dividends even today. One caution: Our efforts should come from our heart, not grudgingly or greedily.

THE BIG PICTURE

> **Genesis 32:1–32** Jacob left Laban and Haran behind and made his way toward his home country. Again he had an encounter with God in the night. This prepared him for the next challenge he faced: seeing Esau again after all those years. Terrified that Esau still wanted to kill him, Jacob prayed for God's protection and sent his family

> ahead of him in the order of the most loved at the back, where there might be protection. Jacob, left alone, had his third encounter with God, which ended with the dislocation of his thigh and being given a new name: Israel.

Terror And Wrestling

Every step Jacob took toward home was another step toward Esau's revenge. Jacob's relationship with God had become essential, and he prayed for deliverance and reminded God of the promises given his father and grandfather for success and countless descendants. He then sent his servants ahead with 550 animals as a present to his brother. Next, he split his family into two different groups to ensure that someone survived the coming attack.

Even so, Jacob was not merely fearful; he was terrified. How like God's provision that Jacob would come across an angel (which was the Lord himself) in the darkness of night. Throughout the night, they wrestled and a supernatural blow to the hip crippled Jacob. Just as the light of day broke, Jacob realized with whom he was wrestling. Jacob clung to his opponent, demanding a blessing. He emerged from that night a changed man, with a changed name: Israel.

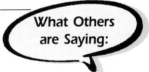

Smith Wigglesworth: Jacob was not dry-eyed that night. . . . He knew he had been a disappointment to the Lord; he had been a groveler. But with the revelation he received as he wrestled that night, there was the possibility of being transformed from the supplanter to a prince of God.[4]

Overcoming Struggles

> The darkness of <u>fear</u> often prevents us from clearly seeing God's best for our lives. God might have sent the fear so that we would wrestle with him. In that case, the fearsome circumstance will not fade until it has changed us. God always has a <u>purpose</u> for our good in the things we go through, even the darkness of fear.

☞ **GO TO:**

Isaiah 21:4 (fear)

Jeremiah 29:11 (purpose)

Genesis 33:1–20 Jacob encountered Esau and was surprised to find that Esau no longer wanted to kill him. Instead, Esau welcomed him into the area and even offered to help. But Jacob refused and they parted company.

Whew! Esau Got Over It!

Jacob's prayer for deliverance from Esau's revenge was answered. Jacob speaks to his brother in humble terms and makes sure his generous gifts are seen as sharing a portion of the blessing he took with him originally.

What Others are Saying:

Bruce H. Wilkinson and Larry Libby: God shows through the life of Jacob the bankruptcy of manipulating people to get your own way. Jacob had manipulation down to a science but it wasn't God's way. Jacob refused God's way, refused God's timing. In so doing, he refused God's best.[5]

Something to Ponder

When fear turns into worry, it makes us focus on the problem rather than seeing the opportunity for God's blessings. When Jacob was fearful, he couldn't imagine his brother could be at peace with him. For Jacob and for us, worry enlarges the problem and diminishes God's abilities. Instead, God wants us to <u>trust</u> him. <u>Faith</u> is the ability to look past the problem and focus on God's great power to help us.

☞ **GO TO:**

Isaiah 41:13 (trust)

1 Corinthians 2:5 (faith)

THE BIG PICTURE

> **Genesis 34:1–31** Jacob's daughter Dinah visited the nearby people of the land and was raped by one of the men there named Shechem. Shechem wanted to marry her but Jacob's sons wouldn't allow it. Instead, Dinah's brothers devised a plan to deceive the men of the country and kill them. Jacob was unhappy about their behavior but seemed **impotent** to control his children.

impotent: powerless

Sons Out Of Control

Jacob missed the opportunity to demonstrate real leadership after his daughter's rape. Justice was needed; however, Jacob was willing to compromise this evil by allowing the rapist to marry his daughter. He failed to take responsibility and exert leadership for his family. As a result, his sons hatched the plan to seemingly permit the marriage. Jacob should have known something was brewing. When his sons acted out their vengeful plan, the result was murderous bloodshed.

KEY POINT

We never need to worry because the God who cares for us is powerful.

What Others are Saying:

Gene A. Getz: Rather than dealing with his sons' murderous actions, Jacob was primarily concerned about his own status and welfare. Consequently, Jacob left the area of Shechem, traveled to Bethel and eventually Hebron.[6]

LEADERSHIP **PRINCIPLE**—As leaders we need to ask the hard questions to ensure the mission and vision for our plans are followed with integrity. Usually those we are responsible for will not directly lie to us, but instead won't volunteer bad news unless directly asked. It is the leader's responsibility to ensure accountability by asking those questions, even if we know the answers will contain information we really don't want to hear.

THE BIG PICTURE 🔍

> **Genesis 35:1–29** God appeared to Jacob and told him to go to Bethel. Because Jacob intended to worship God there, he told his family to rid themselves of all their idols and lucky charms. He arrived in Bethel with his large family and made an altar in honor of God. God, in return, again promised Jacob he would be the father of many nations. Rachel died there giving Jacob his last child: the beloved Benjamin. Isaac, Jacob's father, also died there.

☞ **GO TO:**

1 John 5:21 (idols)

House Cleaning

When Jacob traveled to Bethel with his wife Rachel, he did not know she secretly possessed <u>idols</u> (see illustration, this page). Fortunately, he took a strong leadership position and ordered his household to get rid of their gods.

Charles R. Swindoll: Waste no time in asking God to help you realize and remove any idols that are usurping His place in your heart.[7]

What Others are Saying:

Teraphim

Rachel probably possessed idols like the Assyrian teraphim, whose name means "vile things."

Many in his family gave Jacob their earrings, not because jewelry in itself was evil, but because in Jacob's day they were often worn as good luck charms. His family chose to cleanse themselves of all pagan influences, including reminders of any foreign gods of their old country.

What idols do you have? Idols are not just things. They can be jobs, desires, or thoughts. An idol is anything that is more important to us than obeying or loving God. Like Jacob, we should get rid of anything that can stand between God and us. If we don't, it can ruin our faith.

THE BIG PICTURE 🔍

Genesis 37:1–36 Jacob again experienced deception, but this time, didn't know it. His sons sold one of their youngest brothers, Joseph, into slavery because they were jealous of Joseph's standing in the family. The brothers made it look like a wild animal had killed him. They smeared his coat with blood and showed it to Jacob. When Jacob saw it, he deeply mourned.

Deceived Again

How many times must Jacob be subjected to painful trials? It happened over and over again because of the inner core of his family. His children were acting just like Jacob when he was young. But Jacob kept <u>creating</u> his own troubles through the favoritism he openly demonstrated to his son Joseph.

☞ GO TO:

Proverbs 19:3 (creating)

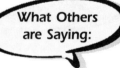
**What Others
are Saying:**

Gene A. Getz: In some respects Jacob knew his sons well. In other respects he did not know them at all. He understood their outward behavior, but he knew little of their inner feelings. If he had, he would not have set Joseph up for such a bad experience.[8]

Grow Your Family

A parent must consider each child unique and different. There isn't any one response that is appropriate for every child in every circumstance. What is appropriate for one may not be right for the other. However, trying to treat each child appropriately may cause siblings to accuse you of favoritism. The different ways we respond to each child need to be handled with great care.

It may be natural for parents to be drawn toward one child over the other because of a preferred personality or skills, but openly demonstrating those feelings without regard to the other children is damaging to the family.

> **Genesis 42–46** Joseph ended up becoming first in command after Pharaoh in Egypt. When there was a famine in the land, Jacob sent his sons to Egypt to buy grain. They encountered Joseph, and he eventually sent them back to bring Jacob along with all he owned to live in Egypt. Jacob was thrilled to see Joseph again.

Family Restored

Imagine losing your favorite son. Things can't get worse, right? Never say that, because the next thing that happened was a devastating famine that made everything die. Faced with starvation, Jacob sent his sons to Egypt to buy food. When they returned, his youngest son had been held hostage. Reaching the end of his emotional and spiritual rope, Jacob heard God's command to go to Egypt. God reassured Jacob He would be with him and take care of him there.

Most of the time when God is leading us, he will give us an assurance of his will through the supernatural <u>peace</u> that accompanies his guidance. That doesn't always happen, but it can be a sign that he is indeed leading us. But we also need to make sure:

- The guidance we're hearing is in line with the Bible.
- It fits with the circumstances that accompany it.
- The direction has been <u>affirmed</u> as being from God.

Remember This . . .

☞ **GO TO:**

Philippians 4:9 (peace)

Proverbs 22:17 (affirmed)

> **Genesis 47:1–31** Joseph introduced Jacob to Pharaoh, and he gave Jacob and his family permission to settle in Goshen where they could raise their flocks. Separated from the Egyptians his family thrived and was not tempted to intermarry with them.

Retirement Home Found

Playing out the last dramatic scene of his life, Jacob was an old man in Pharaoh's court. He had just been embraced by his lost son, Joseph, who was now the number two man in the most powerful country on earth. Jacob's clan had been delivered from the famine, and they had all the food they could eat. He told the Pharaoh his years had been *"few and difficult."* Yet Jacob could tell a story of survival:

- God had delivered him from a family model of deceit and manipulation.

- When Esau threatened him, God protected him.
- When Laban tried to destroy him, God prospered him.
- God delivered his wife, Rachel, and family from idolatry.
- God saved his family from famine.
- God promised that his sons would be the patriarchs of a future land and leaders over their own tribes.

The Lord had kept his every word to Jacob.

What Others are Saying:

Something to Ponder

☞ **GO TO:**

Deuteronomy 32:4 (faithful)

Hebrews 13:8 (never changes)

Psalm 111:5 (forgets)

KEY POINT

Jacob's life demonstrates God's faithfulness.

Something to Ponder

Kay Arthur: When you need assurance that God is there, that He will keep His promises without changing—even though you have wavered in your promises to Him—run to your Jehovah. Trust in His name. It can't change because He can't change.[9]

God is <u>faithful</u> and consistent. He <u>never changes</u> or <u>forgets</u> to keep his promises. He can do that because he has the wisdom to promise the right thing and the power to bring it to completion. Just as he was faithful to Jacob, he is faithful to you.

THE BIG PICTURE 🔍

> **Genesis 48:1–50:3** When he was 147 years old, Jacob called all of his sons to him for the patriarchal blessing. He first prophesied over Joseph's sons and then over each of his own sons. Through God's power and insight, Jacob predicted the future of each of these twelve tribes of Israel. Then Jacob died and was buried.

Predicting The Future Of The Tribes Of Israel

Once a deceitful, independent, and conniving man, Jacob on his deathbed was now marked by total dependence on God. The transformation was complete. Jacob gathered his children and grandchildren around him for a final talk and blessing.

Jacob's life was a constant struggle. As troubles rolled over him, he drew closer to God. Can you trust God when trials are directed at you? Remember, it was the trials that proved God's faithfulness to Jacob. Expect no less in your life. "*A righteous man may have many troubles, but the Lord delivers him from them all*" (Psalm 34:19).

Study Questions

1. Of their sons, whom did Rebekah favor and whom did Isaac favor? Why?
2. How were Rebekah and Jacob able to deceive Isaac into giving Jacob the blessing instead of Esau?
3. What explanation did Laban give for substituting Leah for Rachel on Jacob's wedding night?
4. What does Jacob's new name "Israel" mean?
5. Why did Jacob think Joseph had died?

CHAPTER WRAP-UP

- Jacob was born as a twin and demonstrated his true colors right from the start by grabbing his older brother's heel during birth. God declared to his mother that Jacob would someday be the heir to the birthright instead of Esau. (Genesis 25:19–34)

- Favoritism by the parents found each one manipulating circumstances. Jacob tricked Esau into selling his birthright for some stew. (Genesis 25:29–34)

- After Jacob and his mother deceived Isaac into giving Jacob the patriarchal blessing instead of Esau, Isaac had to run for his life because Esau vowed to kill him. (Genesis 27:1–28:7)

- Jacob arrived in his mother's homeland and immediately met and fell in love with Rachel, his cousin. He worked for seven years to gain her as his wife, but was deceived into marrying her sister, Leah, by their father, Laban. Jacob had to work another seven years to gain Rachel. By being married to both of them and their maids, he became the father of twelve sons. (Genesis 28:10–30:43)

- God prospered Jacob so much that he wanted to return to his home country. He left with his family without telling Laban. While running away, Jacob had an encounter with God and was renamed "Israel." His character had been changed. (Genesis 31–32)

- After reuniting with a forgiving Esau, Jacob settled down. He was deceived again when his sons sold their brother Joseph into slavery. Thinking Joseph was dead, Jacob grieved. Years later he found out Joseph was actually alive in Egypt. Jacob was reunited with Joseph and settled in Egypt, where he died. (Genesis 33–50)

5 JOSEPH: THE OBEDIENT SERVANT

Let's Get Started

No one likes trials. They try our patience and make us wonder if God really loves us (or even likes us). Joseph, the great-grandson of Abraham, could have had those thoughts many times, because he was tested to the ultimate.

Joseph was hated by his brothers, sold into slavery, falsely accused of rape, and forgotten after giving good news. Time after time bad things happened to him, and he never did anything wrong. Talk about being misunderstood!

Yet, Joseph consistently trusted God, didn't complain, stayed pure, and forgave those who meant him harm. In the end, he summarized his life by saying God had it all planned out and meant it for his good and the benefit of many people. Talk about faith! Joseph had a lot of it, and we'll be inspired to have more of it as we learn about him.

> **Genesis 30:22–24** Then God remembered Rachel; he listened to her and opened her womb. She became pregnant and gave birth to a son and said, "God has taken away my disgrace." She named him Joseph, and said, "May the Lord add to me another son."

A Future Prime Minister Is Born

Jacob and Rachel had been married a long time, but Rachel hadn't been able to have children. Leah, Jacob's first <u>wife</u> and Rachel's sister, had given birth to many children and this caused Rachel to feel jealous. She'd even <u>given</u> her maid to Jacob so that she could claim

☞ **GO TO:**

Genesis 29:25 (wife)

Genesis 30:3 (given)

to have children, but she'd never had the satisfaction of holding her own baby. Finally, Rachel became pregnant, and the favored child of the favored wife became a reality. That was Joseph.

What Others are Saying:

Remember This . . .

capriciously: for no good reason

KEY POINT

God is never late and never in a hurry.

Leslie Flynn: For twelve years he was not only the only son of Rachel, but the youngest of all Jacob's sons. He undoubtedly received a lot of attention, for with his half-brothers grown, father Jacob had more time to enjoy the little lad.[1]

God always knows his purposes for everything he does and allows. He doesn't **capriciously** plan to bring harm or trials upon certain people for the fun of it. Instead, *"For I know the plans I have for you," declares the Lord, "plans to prosper you and not to harm you, plans to give you hope and a future. Then you will call upon me and come and pray to me, and I will listen to you. You will seek me and find me when you seek me with all your heart"* (Jeremiah 29:11–13). Always, his intention is to draw us closer to him with everything he does.

THE BIG PICTURE

Genesis 37:1–11 Jacob favored Joseph above his other ten children. That wasn't lost on those other sons. Joseph made the situation worse by voicing his dreams that symbolized his father, mother, and stepbrothers would one day bow down before him.

Joseph, The Naïve Dreamer

Young people often speak their thoughts without realizing the impact their words have on others. Joseph knew his father favored him. As a teenager he likely reminded his brothers of that fact. Who would mentor him toward maturity and gracious behavior? His brothers were older but wouldn't; they were angry because he was the one who was always right. His love of the Lord had caused him to tell his father about his brothers' immoral lifestyle. His heart was sensitive to the God of heaven and was appalled at the sin in their lives. But his report further angered his brothers.

His father, Jacob, was unable to mentor him because he was fueling the conflict with favoritism. Jacob just threw gasoline into the fire by giving Joseph a multi-colored robe. This publicly signified that Jacob favored Joseph and intended to give him all or a larger portion of the inheritance.

Allen P. Ross: God's sovereign choice of a leader often brings out the jealousy of those who must submit. Their actions, though prompted by the belief that they should lead, shows why they should not have led.[2]

Joseph might have contributed to his brothers' envy, but they had already rejected everything their father held dear. In that day, God-given dreams were synonymous with hearing the voice of God. His brothers only heard bitter complaints from each other—blocking out God's voice.

Remember This . . .

BUILD YOUR SPIRIT: When our hearts are focused on the righteousness of God, some resent it. When we make known all that is spiritually dear to us, it may become a **reproach** to others. That shouldn't prevent us from <u>standing</u> for godliness and <u>speaking</u> gently of our faith. We know we will have <u>persecution</u> in this life. Therefore, we shouldn't stop telling what God has done in our lives; however, the Apostle Paul recommends, *"Let your conversation be always full of grace, seasoned with salt, so that you may know how to answer everyone"* (Colossians 4:6).

reproach: reproof

☞ **GO TO:**

1 Corinthians 15:58 (standing)

1 Peter 3:15 (speaking)

1 Thessalonians 3:7 (persecution)

THE BIG PICTURE 🔍

Genesis 37:12–36 The jealousy of Joseph's brothers had increased to the point where they wanted to kill him. They saw their opportunity when Joseph came looking for them out in the wilderness. First, they intended to murder him, but because of Reuben's intervention, they decided to just leave him helpless in a pit. When a train of Midianites passed by, they saw the opportunity to gain some money, and they sold Joseph into slavery. The brothers put goat blood on his multicolored robe and presented it to their father. In great grief, Jacob assumed a wild animal had killed his son. In the meantime, the Midianites sold Joseph to Potiphar in the land of Egypt.

KEY POINT

If we focus on bitterness toward another, we won't hear God.

Sold For Eight Ounces Of Silver

In obedience to his father, Joseph walked 65 miles to find his brothers. Even though he knew his brothers hated him, he went to find them because he wanted to please his father.

Joseph was sold for twenty shekels, which is eight ounces of silver. Once Joseph was sold to the Midianites and then later to Potiphar's household, Joseph began not only slavery, but on-the-job training for maturity and graciousness. He must have wondered how the dreams God had given him squared with being an Egyptian's slave.

What Others are Saying:

Something to Ponder

☞ **GO TO:**

Genesis 27:16
(deceived)

Billy Graham: [Envy] erodes through the soil of the soul, marooning the man who indulges in it on an island of selfishness. In the chemistry of the spirit, no sin is so devastating, no sin can so quickly mar the sweet fellowship between man and God.[3]

How ironic that Jacob was deceived by the goat blood. As a young man, Jacob <u>deceived</u> his father with goat fur to cheat his brother, Esau, out of a blessing. The tables are now reversed. *"A man reaps what he sows"* (Galatians 6:7).

THE BIG PICTURE 🔍

> **Genesis 39:1–6** Joseph served in the home of Potiphar, the Pharaoh's officer and a captain of the bodyguard. Because of God's blessings and divine plan, Joseph had great favor with Potiphar and rose to the position of Potiphar's household manager.

Favor Brings Power

Joseph brought success and wealth to Potiphar's home. His management skills were unsurpassed as he was given control over everything. Potiphar trusted him completely. As Potiphar gave him more power, God blessed Potiphar with more wealth.

What Others are Saying:

Something to Ponder

☞ **GO TO:**

Proverbs 21:1 (king)

Gene A. Getz: It is clear that Potiphar understood that there was a direct cause-effect relationship between Joseph's devotion to God and his successful career as a servant in his household. Consequently, Potiphar looked very favorably on Joseph and promoted him.[4]

When God has a plan in mind that requires you to find favor and value in another person's mind, he can influence that person. Nothing is impossible for God to do—even changing someone's heart and mind. God knew exactly where he wanted Joseph to end up, and it was at the Pharaoh's palace. The favor with Potiphar was one of the steps he was taking to make that possible. No one can escape God's influence, even Pharaoh's officer or a <u>king</u> himself.

Genesis 39:7–23 Potiphar's wife was attracted to Joseph's handsomeness and purity, but when he rebuffed her sexual advances by running away from her, she accused him of raping her. Potiphar believed his wife rather than his servant and threw Joseph into jail. But even in jail, God gave Joseph favor. He became second in command to the chief jailer.

Run, Don't Walk!

Joseph loyally served Potiphar for ten years. The temptation offered by Potiphar's wife was powerful and persistent. He tried to reason with her. He had a duty to Potiphar, and it would be a sin against God. Joseph tried to avoid this woman but ultimately had to run away from her. She struck back (see GWGN, pages 265–266). If she couldn't have him, no one would.

Charles R. Swindoll: Lust is no respecter of persons. No one is immune. You're not. I'm not. And beware—lust never gives up. It never runs out of ideas. How do you handle such an aggressive intruder? Try this: When lust suggests a rendezvous, send Jesus Christ as your representative.[5]

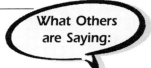

What Others are Saying:

The accusation by Potiphar's wife was likely intended to lead to Joseph's death. Such a betrayal of trust by a slave would normally mean execution. However, Potiphar must have had some doubts because he allowed Joseph to live. Even in jail, his managing prowess caused the chief jailer to promote him. The process started again.

When Joseph first faced temptation he spoke against it. He let Potiphar's wife know that what she proposed was wrong because it would violate the trust her husband held for both of them. He also stressed that it would be an insult and offense to God. When temptation continued to pursue Joseph, he ran! Sometimes reason, prayer, and Scripture quoting are not enough to make people stop tempting us. We must turn, not look back, and <u>run</u>.

Something to Ponder

☞ **GO TO:**

1 Corinthians 6:18 (run)

Genesis 40:1–23 While Joseph was serving in the Egyptian jail, Pharaoh's baker and cup bearer were thrown into jail. They had dreams they couldn't interpret, but Joseph could. He predicted the baker would be hanged, but the cup bearer would be restored to the Pharaoh's favor. Joseph asked the cup bearer to remember him when that happened because, he explained, he had been sold into slavery and imprisoned without just cause. Just as Joseph predicted, the cup bearer was restored; but he forgot about Joseph.

Don't Forget Me When You're Restored To Your Position

Another evidence of God's favor upon Joseph was his remarkable gift of interpreting dreams that no one else could understand (see GWDN, pages 267–271). Joseph clearly sought to faithfully serve others, deriving his sense of significance from his relationship with God. And despite his incredible hardships, Joseph must have sensed that God was truly with him. Joseph's on-the-job training was painful, yet he remained faithful.

Patrick M. Morley: The difference in men is in how we go about satisfying our need to be significant. Some men, eager for the spoils of this life, pursue significance by gratifying only their own ambitions. Others, trained by the scriptures, find it by obeying God.[6]

BUILD YOUR SPIRIT: Like Joseph, we often face troubles in our own lives that are unfair. Just when we think our heartfelt contribution will be graciously accepted, it is misunderstood and thrown back in our face. In those times we are faced with a choice. Everything inside us wants to defend and explain our actions. Our hurt seems to take precedence and self-interest takes over. Joseph was more interested in God's interests. God was with him and gave him strength to persevere. It is no different for us. God promises to be with us and never leave us. When we can set aside our self-interest, we will walk with integrity.

KEY POINT

God wants us to be faithful even when life isn't fair.

What Others are Saying:

Genesis 41:1–36 Two years later, Pharaoh had dreams that his magicians couldn't interpret. The cup bearer then remembered Joseph and told the king about how Joseph interpreted his and the baker's dreams correctly. Joseph was immediately called to Pharaoh's presence and the king explained his dreams to Joseph. Joseph knew God was communicating something important to the Pharaoh and gave God credit for being able to tell him the interpretation of the dream: seven years of bounty and then seven years of famine. Joseph also gave wise advice for managing the coming disaster.

Come! You're Gonna See The Pharaoh!

Joseph put up with two more years of being confined in that stinking, rotten jail before God answered his prayer. Without Joseph's knowledge or influence, God reminded the cup bearer of his experience with Joseph. It was finally the right time for Joseph's deliverance and suddenly he was called before the Pharaoh himself. Joseph must have been relieved but tentative. Was this another ray of hope that would turn disastrous?

Matthew Henry: Great gifts appear most graceful and illustrious when those that have them use them humbly, and take not the praise of them to themselves, but give it to God. To such, God gives more grace.[7]

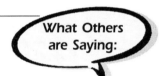

What Others are Saying:

Joseph took a great risk by speaking of Jehovah, the Hebrew's God, when Pharaoh didn't believe in him. Pharaoh could have immediately scoffed at such nonsense and thrown the Israelite back into prison. But Joseph's integrity remained intact, and he again faithfully told the truth as he had so many times before.

Remember This . . .

BUILD YOUR SPIRIT: When bringing problems to others, particularly your superiors, give some thought to the solution. Be willing to offer your suggestions to resolve the issue. Ask if they would be interested in your opinion. This accomplishes four things:

- Dilutes the appearance of finger pointing
- Demonstrates your willingness to work as a team member

- Shows respect for the other person
- Allows you the opportunity to contribute to the success of the job or project

THE BIG PICTURE 🔍

> **Genesis 41:37–57** The Pharaoh recognized Joseph's wisdom and godliness and put him second in command to manage food for the coming fourteen years. Additionally, Pharaoh gave Joseph the daughter of one of his priests in marriage and two sons were born to him. Just as Joseph predicted, the seven years of bounty arrived and then the seven years of famine. It affected all the known earth.

From Prison To The Palace

Pharaoh asked his advisors, *"Can we find anyone like this man, one in whom is the spirit of God?"* (Genesis 41:38). When everyone admitted no one was as wise as Joseph, Pharaoh promoted Joseph by:

- Giving him his signet ring
- Dressing him in expensive clothes and jewelry
- Naming him second in command
- Giving him permission to ride in the second chariot and receive everyone's adulation
- Presenting his daughter, Asenath, to him as his wife
- Giving him an Egyptian name, Zaphenath-Paneah

All this happened when Joseph was only thirty years old.

What Others are Saying:

☞ **GO TO:**

Romans 8:11 (dwells)

Something to Ponder

Merrill F. Unger: A seal is a portable instrument used to stamp a document or other article, instead of or with signing manually. The impression made therewith had the same legal validity as an actual signature, as is still the case in the east. Indeed, the importance attached to this method is so great that, without a seal, no document is considered authentic.[8]

Picture standing in front of the President of the United States. He points at you and tells his advisors that the Spirit of God is in you, then appoints you to a Cabinet post. What an honor for you and God. The Bible tells us the Spirit <u>dwells</u> within us when we accept Christ. It is only when we yield our will and behavior to the Spirit that God will use us to influence others as he did with Joseph.

It took thirteen years for Joseph to go from slave to servant/manager, then to inmate/manager, and finally to prince/manager. The on-the-job training was over and God was ready to <u>complete</u> his plan through Joseph. He had been faithful in all the little things he experienced throughout the long years that he'd been separated from his home and family. Now his integrity and faithfulness were paying off with great interest. God always rewards his children who serve him faithfully; if not here on earth, for sure in heaven.

THE BIG PICTURE

> **Genesis 42:1–24** The famine also affected Jacob and his family back in Canaan. When they heard there was food in Egypt to be bought, Jacob sent his ten oldest sons to buy grain for them. When they arrived, Joseph saw his brothers and recognized them, but they didn't recognize him. (He would have been groomed in Egyptian fashions, including face makeup.) He accused them of being spies and put them in prison. Later, he released them, ordering that one of the brothers must remain to guarantee the other brothers would return later. Plus, the youngest brother must return with them if they wanted any future grain purchases. While there, the brothers became sorrowful for what they did to Joseph many years earlier.

The Testing Of The Brothers Begins

What went on in Joseph's emotions when he saw his brothers? **Ambivalence**? Joy? Defensiveness? He must have been greatly suspicious when his full brother, Benjamin, wasn't with them. Had the brothers attacked—even killed—him too?

Since his half-brothers did not recognize him, Joseph devised a plan to return the family to Egypt and test the hearts of his brothers. Joseph caused them to experience what he had experienced—prison, false accusations, and fear.

Leslie Flynn: Some argue that Joseph could have dispatched a messenger to tell Jacob that he was alive, but such news might have incited revenge by the father on the brothers. Also, didn't Joseph's dreams indicate his family would some day bow down to him? Joseph suspected that sooner or later the famine would drive the brothers down to Egypt to come knocking at his door for grain. Then he could seek reunion with his father.[9]

Remember
This . . .

☞ **GO TO:**

Philippians 1:6
(complete)

ambivalence: simultaneous contradictory feelings

What Others
are Saying:

☞ GO TO:

Genesis 37:6–8
(dreams)

When the brothers appeared before him and bowed down to him as ruler, Joseph's <u>dreams</u> from many years earlier were fulfilled. The brothers had mocked him for his "foolish" notions of grandeur, but Joseph carried the confidence all those years that God's revelation to him would be carried out. And it was.

THE BIG PICTURE 🔎

> **Genesis 42:25–43:15** When Joseph dismissed the brothers from Egypt, he kept Simeon imprisoned and put the money they paid for the grain back into their sacks. One of the brothers discovered it while returning home; the rest found theirs when they arrived home. They told their father about their experience and wanted to go back to get Simeon, but Jacob refused to allow his youngest son to be taken from him. Eventually, the grain the brothers brought from Egypt ran out, and they were forced to return. Jacob finally agreed to allow Benjamin to join them, only after one of the brothers, Judah, guaranteed he would bring Benjamin home safely.

The Return Trip With Benjamin In Tow

The insight, courage, and thoroughness Joseph put into his plan was remarkable. His arrangement of the money in the sacks guaranteed the brothers would feel the same kind of fear he had experienced when sold into slavery. The tables had turned. Suffering and conflict found their way into the lives of his brothers. Joseph used this opportunity to effectively bring them to a point of **repentance** with the threat of a spying conviction. The final exam was about to be administered.

repentance: turning away from sin

What Others are Saying:

KEY POINT

Guilt is God's way of motivating us to repent and seek forgiveness.

Patrick M. Morley: Men suffer for seven reasons:

- An innocent mistake
- An error in judgment
- An integrity problem
- The environment changes
- Evil happens
- God disciplines
- God tests.[10]

The brothers were being tested as Joseph had been tested over the years. Would they refuse to return to Egypt, sacrificing the brother left behind? When they found the money in their sacks, would they take it for themselves or report it to Joseph? They were beginning to make right choices. They were willing to return to Egypt with Benjamin, and they reported finding the money to Joseph.

THE BIG PICTURE 🔍

> **Genesis 43:16–44:34** Back in Egypt, Joseph saw the brothers arrive, with Benjamin. Joseph commanded that they be brought to his home for the noon meal where he accepted their gift and asked them about their father. Seeing his blood brother, Benjamin, made Joseph cry, and he had to excuse himself. But after controlling himself he returned to finish the meal. Joseph dismissed all the brothers but arranged for one of his silver cups to be put into Benjamin's sack. When they had gone a short distance, Joseph sent his steward to intercept them, find the cup in the sack, and accuse Benjamin of stealing. This was a test of the brothers' loyalty to their stepbrother, something they'd lacked with Joseph. When they were brought before Joseph again, Judah demonstrated he had changed because he offered to become a slave in Benjamin's place.

Another Test

When Joseph's servant made the accusation against Benjamin, the brothers were shocked. They tore their clothes in grief, the very thing their <u>father</u> had done when he learned of Joseph's bloodied coat. Judah, who promised Jacob he would be responsible for Benjamin, begged Joseph to take him as a slave in the place of the youngest brother. It had been Judah who suggested selling Joseph into slavery years before. Now he willingly sacrificed himself. There was no finger pointing from any of the brothers. They didn't try to justify what had happened. God's plan to bring them to a point of submission, sorrow, and ultimately repentance for selling Joseph into slavery was effective.

Gene A. Getz: Joseph had no doubt instructed the steward to tell them before he conducted his investigation that whoever had the cup would become a slave and the rest were free to go. Twenty-two years before, there was no question what they would have

Something to Ponder

☞ **GO TO:**

Genesis 37:34 (father)

What Others are Saying:

done. And Judah would have taken the lead in suggesting that Benjamin bear the blame and become a slave. But their reactions this time were different. Together they returned to Egypt.[11]

BUILD YOUR SPIRIT: We have sinned against God time and again. But each time God graciously forgives us if we turn from our sin. *"For as high as the heavens are above the earth, so great is his love for those who fear him; as far as the east is from the west, so far has he removed our transgressions from us"* (Psalm 103:11–12).

THE BIG PICTURE

Genesis 45:1–20 At Judah's sacrificial offer, Joseph became emotionally overwhelmed and revealed himself to his brothers. He immediately tried to comfort them, knowing they would be upset with themselves over their past choices. He didn't want them to mourn past sins. He expressed his faith and knowledge that God had used their cruelty for the good of the people of the land by giving him the wisdom to deal with the famine. He told them to bring his father, Jacob, to him in Egypt so that they all would be safe in the remaining five years of the famine.

Joseph's Shocking Revelation

Joseph told his brothers that God was behind all these events! *"And now, do not be distressed and do not be angry with yourselves for selling me here, because it was to save lives that God sent me ahead of you. So then, it was not you who sent me here, but God"* (Genesis 45:5, 8). What a scene that must have been. Like a deer frozen in approaching headlights, the brothers probably stood with open mouths. They heard the words, but I doubt they grasped their significance. Even though Joseph kissed and hugged them, deep down inside they probably still feared him.

What Others are Saying:

Max Lucado: Because Jacob's boys are as greedy as they are mean, Joseph is sold to some southbound gypsies and he changes history. Joseph eventually stands before his brothers—this time with them asking for his help. And he is wise enough to give them what they ask and not what they deserve.[12]

As a symbol of Christ, Joseph represented how Jesus was willing to endure the great suffering of dying on a <u>cross</u> knowing it was all part of his Father's plan for the <u>salvation</u> of the people of the world. It also gave Jesus the ability to <u>understand</u> the temptations and difficulties that humans face. As a result, he is better able to pray for us as our <u>intercessor</u> before God's throne.

☞ **GO TO:**

Matthew 27:38 (cross)

Luke 1:77 (salvation)

Hebrews 4:15 (understand)

Romans 8:27 (intercessor)

James 1:2–4 (stronger)

BUILD YOUR SPIRIT: Remember: the ugliest, most painful, and most ragged spots in our lives can be changed into glory for God. The failures we face today are often the foundation God uses to build a positive impact in the lives of others. Rarely do we reflect on how the good times shaped our lives. It is always the trouble we walk through that makes us <u>stronger</u>.

THE BIG PICTURE 🔍

Genesis 45:21–47:12 The brothers returned home and gave the amazing news to Jacob that his son, Joseph, was still alive. Jacob was shocked to find out Joseph was second in charge in Egypt and overwhelmed with joy to know he would see his favored son again. Jacob took his family to Egypt where he saw Joseph again and rejoiced in God's blessings. Joseph arranged for his family to meet Pharaoh. Taking advantage of an Egyptian prejudice, Joseph ordered his clan to say they were shepherds. That way, they would live separately from the other Egyptians. The Pharaoh placed them in charge of his own livestock.

Movin' Time!

Jacob moved everything he owned from the land he knew to Egypt. He saw Joseph, the son he thought long dead, for the first time in thirteen years. The fulfillment of God's plan was occurring just as intended. All that had happened was God's way of pulling his chosen people out of the land of the Canaanites, so he could grow them into a huge nation without evil influence. And grow they did! For the next two centuries the Israelites lived in Goshen while their population grew to about two million. God used Joseph's faithfulness and willingness to work for the greater good of others.

What Others are Saying:

Overcoming Struggles

KEY POINT

God's ways are mysterious and sometimes beyond our <u>comprehension</u>.

☞ **GO TO:**

2 Corinthians 1:3, 4 (share)

Isaiah 55:3 (comprehension)

Canaan: the territory promised to Abraham's descendants; thus, "the promised land"

What Others are Saying:

Remember This . . .

Philip Yancey: Through all his trials, Joseph learned to trust, not that God would prevent hardship, but that he would redeem even hardship.[13]

Although God can give instantaneous deliverance from the struggles we face, it is often his plan to have us go through pain and slowly learn ways of deliverance from the journey. As a result, we'll gain more and have something to <u>share</u> with others in their journey.

THE BIG PICTURE 🔎

Genesis 47:13–49:33 Joseph continued to prove himself an effective and efficient manager, bringing great wealth into Pharaoh's administration as people from all over the world came to Egypt to buy food. Eventually, as the famine got worse, the people were forced to sell their land to Joseph. Joseph then rented the land back to them to farm it.

A Drive Down Memory Lane

Before Joseph died, he requested that when his father's descendants returned to **Canaan**, his bones be carried back to be buried there. This confirmed his belief that the children of Israel would one day fulfill God's promise to Abraham that they would own a great amount of land and be a great nation of people.

Joseph was trained in pain. He was strengthened by deception and became patient through imprisonment. Troubles seemed to wash over Joseph most of his life. After all the affliction and his rise to power, he was faced with the emotionally painful challenge of testing and reuniting his family. Yet faith (see GWGN, pages 296–297), skill, and integrity marked his life. God gave him favor and under the Lord's guidance, Joseph developed the character to persevere.

Edwin Louis Cole: Every man is limited by three things: The knowledge in his mind. The strength of his character. The principles upon which he builds his life.[14]

Stephen, one of the New Testament followers of Jesus, used an example from Joseph's life in his <u>sermon</u> to defend his faith before the Jewish High Council. Joseph is also mentioned in the Hebrews book of <u>Hall of Faith</u>. Just as Joseph's example of integrity and trust in God has inspired many through the ages, God wants to use our lives to represent him.

🚸 **BUILD YOUR SPIRIT:** One of the keys for building our spiritual strength is to <u>review</u> how God has been faithful in the past. That will strengthen our faith and dependence upon him. The Bible is basically a record of God's workings and a revelation of his character. As we review what he did in the lives of Biblical characters like Joseph, and then what he has done in our own life, we'll become spiritually strong, knowing we can face any situation, just like Joseph did.

Study Questions

1. Why did Jacob love Joseph more than his other sons?
2. How did Reuben save Joseph's life?
3. What means did God use to bring Joseph to the attention of Pharaoh?
4. In what two ways did Joseph cause his brothers to come to a point of surrender?
5. When Joseph revealed himself to his brothers, what were they afraid of?

CHAPTER WRAP-UP

- Joseph's father Jacob favored him over his brothers. Joseph had a dream that indicated his father and brothers would bow down to him, and he told them about it, making the brothers jealous. (Genesis 37:3–11)

- All that favoritism poisoned the family relationships and created distrust, unhappiness, and anger. Without Jacob's knowledge, Joseph's brothers sold him into slavery for eight ounces of silver. (Genesis 37:18–28)

- From slavery Joseph rose to managing an important household. He was falsely accused of rape by his employer's wife and thrown into prison. While there, he interpreted the dreams of some of the Pharaoh's employees, and when Pharaoh had a dream, Joseph was brought to the palace to interpret it. Through all the difficulties Joseph faced, he didn't complain to God. (Genesis 39–41)

☞ **GO TO:**

Acts 7:13 (sermon)

Hebrews 11:22 (Hall of Faith)

Romans 15:4 (review)

KEY POINT

Character does count, but it takes work.

- While in charge of Pharaoh's food program during a famine, Joseph saw his brothers come to buy grain. He tested them to make sure they had changed their attitudes. He engineered a plan that revealed that the brothers were willing to sacrifice themselves for each other. (Genesis 42–44)

- When Joseph knew they had changed, he revealed himself as their long-lost brother and restored the family by bringing everyone together in Egypt. After Jacob died, the brothers feared Joseph would take revenge on them. But Joseph showed his faith by telling them God meant everything that had happened to work for their good. (Genesis 45–47)

6 MOSES: THE MAN OF HUMILITY AND STRENGTH

CHAPTER HIGHLIGHTS

- Moses Saved as a Child
- Moses Flees Egypt
- Moses Meets God
- Moses Confronts Pharaoh
- Moses Leads the Israelites

Let's Get Started

Humility and strength are elusive yet important character traits that develop while we're not even trying for them. God performed that kind of development in Moses by taking him through many difficult trials. He had an encounter with God, was challenged to become a leader when he didn't believe he could, led a huge group of people who didn't want to follow, and communicated God's important Law to a skeptical, burgeoning Israelite nation.

Yet, in the midst of so many challenges, Moses stayed faithful and true. Of course, he had his ups and downs, at times feeling discouraged and even wanting to quit, but he was always willing to do what God wanted. Because he was more concerned about God's reputation than his own, God called Moses the most humble man on earth. What a distinction—one we all should shoot for.

THE BIG PICTURE

> **Exodus 2:1–10** A Levite and his wife gave birth to a son, who, according to Pharaoh's instructions, should have been killed (see illustration, page 72). But they courageously kept him hidden until he was too old to hide any longer. Moses' mother, Jochebed, put him in a basket and then into the Nile River. The Pharaoh's daughter found him on the river and adopted him as her son, calling him Moses.

From Death Row To The Palace

The Israelites in Egypt had grown to such proportions that they were perceived as a threat by their Egyptian neighbors. Therefore,

☞ **GO TO:**

Exodus 1:14 (serve)

they were put into bondage to <u>serve</u> as brick-makers and field hands. They continued to multiply anyway. To stop this, Pharaoh made a law that all of the male babies born to the Hebrew women must be killed. Abraham's descendants cried out to God to help them. That's why God raised up Moses.

What Others are Saying:

Bruce H. Wilkinson and Larry Libby: At the age of 40, when Moses faced a major crossroads, the simple values instilled by his Hebrew mother when he was still a young child outweighed the influence of a prestigious education.[1]

Something to Ponder

Moses' mother, Jochebed, was brave in hiding her son and then trusting God enough to let him float down a river. After he was plucked from the river and made the son of the Pharaoh's daughter, Jochebed became his wet nurse. We don't know how many years she had contact with him, but evidently she must have instilled into him some of her courage. Plus, she must have instructed him in the ways of the Lord because Moses <u>knew</u> he was really a Hebrew and not Egyptian in his early years.

☞ **GO TO:**

Exodus 2:11 (knew)

BUILD YOUR SPIRIT: <u>Courage</u> is a sometimes subtle and **elusive** characteristic that can't be developed without having an opportunity to choose it. Courage grows only through facing danger or discouragement and then choosing to continue.

THE BIG PICTURE 🔍

> **Exodus 2:11–25** Moses knew of his heritage. When he had grown, he tried to defend a Hebrew who was being beaten by an Egyptian. He killed the Egyptian and hid the body. Later two Hebrews confronted him about it; then Pharaoh tried to kill him. Afraid, he ran for his life. He ended up in Midian where he found favor with Reuel and married his daughter, Zipporah. In the meantime, the Hebrew people, the Israelites, were tired of being slaves to the Egyptians and kept asking God to deliver them.

From Prince To Shepherd

Privilege and power marked Moses' life. However, when he was faced with the brutal beating of a Hebrew slave, principle overcame preference. In that moment, his passion placed his comfort and position into secondary priorities. When he rescued the slave, Moses knew he put his preference for the palace on the line. But he wasn't quite ready to forsake that privilege and power. He tried to hide the evidence of his crime, hoping to maintain his lifestyle.

But when the crime was revealed and his life was in danger, Moses ran over three hundred miles to Midian. At a well there, he rescued several women from some aggressive shepherds. Those women turned out to be the daughters of Reuel, also known as Jethro. Moses married one of them, Zipporah. As a result, Moses began his family life as a shepherd, far from his destiny in Egypt.

Jamie Buckingham: Jethro, with warm, simple hospitality, helped the former prince of Egypt emerge from his shell of grief and self-pity and enter a world of preparation, a world designed by God to train him for the time he would return to Egypt for a far greater purpose.[2]

LEADERSHIP 🦅 **PRINCIPLE**—Moses' <u>forty</u> years in the wilderness taught him the topography of the land. It would be that very same kind of land that he and the Israelites would travel through during their forty years of wandering in the wilderness. The knowl-

☞ **GO TO:**

Acts 4:13 (courage)

courage: bravery in the face of danger

elusive: hard to find

KEY POINT

Courage is developed as we face difficult choices.

What Others are Saying:

☞ **GO TO:**

Exodus 16:35 (forty)

edge he had gained as a shepherd would be valuable. In the same way, the difficult things we learn as lowly employees later become the valuable information God uses to empower us as leaders.

> Moses must have been discouraged when he ran for his life. But God had a bigger plan, unimaginable to Moses. In the same way, when you and I are discouraged and feel like we've let ourselves or others down, we need to be <u>patient</u> with God's pruning of our character and skills. It takes time to become who God wants us to be. And God isn't impatient about doing that.

Sometimes we forget that our children need to develop slowly. We become <u>impatient</u> with their growth and maturity, thinking they should be like our neighbor's brilliant daughter or our brother's athletic son. <u>Comparing</u> our children to others won't encourage them to grow. We can't force it. All we can do is encourage them with praise and give them consequences for poor choices.

THE BIG PICTURE 🔍

Exodus 3:1–11 God unexpectedly appeared to Moses one day while Moses was up in Mount Horeb tending his flocks. God identified himself as he spoke from a bush that was on fire but didn't burn up. God told Moses that he had picked him to deliver the Israelites from their Egyptian bondage. Moses replied, "Who am I?"

From Shepherd To Seeker

Moses spent his first forty years as a prince and the next forty as a shepherd. That made him eighty years old the day he walked toward the fire of the burning bush. Moses knew something **supernatural** was happening because the bush wasn't **consumed**. Through it, God revealed a portion of his glory to Moses. He told him to return to Egypt and deliver the Hebrews. Moses' reaction? He asked, "Who, me?" Moses immediately recognized even his princely training had not prepared him for this role.

Bruce H. Wilkinson and Larry Libby: In this, Moses' second glimpse of God, he saw a God of grace. A God who not only remembered the anguish of his people back in Egypt, but also the discarded dreams of a discouraged servant. Moses had wanted so much to do something for God. Tried so hard. And failed so mis-

---

Overcoming Struggles

☞ **GO TO:**

Philippians 1:6 (patient)

Grow Your Family

☞ **GO TO:**

Ephesians 6:4 (impatient)

Galatians 6:4 (comparing)

supernatural: *something outside the normal*

consumed: *burned up*

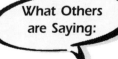
What Others are Saying:

---

erably. But God hadn't written him off as an impetuous bumbler—a hopeless case. Instead, he sent Moses to school.[3]

What Others are Saying:

Jamie Buckingham: At the age of forty, Moses entered God's graduate school. The next forty years were spent in the deprivation of the wilderness. These were years in which his rough edges were sanded smooth. The literal blast of the furnace of the Sinai refined the character of a man God was going to use. There he learned to pray and learned the value of solitude. There, sitting with a few sheep and goats, he learned the principles of leadership.[4]

Something to Ponder

Forty years in Midian prepared Moses for this meeting. Forty years of relative obscurity had readied Moses for a change. Forty years of tending sheep had developed patience and meekness. Those are perfect qualities to lead a multitude for God. The prince turned shepherd was ready to depend upon something other than his own wits.

LEADERSHIP PRINCIPLE—In the hard-charging world of business we hear little of building character traits like patience and meekness. Humility is not embraced by many. However, looking at the enormous job asked of Moses, it was a good thing that those traits were so ingrained they became foundational in his character. On this foundation the strong, confident, and bigger-than-life leader developed. It should be no different for us.

THE BIG PICTURE

> **Exodus 3:12–4:17** Moses was shocked that God had picked him to be the Israelites' deliverer. He argued with God that he wasn't qualified. God answered all his arguments patiently and insisted that Moses would indeed be the person he used.

Not Me, Lord!

Moses said "<u>Here</u> I am," but then he argued with God about how he chose to use him. Moses developed argument after argument against the very goal he'd originally wanted to see happen. Yet God was persistent and didn't give up on Moses. God did end up getting angry with him because Moses' final arguments were no longer out of fear but disobedience.

☞ **GO TO:**

Exodus 3:4 (here)

How God Dealt with a Reluctant Leader

Exodus	Moses' Objection	God's Answer
3:11, 12	I'm not anyone special.	I will be with you.
3:13–22	Who shall I say sent me?	Say, "I AM WHO I AM" sent you.
4:1–9	What if they won't believe me?	Take your staff and I will use it to perform miracles.
4:10–12	I am slow of speech and slow of tongue.	I will teach you what to say.
4:13–17	Send someone else, please!	Your brother, Aaron, will assist you, but you will do it.

BUILD YOUR SPIRIT: Although it shouldn't make us feel free to argue with him, we can count on God being persistent and <u>faithful</u> as he works in our lives. But we'll be happier if we add to our "Here I am," an immediate, "I'll do whatever you say." Arguing will only make us miserable. Why not obey instantly and see God's blessings sooner?

What Others are Saying:

Max Lucado: Do something that demonstrates faith. For faith with no effort is no faith at all. *God will respond.* He has never rejected a genuine gesture of faith. God honors radical, risk-taking faith.[5]

THE BIG PICTURE

☞ **GO TO:**

Deuteronomy 7:9
(faithful)

> **Exodus 4:18–31** Moses obeyed God and after informing his father-in-law of his intentions, took his family back to Egypt. On the way, God almost killed him because Moses hadn't yet circumcised his son. When he wanted to do it, Zipporah became angry and did it herself. As they continued traveling, Aaron met Moses in the desert as God had said he would, and when Moses explained what had happened, Aaron joined him to call the elders together. Those Hebrew leaders believed Moses' account.

Steppin' Out In Faith

God assured Moses that the Pharaoh who had wanted to kill him was now dead. That may have given him more courage to go back. Moses asked for his father-in-law's permission to take his daughter and grandsons with him. Jethro agreed. As Moses traveled, God explained more of the plan that he had in mind. He said to Moses:

- You will perform miracles and wonders.
- I will harden Pharaoh's heart so that he won't let you go.
- You will say to Pharaoh to let the Israelites serve me.
- I will arrange for Pharaoh's firstborn son to be killed.

All those things happened.

John Hercus: Moses was to learn, but he hadn't then learned, that if God asks a man to do something, it is up to God to provide the equipment needed.[6]

When God said he would harden Pharaoh's heart, he was predicting Pharaoh's natural and selfish reaction. He would use that to give Moses an opportunity to perform miracles and thus have God glorified. God didn't remove the ability of Pharaoh to make his own decisions but he knows the condition of everyone's heart, including Pharaoh's. As the encounters between Moses and Pharaoh went along, God would then harden Pharaoh's heart so that further miracles could be done. Eventually, though, when God's purposes were fulfilled, Pharaoh's heart softened, and he let the Israelites leave. Everything that happens in Exodus and in all of our lives is controlled by God's **sovereignty**, while at the same time, he gives us freedom to make our own choices. It's a paradox no one can explain.

Crisis In The Desert

Many commentators are uncertain about the meaning of the experience when Zipporah circumcised Moses' sons. But many agree that Moses became sick, and God revealed that it was because Moses had not circumcised his sons. Since he was going to die, Zipporah circumcised the boys herself even though she didn't agree with the practice. She threw the boys' foreskins at Moses' feet and that symbolized a sort of substitution: obedience for the previous disobedience.

What Others are Saying:

Something to Ponder

☞ **GO TO:**

Habakkuk 3:19 (sovereignty)

sovereignty: totally in control

BUILD YOUR SPIRIT: One of the ways God empowered Moses was to assure him that the Pharaoh who had wanted to kill Moses was now dead. God often deals with our real fears and gives us assurances of how he wants to help us. But if he has answered our fears, and we are being disobedient, God usually isn't quite as quick to give us assurances. He just wants us to obey!

THE BIG PICTURE

> **Exodus 5:1–23** Moses and Aaron went to Pharaoh and demanded that God's people should be allowed to travel three days into the wilderness to sacrifice to their God. But the king didn't like the idea of the Hebrews leaving their work, so he refused and put even more strict requirements upon them. Now they had to find their own straw for making the bricks while keeping the same production quota. When the people's work increased, they blamed Moses, and Moses cried out to God. He couldn't understand why he was encountering obstacles to God's plan.

From Shepherd To Deliverer

Moses knew God had brought him before Pharaoh to deliver the Hebrews from slavery. It was pretty heady stuff and he expected quick results. Moses marched up to Pharaoh, and in the name of the Lord, asked him to free the Hebrews. Shock and dismay swept over Moses when his intervention caused more harm to those he came to help. Not only was Pharaoh resisting him, but also his own people became angry and questioned his mission.

What Others are Saying:

Oswald Chambers: God's Spirit alters the atmosphere of our ways of looking at things, and things begin to be possible which never were possible before. If you are going through a period of discouragement there is a big personal enlargement ahead.[7]

Something to Ponder

Moses' prayer to God demonstrated how he wanted a smooth deliverance and a quick fix to this problem. He couldn't understand why he'd encountered this glitch. He must not have remembered God's previous prediction. God had already told him that Pharaoh's heart would be hardened to the point that his firstborn son would be killed. That hadn't happened yet. To his credit, Moses did immediately seek God.

☞ **GO TO:**

Exodus 4:21 (prediction)

LEADERSHIP 🦅 **PRINCIPLE**—When leading others, sometimes your choices will make things worse. The results of discipline, cutbacks, and even dumb decisions will test your leadership resolve or weaken your confidence. The principles of obedience in Moses' leadership were momentarily overshadowed by this setback even though those principles had moved Moses to Egypt from Midian. When we suffer bad outcomes, we need to make sure our moral compass is still pointing toward the principles and values that honor justice, service, and integrity. If not, correct your course.

THE BIG PICTURE 🔍

Exodus 6:1–12 God replied to Moses' complaint that he was indeed God and in charge of what was happening. God confirmed that he would deliver the Israelites and take them to a new land. When Moses tried to tell the elders about it, they couldn't listen because they were so depressed. So when God told Moses to go back to Pharaoh, Moses again objected, saying he wasn't skilled in his speech.

From Deliverer To Reluctant Leader

God quieted Moses' complaints with detailed instructions on how to lead the children of Israel and deal with Pharaoh. Moses was devastated and his confidence weakened after his attempts to rally the Israelites failed. Moses wasn't the most articulate speaker and again pointed this out to God.

BUILD YOUR SPIRIT: Losing hope creates spiritual deafness. Depression weakens our resolve and makes circumstances appear larger, darker, and more powerful than even God can handle. The Israelites heard a direct promise of deliverance, yet were unable to believe it. We must never allow circumstances to make us deaf to the Word of God.

KEY POINT

If we'll listen, God will tell us his plan. Our job is to stick to it.

THE BIG PICTURE 🔍

Exodus 7:1–11:10 God reassured Moses that he would indeed use him even with unskilled speech, and Aaron would help him. God also explained that even though he would empower them, they would still encounter difficulties because God intended for Pharaoh to be stubborn. That way, God would receive greater glory as he performed miracles that would show his own great power.

Reluctant Leader Sends The Message

Moses and Aaron began their effective ministry with Pharaoh with a string of ten miracles. One of them turned the Nile River's water into blood. With each miracle, the power and influence of God was revealed. Moses' reputation with the Egyptians grew while he led this miracle campaign. The Egyptians worshiped many gods and each miracle revealed how weak their gods were. Since the masses believed that Pharaoh was also a god, the miracles demonstrated his weaknesses. The ten miracles came after Aaron's rod swallowed Pharaoh's magician's rods. This represented God's superior power.

Throughout God's work in the miracles, Moses maintained a consistent trust in God, going back again and again to Pharaoh to tell God's next judgment. Whereas he had been discouraged in the past when God's plan didn't bring immediate results, Moses had developed a strength that believed God was truly in control of everything that was happening.

What Others are Saying:

Charles R. Swindoll: The attack on the Nile struck even deeper at Egypt's spiritual roots. The Nile god, Hapi, was their supreme deity, and the Egyptians, including Pharaoh, often came to the river to worship him. By turning this life source into a bloody stream of death, the Lord stated unequivocally that He was superior to Egypt's greatest deity.[8]

Remember This . . .

The most important purpose of these miraculous plaques was revealed when God said, " . . . *I performed my signs among them, and that you may know that I am the Lord*" (Exodus 10:2). God yearns for relationship with his creation. Miracles and deliverance throughout history are evidence of his efforts to reach out to mankind. Though the deliverance of the Hebrews was mighty, God's greatest act of deliverance came fourteen hundred years later when he allowed Jesus Christ to die on our behalf.

Overcoming Struggles

Moses had become strong in his faith and endurance because of the trials he had faced. God wants us to experience the same thing—even to the point of looking positively on our struggles. "*Consider it pure joy, my brothers, whenever you face trials of many kinds, because you know that the testing of your faith develops perseverance. Perseverance must finish its work so that you may be mature and complete, not lacking anything*" (James 1:2–4).

KEY POINT

When God does miracles, they are intended to reveal him as Sovereign God.

Exodus 12:1–13:16 Even though God caused the first-born sons of the Egyptians to die, he spared the Israelites' homes when they obeyed him and performed the **Passover** feast. Each family sacrificed a lamb and covered the door posts of their houses with the lamb's blood. Additionally, they performed a ceremony of eating unleavened bread and other food in a specific way. These ceremonies became a festival the Israelites celebrate to this day.

When Pharaoh realized his own son and the firstborn sons of all the Egyptians had died, he allowed the Israelites to leave Egypt. The Israelites quickly packed up everything and left Egypt, bringing along some who weren't Hebrews. God gave Moses further instructions about the Passover and how he wanted it to remind them of what God had done in delivering them from their bondage.

Passover: when God "passed over" the Hebrew homes and spared their firstborn sons

Death And Deliverance

The Hebrews were to kill a male lamb that was one year old and put its blood on two door posts of each home. Then they were to eat the meat with unleavened bread and bitter herbs. They were to dine with all their clothes on—ready for the deliverance God was about to do. The blood on the door posts caused God's Spirit to "pass over" those homes when God's judgment of death for the firstborn sons in the Egyptian homes came through the towns.

Not only did God give the Hebrews instructions for fleeing from Egypt, but the instructions included future observance of the Passover Festival. They were instructed to celebrate it every year as a memorial of God's great work on their behalf. Moses made sure the Israelites followed God's command both then and in the future.

The use of blood on the door posts and the Passover celebration all point to the coming Messiah who would shed his blood for the sins of the world. That is why Jesus is called the "Lamb of God." "*In fact, the law requires that nearly everything be cleansed with blood, and without the shedding of blood there is no forgiveness*" (Hebrews 9:22). Jesus **shedding** his blood on the cross made our forgiveness possible.

Something to Ponder

shedding: pouring forth in a stream

> **Exodus 13:17–14:31** Moses led the Israelites out of Egypt, but Pharaoh changed his mind and tried to catch them at the Red Sea. It looked like the Israelites were trapped. God directed Moses to use his staff to divide the waters of the Red Sea. The Israelites crossed over on dry ground. The Egyptians tried to follow, but they drowned when the waters covered them. The Israelites were again saved.

KEY POINT

God wants us to celebrate his work in our lives.

Leader Challenged Again

Two million people were trapped between the Red Sea and the Egyptian army. Duty pressed the Egyptian army forward, but fear and loathing filled most of their hearts. During the past nine months, ten different miracles convinced these Egyptians that the God of Abraham, Isaac, and Jacob was the Hebrews' protector. The facts were clear to them. Their belief was echoed by the fear in their hearts.

Something to Ponder

The Hebrews were also filled with fear as they looked one way and saw the Red Sea and then looked the other way and saw the dust of the massive army closing in. Unlike the Egyptians, they forgot God's miracles and angrily confronted Moses. Imagine the many times he had proved God was with them. Once more his own people turned against him. Moses spoke up and told them, *"Do not be afraid. Stand firm and you will see the deliverance the Lord will bring you today. The Egyptians you see today you will never see again. The Lord will fight for you; you need only to be still"* (Exodus 14:14).

WARNING

As soon as we start fearing, like the Israelites, we are replacing our faith in God with doubt.

LEADERSHIP PRINCIPLE—The importance of Moses' years of humbling in Midian becomes evident, as time and again Moses is the focus of attack. His patience can only be explained as God-inspired. All leaders must be prepared for the criticism, judgment, and anger from those following them. It will come. Just like a toad in a hailstorm, we will have to dodge those missiles of critical comments. To have the strength that Moses had, we need to realize that the comments are not usually personal, but reflect the discomfort of the people.

KEY POINT

Fear feeds on forgetfulness. Remember God's past faithfulness.

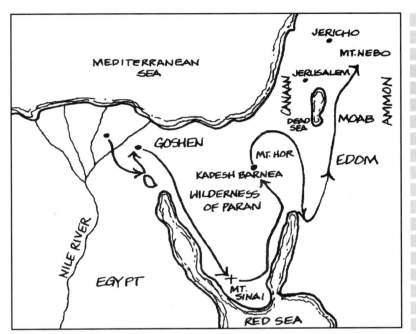

THE BIG PICTURE 🔍

Map of Wilderness Wanderings

When the Israelites left Mount Sinai they traveled to Kadish Barnea, where they rebelled against God. After wandering in the desert for thirty-eight years they traveled north to the plains of Moab. There, just across the Jordan River from the Promised Land, Moses reviewed God's law.

Exodus 15:1–40:38 When Moses and the sons of Israel saw God's deliverance in another miraculous way, they composed a song of praise to God. The women joined them in singing and by playing the timbrel and dancing. Everyone rejoiced because they were finally set free from their bondage in Egypt. Moses continued to lead the Israelites toward the land that God had promised them, a land with *"milk and honey."* As they traveled, they encountered many difficulties that were trials sent by God to make them seek him and depend upon him. Because of that, Moses, as their leader, was challenged over and over again. Each time he asked God for guidance. God always helped him to deal with each situation. During this time in the desert, God also delivered the Ten Commandments to Moses on Mt. Sinai (see illustration, this page).

The Challenges Never Stop Coming

As the Israelites traveled, they weren't a happy group. They complained and blamed Moses for everything. They were unhappy when they didn't have water or food, and they disobeyed God repeatedly. Yet, Moses stayed consistently faithful in representing

God and responding to the people with patience and humility. He resisted taking on the responsibility that only God could shoulder. That's hard to do. If he hadn't resisted, he would have shifted the focus off God and onto himself.

What Others are Saying:

Something to Ponder

Max Lucado: I know what it's like to set out to serve God and end up serving self. I've spoken to conference audiences about the sufferings of Christ and then gotten frustrated that the hotel room wasn't ready. It's easy to forget who is the servant and who is to be served. Satan knows that. This tool of distortion is one of Satan's slyest.[9]

As the Israelites traveled, God communicated with Moses and gave many guidelines for his people, who would occupy the future land of Israel. In each case, Moses passed those rules along to the people clearly and honestly.

THE BIG PICTURE

Numbers 11:1–15 The Israelites continued to travel, and they easily slipped into a negative mindset when they weren't comfortable or happy. In this instance, God disciplined them with a fire that only stopped when Moses prayed. After that, those who weren't Israelite by birth created problems when they affectionately recalled (no doubt with some exaggeration) the different foods that were available to them back in Egypt. They had grown tired of eating the wonderful sweet manna, which God provided daily. Moses also grew tired—tired of the complaints of God's people. He even asked for God to kill him so that he wouldn't have to deal with it anymore.

I Want To Quit, Now!

It's hard to understand why the Israelites continued to be so unhappy. All their physical needs were met by God's direct provision. They were marching to the Promised Land. They could remember miracle upon miracle where God had freed and delivered them, and lit their path. Everything God had promised came true, yet still they grumbled. As a result, Moses was sick of the whining, sniveling malcontents he was leading. He wanted to die rather than lead this ungrateful mob one more step. The only thing that had changed was Moses; the people had grumbled all along. He had hit a dead end (see illustration, page 85).

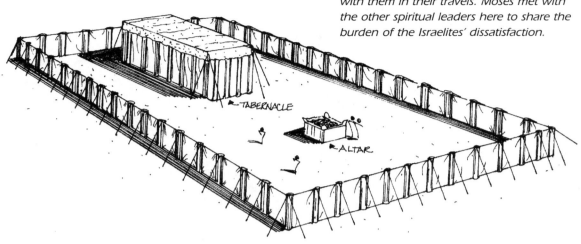

The Wilderness Tabernacle

The Israelites carried a portable tent church with them in their travels. Moses met with the other spiritual leaders here to share the burden of the Israelites' dissatisfaction.

What Others are Saying:

Oswald Chambers: We may have a vision of God, a very clear understanding of what God wants—wrongs to be righted, the salvation of sinners, and the sanctification of believers; we are certain we see the way out, and we start to do the thing. Then comes something equivalent to the forty years in the wilderness: discouragement, disaster, upset, as if God has ignored the whole thing. When we are thoroughly flattened out, God comes back and revives the call.[10]

Moses' cried out to God (Numbers 11:10–15). His discouragement had the common symptoms of burnout and depression. They are:

- Exaggerating the problem
- Blaming God
- Taking responsibility for something that he shouldn't
- Thinking he is responsible to provide for the people
- Focusing on himself
- Forgetting who God is
- Forgetting God's original purpose, provision, and promises

Something to Ponder

☞ GO TO:

Philippians 4:13
(strength)

LEADERSHIP PRINCIPLE—Moses was ready to remove the mantle of leadership that God had given him. He even wanted to die. But God wouldn't allow it. And at times, a leader wants to give up and resign from his position. But if that's not God's will, he shouldn't. Instead, by seeking God as Moses did, he will find God's renewed <u>strength</u>.

THE BIG PICTURE

> **Numbers 12:1–16** Miriam and Aaron, Moses' sister and brother, also began to complain. They were dissatisfied with Moses' leadership because they were jealous that he was in control and honored. God corrected them in person and caused Miriam to have a skin disease that required her to be in solitude outside the camp. She was healed only when Moses prayed for her healing.

Most Humble On Earth

Throughout all the trials and troubles of the past, Aaron and Miriam, Moses' brother and sister, had stood at his side. Aaron was the high priest (see GWBI, page 36) and Miriam a prophetess. They were both joint-commissioners with Moses for the deliverance of Israel. Yet, these trusted siblings and co-laborers chose to criticize Moses' wife instead of dealing with the real issue—their jealousy.

God reacted immediately because the core of his leadership team was about to come apart. This affront demonstrated poor character and poor role modeling because this team lead a people who were disposed to rebellion. He brought all three together and spoke of his special relationship with Moses. Then he dealt with Aaron and Miriam (see GWWB, page 243).

What Others are Saying:

Gene A. Getz: Moses' response to this false criticism immediately revealed who was right and who was wrong. Self-defense is not necessarily wrong, but there are times when it's better to let the truth win out in other ways. Because of his humility and meekness, he did not try to justify himself or to put his brother and sister down.[11]

☞ GO TO:

Exodus 32:4 (golden calf)

LEADERSHIP PRINCIPLE—Moses had boldly defended the honor of God during the <u>golden calf</u> incident. But in this incident, Moses reacted mildly when his own character was attacked. *"Seek the Lord, all you humble of the land, you who do what he com-*

mands. *Seek righteousness, seek humility; perhaps you will be sheltered on the day of the Lord's anger*" (Zephaniah 2:3). Moses was content to battle for the Lord's honor but let his own honor rise or fall on its own merits. Real strength of character is demonstrated when we spend more time building up others, rather than defending ourselves.

THE BIG PICTURE

Numbers 13–36 Moses faithfully guided the Israelites toward the Promised Land even though they disobeyed God many times. They should have immediately gone into the Promised Land, but because of their lack of faith in God's power, they were destined to wander for 40 years in the wilderness. During the wandering, Miriam and Aaron died. Moses continued to lead alone, even though originally he feared he could not.

Keep On Keepin' On

Just before entering the Promised Land, Moses sent twelve leaders into the area to spy out the territory. Ten of them returned with scary tales of giants. The Hebrews grew fearful and had a great meeting where they talked about getting a new leader. Moses and Aaron fell on their faces and only two of the spies, Joshua and Caleb, spoke against the rebellion and challenged the crowd to enter the Promised Land. Their words fell on fearful, deaf ears. The crowd talked of stoning them. Only God's intervention once again saved the faithful few. For their unbelief, God promised that the rebellious adults would never enter the Promised Land. They would die in the desert.

If anything should be remembered about Moses, it's that he persevered! He was a faithful servant of God who was more interested in God's reputation than his own. Even though the Israelites continued to rebel, Moses kept going, until the very end.

Remember This . . .

> **Deuteronomy 1–34** This book of the Bible is a record of three sermons that Moses gave to the Israelites as they prepared to enter the Promised Land of Canaan. Because all the Israelites who had started out from Egypt had died, a new generation was entering the land God had promised to Abraham so many years earlier. Moses' three sermons reminded that new generation of what God had done in the past, what God expected of the Israelites, and what God wanted to do in the future.

Sit Down For Some Long Sermons

The unfaithful parents of those about to enter Canaan were gone. Moses was faithful to the end and in his final acts as a leader, reminded the Hebrews of God's mighty deeds and the covenant obligations.

Here is an outline of the three sermons that Moses gave in the book of Deuteronomy:

Deuteronomy 1:1–4:43   A reminder of what God had done in the past

Deuteronomy 4:44–26:19   A review of the laws God expected the people to keep in the new land

Deuteronomy 27:1–34:12   A revelation of what God promised to do for Israel in the future

And That's All He Has To Say!

In Moses' final comments, he gives:

- A final challenge to the Israelites (Deuteronomy 31:1–33)
- A final song of praise to God (Deuteronomy 32:1–43)
- A final blessing of the tribes of Israel (Deuteronomy 33:1–29)

Remember This . . .

What Others are Saying:

Gene A. Getz: Perhaps the greatest lesson we can learn from Moses' final days is that a person never gets too old to fail. Therefore we must be on guard against Satan and his subtle attacks at all times.[12]

It has been said Moses spent forty years in Pharaoh's court, learning he was somebody. Then he spent forty years in Midian, learning he was nobody. Finally he spent the last forty years of his life learning what God can do with a somebody who finds out that he is a nobody.

Something to Ponder

LEADERSHIP PRINCIPLE—The traits of Moses' life are rarely found in today's leaders. There are plenty of confident and powerful leaders who feign humility, but their motives are so evident that nobody believes their false modesty. It is difficult to fake humility. Just as courage springs spontaneously from the heart, humility flows freely because it represents an inward commitment that transforms the outward behavior.

Study Questions

1. Why did Moses run away from being a prince in a palace?
2. What were some of the objections Moses gave for not wanting to become Israel's deliverer?
3. What are some of the miracles God did to deliver the Israelites from the Egyptians?
4. When Moses was burned out and wanted to quit what solutions did God provide?
5. How did Moses show his humility when God struck Miriam with leprosy?

CHAPTER WRAP-UP

- Moses' life was in danger as soon as he was born because all Hebrew boys were to be killed. His mother, Jochebed, had great faith in God, and rather than see him die, she put him in the river in a basket. Downstream, he was found by Pharaoh's daughter and adopted as a prince of Egypt. (Exodus 2:1–10)

- Moses killed an Egyptian who was attacking an Israelite and then ran away because Pharaoh wanted to kill him for it. Moses became a shepherd with the Midians and in the solitude of the desert, God prepared him for future leadership. (Exodus 2:11–22)

- God appeared to Moses in a burning bush and told him he would deliver the Israelites out of their Egyptian bondage. Even though Moses argued, God won and Moses agreed to lead the Israelites. Moses learned God could enable him. (Exodus 3–4)

- Moses performed many miracles in God's power in order to convince Pharaoh to release God's people from their bondage. When Pharaoh finally let the Israelites leave Egypt, Moses led them through the desert and Moses had to constantly use God's power to keep them in line. (Exodus 5–18)

- The people rebelled against going into the Promised Land, so Moses had to lead the Israelites around in the wilderness for 40 years until the unbelieving generation died out. God entrusted Moses with his Law for the people to follow, starting with the Ten Commandments. (Exodus, Leviticus, Numbers, and Deuteronomy)

7 DAVID: A MAN AFTER GOD'S OWN HEART

CHAPTER HIGHLIGHTS

- David Kills Goliath
- David Refuses to Kill His Stalker
- Faithfully Keeping a Promise
- David: Murderer and Adulterer
- A Weak King
- David Dies

Let's Get Started

David, an ordinary shepherd, was chosen by God to be king of Israel. Saul, the current king, had disobeyed God. Therefore, even before Saul died—which was the usual way a king was replaced—God directed the prophet Samuel to anoint David as the new king.

David was a gifted king. But he was not a perfect man. He lied, committed adultery, and murdered. He was responsible for the suffering of many people. Still, God used him in incredible ways, and the Scriptures ensure he'll always be remembered as a man after God's own heart.

THE BIG PICTURE

> **1 Samuel 16** Because the first king of Israel, Saul, had displeased God so greatly, David was chosen by God to replace him (see illustration, page 92). God directed his prophet, Samuel, to anoint David king even though the shepherd boy's appearance and stature were not kingly looking. Saul became emotionally unbalanced. David was called to the palace to play his harp to calm him. Saul, not knowing of David's anointing, delighted in David and assigned him as the king's own armor bearer.

☞ **GO TO:**

Acts 13:22 (after God's own heart)

Bad King, Good Shepherd

Saul, who physically was a superior man, made a poor king. Anger, depression, and open disobedience to God marked his reign.

King David expanded Israel's borders to give his people ten times as much land as they occupied when Saul became king. The striped area of land indicates the extent of Israel's kingdom before David's reign. The dashed line indicates the extent of Israel's kingdom at the end of David's reign.

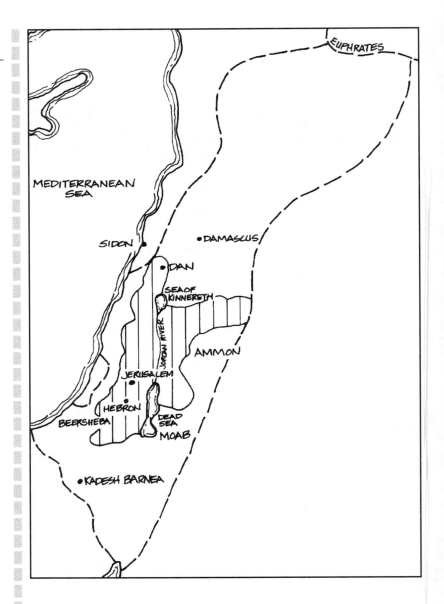

God sent a message to Saul through the prophet Samuel. *"You acted foolishly,"* Samuel said. *"You have not kept the command the Lord your God gave you; if you had, he would have established your kingdom over Israel for all time. But now your kingdom will not endure; the Lord has sought out a man after his own heart and appointed him leader of his people, because you have not kept the Lord's command"* (1 Samuel 13:13–14).

The prophet Samuel was sent to David's family home to pick out the next king. He looked at each of David's impressive brothers, but God said, *"Do not consider his appearance or his height, for I have rejected him. The Lord does not look at the things man looks at. Man looks at the outward appearance, but the Lord looks at the heart"* (1 Samuel 16:7). It turned out that David was *"ruddy, with a fine appearance and handsome features"* (1 Samuel 16:12), but appearances didn't interest God. He looked into David's heart.

David, the youngest son in the family of Jesse, trained in solitude to be a king. While tending sheep in the isolated plains and mountains, this musician, songwriter, and godly man developed a heart for God. His psalms of praise scattered throughout the book of Psalms reflect a man who longed for God. It was these songwriting and musical skills that brought him to the palace as Saul's harpist.

Remember This . . .

KEY POINT

To know God's heart, we must spend time alone with him.

Something to Ponder

BUILD YOUR SPIRIT: David's isolation was used to build his spiritual life. Although corporate worship in our church is great and fellowship with other Christians is encouraging, time alone with God is essential. It's in the times of being <u>still</u> and focusing on him that our hearts get to know him best.

☞ **GO TO:**

Psalm 46:10 (still)

THE BIG PICTURE 🔍

1 Samuel 17 David's father sent him to check on his brothers who were at the battlefront in Israel's fight with the neighboring Philistines. When David arrived, he found the battle was at a stalemate because the Philistine giant, Goliath, had challenged the Israelite army to fight him. David couldn't understand why his countrymen were so afraid. He used his slingshot and killed Goliath with a single stone (see illustration, page 94). As a result, the Israelites were victorious in the battle.

He Is Too Big To Miss

The solitude that surrounded David's early life also taught him responsibility and gave him courage. As a shepherd, it was necessary to protect the flock from predators. Standing toe to toe alone with a lion put steel into the backbone of this little shepherd. One sage said, "Not the size of the dog in the fight, but the size of the fight in the dog determines the outcome."

What Others are Saying:

Something to Ponder

☞ **GO TO:**

1 Samuel 17:33
(ridiculed)

F. B. Meyer: You may have nothing in the outward semblance, nothing in your surroundings or circumstances, to indicate the true royalty within; but if you bare your heart to God, you shall stand revealed as his son, as a priest and king unto himself.[1]

King Saul was a seasoned warrior, and he was taller than most Israelites. He should have been the man to face Goliath. When David offered to fight Goliath, Saul <u>ridiculed</u> David because of his size and youth.

LEADERSHIP 🦅 **PRINCIPLE**—As a leader, it is your responsibility to encourage and challenge those who are under your leadership. If you belittle the faith or courage or vision of your "troops" like Saul did David, you may find they lack courage and the ability to think for themselves.

BUILD YOUR SPIRIT: When facing fearful giants in our lives, we normally draw upon our experience. Take a lesson from David and remember our real strength comes from knowing Whose we are, rather than what we are.

How Tall Was Goliath?

At six cubits and a span, Goliath was over nine feet tall!

What Did a Sling Look Like?

It looked like a doubled rope with a leather pocket in the center.

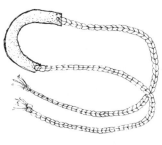

How Heavy Were Sling Stones?

Sling stones found on Israelite battlefields were the size of tennis balls.

Don't belittle your children for their awkwardness, sports inability, struggle with academics, or tender heart. You may crush their spirits and make them fear trying new things. If you give them the feeling that they can never please you no matter how much they try, they'll give up trying.

Grow Your Family

THE BIG PICTURE

> **1 Samuel 18–24** When introduced to King Saul as Goliath's conqueror, David met Saul's son, Jonathan, and they became best friends. Everyone in the country heard about David's courage, and they lifted him up in song as a great hero, even above Saul. That made Saul so jealous that he tried to kill David by spearing him.
> Failing in this, he developed another plan. He would give his daughter Michal's hand in marriage to David, if the upstart warrior brought back the foreskins of a hundred Philistines. David successfully completed his task and married Michal. Over time, Saul tried various ways to have David killed. Yet God always protected the up-and-coming shepherd king from the down-and-sinking coward king.

Spears Keep Whizzing By My Head

The prophet Samuel had already anointed David as the next king, but while he waited in the wings for the promotion, David found himself dodging spears chucked by a demented Saul. David fled and gathered a loyal following of six hundred fighters. His relationship with Jonathan gave him intelligence information from inside the palace.

Charles R. Swindoll: David became a sort of Robin Hood. His Sherwood Forest was the rugged Judean wilderness, with its mountains, caves, and deep wadis. There, he commanded a group of mavericks because God wanted him to become a maverick king.[2]

What Others are Saying:

David must have lived a stressful life. Saul threw spears at him, tricked him into potentially getting killed by Philistines, commanded his servants to kill him, sent messengers to kill him in bed, and arrived at Samuel's house to do it himself. He even commanded his son, Jonathan, David's best friend, to kill him. Talk about pressure! David was forced to grow closer to God.

Something to Ponder

> **1 Samuel 25** After David's trusted friend, Samuel, died, he moved out into the desert. As David traveled around trying to keep his distance from Saul, he encountered the servants of a man named Nabal. When he sent his servants to ask for a donation in exchange for helping Nabal's sheep shearers, Nabal rebuffed him. An angered David determined to destroy Nabal and all he owned. But Nabal's wife, Abigail, heard about the situation, intercepted David, and placated him by apologizing and providing food and drink. David relented from his deadly plans. When David later heard that Nabal had suddenly died of heart failure, David proposed marriage to Abigail and she accepted.

Labor/Management Conflict

David had been providing protection for Nabal and so David sent some of his men to the rich rancher requesting provisions. Nabal rudely rejected this request, even though he benefited from David's protection. David was so furious that he took four hundred armed men to kill Nabal. David, the man after God's heart, had lost it.

What Others are Saying:

Alan Redpath: David! David! What is wrong with you? Why, one of the most wonderful things we have learned about you recently is your patience with Saul. You learned to wait upon the Lord, you refused to lift your hand to touch the Lord's anointed, although he had been your enemy for so many years. But now, look at you! . . . Your self-restraint has gone to pieces and a few insulting words from a fool of a man like Nabal have made you see red? David, what's the matter?

"I am justified in doing this," David would reply. "There is no reason why Nabal should treat me as he has. He has repaid all my kindness with insults. I will show him he can't trifle with me. It is one thing to take it from Saul, who is my superior at this point, but this sort of man—this highhanded individual must be taught a lesson!"[3]

Overcoming Struggles

David's anger at Nabal is what most of us feel when we are rejected or mistreated. Yet, it's not the way God wants us to respond. We will show more forcefully that we are Christians by responding with kindness and gentleness. Besides, more people are convicted of their sin by our gracious response than an angry one.

David Pours Out His Fear

While David was on the run from Saul and his life was in danger, he expressed his emotions by writing more songs and verse. These portions of poetry were David's way of dealing with his fear and of continuing to develop his trust in God. Many of his psalms also expressed his joy at knowing God would protect him.

Today, these songs and poetry have become what we call the "Psalms" in Scripture. David didn't write all of the 150 psalms in our Bible, but the majority are his. People through the centuries have identified with David's heartfelt cries. They have found that joyful moments are enhanced and sorrowful ones softened.

Psalms of Comfort

Psalm	What It's About
59	When Saul had sent men to watch David's house in order to kill him
56	When the Philistines seized David in Gath
34	When David pretended to be insane before Abimelech
142	When David was hiding in a cave

THE BIG PICTURE 🔍

1 Samuel 26–27, 29–31 For a second time, David had the opportunity to kill Saul, but he refused to dishonor God. When Saul realized what had happened, he acknowledged his guilt in trying to kill David. But David, knowing Saul's moods were changeable, joined the Philistines. But they didn't trust him, so they wouldn't let him fight with them. That was God's plan. When David's family was captured by the Amalekites, he was available to rescue them. Shortly after that, King Saul and Jonathan were killed.

Returning Good For Evil

David resisted the temptation to kill Saul, faithfully waiting for God's timing to place him on the throne. This demonstrated David's commitment to God.

Oswald Chambers: Every temptation of the devil is full of the most amazing wisdom and the understanding of every problem that ever stretched before men's view. . . . No matter what your circumstances may be, don't try to shield yourself from things God is bring-

KEY POINT

Many who feel their lives are spent on the run have found comfort in the book of Psalms.

What Others are Saying:

ing into your life. God engineers circumstances; we have to see that we face them abiding continually with Him in His temptations.[4]

Something to Ponder

David had every opportunity to accelerate God's plan. The throne had been promised to him, and this man Saul was out to kill him. He had opportunity, just reasons, and loyal followers to take the kingdom. He resisted those ungodly temptations.

THE BIG PICTURE

> **2 Samuel 1–8, 10** Although Saul had died, David didn't take the throne in both Judah and Israel without opposition. He was easily crowned king in Judah because that was where he was from. But in the land of Israel, Saul's relatives crowned Saul's other son, Ish-bosheth, to be king over them. In time, some of Ish-bosheth's commanders turned against him and killed him. That opened the door for David to become king over all of Israel. Years earlier, Saul had given Michal, David's first wife, to be another man's wife. Now, David demanded that she be returned to him. She was, but her heart was no longer entwined with his as at the beginning. Later, she grew to hate him, especially when she saw him dancing in the streets of Jerusalem over the return of God's Ark.

David's Victories

After Saul died, you might expect David to march into the palace and fulfill his destiny. Instead, we find a man who was in a hurry to know more of his God. *"In the course of time, David inquired of the Lord. 'Shall I go up to one of the towns of Judah?' he asked. The Lord said, 'Go up.' David asked, 'Where shall I go?' 'To Hebron,' the Lord answered"* (2 Samuel 2:1).

Notice the statement *"in the course of time."* Saul is dead and David takes the time to ask God what he should do. The humility and patience developed in the pastures have cashed in dividends. Success is at hand but David didn't let this future power go to his head. David lived in Hebron for seven and a half years, where he reigned over Judah.

But the darker side of David started to appear. He married six women, and six children were born to him in Hebron. David's move into polygamy started him down the road of poor choices.

One of his top army commanders, Joab, began killing potential opponents against David's wishes, yet David seemed unwilling to deal with this skilled but ruthless leader.

David's conquests brought power and prestige to his kingdom. General prosperity arrived for all his people.

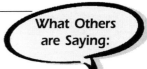

What Others are Saying:

Thomas Carlyle: But for one man who can stand prosperity, there are a hundred that will stand adversity.[5]

Remember This . . .

David began his reign with a wonderful heart for God. He wanted God's will to be done, and he became highly successful against the enemies of Israel. When peace came because of those victories, David wanted to build a house for God. But God communicated to him through the prophet Nathan that David wouldn't build such a house—but his son would. David obeyed God instead of forcing his own will.

THE BIG PICTURE

> **2 Samuel 11–12** One spring when David should have been on the battlefield fighting, he was walking on the roof of his palace and saw a beautiful woman on a neighboring rooftop bathing. He called for her. Her name was Bathsheba and they committed adultery. When she sent word that she was pregnant, David called her husband, Uriah, home from the battlefield, hoping Uriah would sleep with Bathsheba and believe he was father of the coming child. When Uriah wouldn't go home to be with her, David had him put into a position on the battlefield where he would be killed. Then David took Bathsheba for his wife. Their son was born, but God disciplined them by causing the child to die. David repented of his sin after Nathan, the prophet, confronted him. A second son was born to him and Bathsheba. They named him Solomon.

A Moment Of Pleasure, Years Of Pain

David was on top of the world. In younger years he had written, *"I will be careful to lead a blameless life . . . I will walk in my house with a blameless heart. I will set before my eyes no vile thing. The deeds of faithless men I hate; they will not cling to me"* (Psalm 101:2–3). But now he was around fifty years old and had been king for twenty years. Everything was going his way. That godly desire began to slide when he began taking more wives and concubines. In Deuteronomy 17:14–17, God set three rules for the kings of Israel. They must not multiply horses for themselves, they must not enrich themselves with gold and silver, and, finally, they must not take multiple wives. David failed the last requirement. David's lust for women began to weaken his ability to make wise, godly choices.

His next slide into sinful passion came with one glance at Bathsheba's beautiful body. The next thing he knew, he was telling his ruthless commander Joab to arrange the death of her husband. After the news of Uriah's death reached David, he took Bathsheba as his wife. The cover-up worked, except that the secret sin ate away at a heart that once was only devoted to God. David wrote of that time, "*When I kept silent, my bones wasted away through my groaning all day long. For day and night your hand was heavy upon me; my strength was sapped as in the heat of summer*" (Psalm 32:3–4).

After Nathan's finger of blame pierced David's heart, the king repented and finally found forgiveness. However, the consequences of the sin rocked David until his death.

What Others are Saying:

Max Lucado: Those who rebel—those who choose to roam the back alleys of escape—are prime candidates to stumble into one of the Satan's oldest pits . . . adultery. The David in us calls for Bathsheba. A romp is taken in the greener grass and the hurt begins.[6]

WARNING

☞ **GO TO:**

Isaiah 57:15 (contrite)

Psalm 103:12 (forget)

contrite: *repentant*

Overcoming Struggles

David's **contrite** heart existed because it hadn't suffered "hardening of the attitudes" yet. His conscience was still tender and open to identifying the sickness of sin. He felt spiritual chest pains with every pulse of God's conviction coursing through his heart. David had a godly sorrow! How about you? Are you numb to the things you know are wrong? Is there a small corner in your heart still soft enough to feel the pain of conviction? God is ready to finish the heart surgery for your soul. Humbly approach the great physician and admit, "I have sinned."

The healing touch of forgiveness only comes from a contrite heart. We can escape the penalty of the sin through forgiveness, but the painful consequences of our sin will often follow us. We will remember our sin and so will those we hurt. Only God will <u>forget</u> it.

> **2 Samuel 13–15:12** After David sinned, his life and reign began to crumble. His son Amnon raped his step-sister Tamar, the sister of Absalom. Two years later, Absalom, who had vowed to take revenge on Amnon, murdered him. David, crushed by all this conflict, wept along with all his sons. Absalom fled and for three years, David refused to reach out to him. Only after Joab concocted a plan to force David to see his error did David allow Absalom to return to the area. Still David wouldn't see him personally. Two years later, Absalom rebelled against his father and set himself up as king.

Like Father, Like Sons

David saw his sins mirrored in the lives of his children. Consequences of adultery are costly. The Bible says, *"Do not be deceived: God cannot be mocked. A man reaps what he sows. The one who sows to please his sinful nature, from that nature will reap destruction; the one who sows to please the Spirit, from the Spirit will reap eternal life"* (Galatians 6:7–8). David's life began to spin deeper into trouble.

John W. Lawrence: When David sowed to the flesh, he reaped what the flesh produced. Moreover, he reaped the consequences of his action even though he had confessed his sin and been forgiven for it. Underline it, star it, mark it deeply upon your conscious mind: Confession and forgiveness in no way stop the harvest. He had sown: he was to reap. Forgiven he was, but the consequences continued. . . . What we sow we will reap, and there are no exceptions.[7]

What Others are Saying:

KEY POINT

The only way to escape sin's consequences: don't sin.

Greg Laurie, author of *The Great Compromise*, says there are six reasons to avoid the compromise of adultery:

1. You damage your spouse.
2. You damage your self.
3. You damage your children.
4. You damage your church.
5. You damage your witness, as well as the cause of Christ.
6. You sin against the Lord.[8]

Remember This . . .

Although we can always receive forgiveness from God's gracious hand, we won't be able to avoid the consequences of our sin.

WARNING

2 Samuel 15:13–19:43 David was so upset by Absalom's disloyalty that he surrendered his reign to his son and left with his entire household. Absalom set up his reign in Jerusalem and demonstrated his newfound power by having sex with his father's concubines on top of a roof, in the sight of all Israel. He also took counsel from one of David's former counselors, Hushai, who was secretly loyal to David. Hushai told him to delay in pursuing David. Absalom followed his advice and lost the advantage. As a result, David had time to organize his defenses. Absalom eventually pursued David. Joab, thinking he would please David, killed Absalom. Instead, David was grieved. But after Joab reproved him for being insensitive to the needs of his loyal followers, David addressed them. David was restored to his kingly position and forgave those who had treated him badly when he was forced to leave.

Let's Just Throw In The Towel

In direct violation of David's orders, Joab killed Absalom. David's earlier neglect and unwillingness to control his military commander contributed to the death of his son.

What Others are Saying:

Charles R. Swindoll: Absalom is dead—murdered. This happened before [David] had a chance to clear up several unresolved conflicts between father and son . . . before he and his son could sit down and come to terms with their differences. Even before David could tell him how sorry he was for being so busy, so preoccupied, so negligent as a dad—BOOM! The news of Absalom's death hits him in the face.[9]

Something to Ponder

David's inability to hold others accountable weakened his authority. His conflicting emotions overwhelmed his management skills. Now with Absalom dead, David's grief had built a wall between him and the warriors who fought for him. So great was the affront and rebuff to these loyal troops that Joab feared another rebellion could occur. As the military leader, Joab knew the king must address his troops. Joab challenged the king to do his duty and shake off his grief. David obeyed even though his heart wasn't in it.

> **2 Samuel 20–24** David was reinstated as king. A famine, caused by Saul's mistreatment of the Gibeonites years earlier, was corrected when David cooperated with the Gibeonites' demand that Saul's sons by his wife Rizpah be hanged. Israel was again victorious against the Philistines even though the Philistines had more giants like Goliath. David remembered God's provision over the years and wrote a song of thanksgiving. Then, against God's specific command, David insisted in making a census of the people to discover how many warriors he could draft. When he realized that was a sin, he accepted God's discipline of a plague that killed seventy thousand Israelites. It only stopped after David offered a sacrifice on an altar built at the threshing floor of Araunah the Jebusite.

David Was Dangerous To Be Around

In 1 Chronicles 21:1, we get another glimpse into this census story. We learn that Satan planted this little temptation in David's mind. Satan whispered to David's prideful side, "You are the great king of Israel, why don't you find out just how big you are?" This census amounted to a draft for the army. There was no need to enlist men because Israel was at peace, and David was solidly in power. But David's pride wanted it done. Even Joab knew the idea of a census was wrong and advised against it. David ignored Joab and ordered it done.

David's pride had caused his downfall in the past, and now God was giving him another opportunity to show he had changed. Unfortunately, he hadn't.

What Others are Saying:

Steve Farrar: The Lord disciplines every one of us as a father would discipline a young, immature son. God is disciplining us because He wants to give every one of us spiritual responsibilities. But first we have to take some character examinations. If you don't pass on the first try, you'll take it again, and again, and again, until you do pass and God can entrust leadership into your hands.[10]

Something to Ponder

After David's disobedience, we find him conscience-stricken. *"I have sinned greatly in what I have done. Now, O Lord, I beg you, take away the guilt of your servant. I have done a very foolish thing"* (2 Samuel 24:10). His heart troubled him and soon we find him on his knees again confessing his foolish sin. This time the consequences led to a plague for his people. David was in great distress.

Throwing a pebble into a calm pond causes a rippling of waves. The foolish choices we make are like that point of impact. Just one peek into the consequences of our choices would restrain our impulsive side. In fact, we are allowed that peek through the life of David. Great success, painful sin, and profound forgiveness marked his life. Each time he sinned, a price was paid that compounded in misery and troubles—even in the lives of others.

THE BIG PICTURE

> **1 Kings 1–2:11** David was dying and Adonijah, a son of David's through his wife Haggith, declared himself the next king, even though David had previously determined that Solomon would follow him as king. When Bathsheba saw what was happening, she recruited the prophet Nathan to help her to establish Solomon as the rightful heir. After David died, Solomon became king.

"A Heart After God" Dies

David was near death. Another son attempted to take the throne instead of Solomon. David pulled Solomon to his side for some kingly advice. David encouraged a spiritual dependency within Solomon so that his son would walk in God's ways. Interestingly, he then asked Solomon to do what he had been unwilling to do: hold Joab accountable for murder. David had been willing to keep Joab near for his skills as an army commander, but he knew justice required Joab's death.

What Others are Saying:

Steve Farrar: David was a real man, a man after God's own heart. But after committing adultery, he was never again quite the same. He was forgiven, but the aftershocks devastated his family. Apparently he lost his razor-sharp edge of credibility, and until his dying day he never completely got it back.[11]

David charged Solomon as the next king to:

- Be strong
- Show himself a man
- Observe what the Lord your God requires
- Walk in his ways
- Keep his decrees and commands

David told Solomon that if he would do those things, he would *"prosper in all you do and wherever you go"* (1 Kings 2:3).

David's instructions to his son for his kingship could also be applied to a father blessing his son or daughter (with some appropriate word changes for a female). As we encourage our children to obey God and be strong in the Lord, and we model it ourselves, they will want to seek him like we do.

Something to Ponder

Grow Your Family

Study Questions

1. What was Saul's response to David's offer to fight Goliath?
2. Who became David's best friend and helped to protect him?
3. How did David keep his covenant with Jonathan after Jonathan died?
4. Where should David have been when he was tempted to have adultery with Bathsheba?
5. What advantage did David have when he fled from Jerusalem because Absalom had staged a rebellion?

CHAPTER WRAP-UP

- David was chosen as king to replace Saul even though David was young. God chose David as the next king because David trusted him, demonstrated when David killed Goliath. (1 Samuel 16–17)

- Once Saul knew David would replace him as king, he tried many times to kill David. David trusted God so much that when he had the opportunity to kill Saul, he didn't. David believed God would install him as king in his own timing. (1 Samuel 24:1–22)

- When Jonathan died, David kept his promise to care for Jonathan's family by taking Mephibosheth into the royal household. David proved he kept his promises and was a loyal friend. (2 Samuel 9:1–13)

- When David stayed home from the battlefield, he saw Bathsheba bathing, and committed adultery with her. When she became pregnant, he had to have her husband, Uriah, killed in order to take her as his wife. David fell hard, but repented harder. (2 Samuel 11:1–27)

- When Absalom, David's son, staged a rebellion, David meekly submitted, trusting God could reestablish him if God still wanted him as king. Later, David won back his position. David still loved Absalom so much that he was saddened to hear that his son had been killed. (2 Samuel 16–18)

- David died after forty years of serving as Israel's king. He was considered a man after God's own heart, even though he made many mistakes. (2 Kings 2:10–11)

8 MEN OF STRONG FAITH: LESSONS IN PERSEVERANCE

Let's Get Started

Two men with great faith stand out among the men of the Bible, even though they didn't hold prominent positions, nor were they patriarchs of the faith. But they believed God would fulfill his purposes through them. Noah labored for 120 years at a God-given task everyone laughed at. Job suffered under the most incredible personal and physical difficulties, and yet he kept his faith in God's goodness.

Both of these men had enough faith to hold firm in God's promise until they experienced God's solution. That attitude gave them the power they needed to take action as God directed. We'll be able to do the same if we learn from these men of faith.

Noah

. . . One Hundred Twenty Years of Faithfulness

THE BIG PICTURE

> **Genesis 6:5–12** After God created the earth and mankind, and as men became more numerous on earth, their sins multiplied. God grieved over their disobedience but saw in Noah a man who served him and was righteous.

And Then There Was One

We are first introduced to Noah when he was nearly five hundred years old. For five centuries, he had a good relationship with God. Yet sin was running rampant around him, and God saw Noah as the only one faithful to him. Because the people were so wicked, God decided to wipe out everyone except Noah's family.

**What Others
are Saying:**

**Something
to Ponder**

**Remember
This . . .**

☞ **GO TO:**

Psalm 14:2 (looking)

Jeremiah 29:13 (seeks)

Matthew 7:7–8 (find)

Hebrews 10:25
(church)

Max Lucado: Do something that demonstrates faith. For faith with no effort is no faith at all. God will respond. He has never rejected a genuine gesture of faith. Never. God honors radical, risk-taking faith. When Arks are built, lives are saved.[1]

Try to imagine you are the only person on the earth who believes in God. That is what Noah faced. The Bible tells us, *"Noah was a righteous man, blameless among the people of his time, and he walked with God"* (Genesis 6:9). Now this doesn't mean he never sinned, but it does mean he loved, obeyed, and most importantly, walked with God.

God was seeking those who were faithful to him. Throughout the Bible, there are examples of God <u>looking</u> for a relationship with his created. During Noah's time, the rest of the world was filled with evil men and women seeking fulfillment apart from God. But anyone who <u>seeks</u> God sincerely can <u>find</u> him.

⚠ **BUILD YOUR SPIRIT:** Noah must have felt lonely in his faith. His immediate family may have helped, but he didn't have any friends to share the Lord with. If we feel that way too, we can be encouraged that when we face spiritual isolation, we can still walk with God. Thankfully, other Christian men are available and God wants to provide Christian friendships. Be sure to attend <u>church</u> and ask God to guide you to those who can offer godly encouragement.

THE BIG PICTURE 🔍

> **Genesis 6:13–22** God told Noah to build an Ark of very specific materials and dimensions (see illustration, page 109). He wanted to provide protection for those who were righteous on the earth but he intended to destroy everything and everyone else.

Midlife Career Move

Noah started his boat-building career out of obedience to God. God told him to build a boat—but this was no ordinary boat. It was made of "gopher" wood, 450 feet long, 75 feet wide, and 45

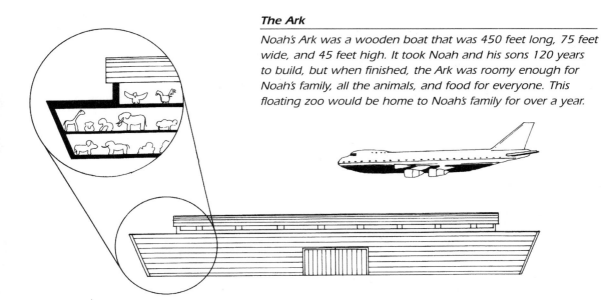

The Ark

Noah's Ark was a wooden boat that was 450 feet long, 75 feet wide, and 45 feet high. It took Noah and his sons 120 years to build, but when finished, the Ark was roomy enough for Noah's family, all the animals, and food for everyone. This floating zoo would be home to Noah's family for over a year.

feet tall. It was the length of one and a half football fields and as tall as a four-story building. No wonder Noah took 120 years to build it. This project announced God's coming judgment.

Herschel H. Hobbs: The word *gopher* appears nowhere else in the Bible, and its meaning is uncertain. Since the Phoenicians used cypress for shipbuilding due to its lightness and strength, this probably was the wood used. To make it watertight, the Ark was to be covered inside and out with "pitch," a material that abounded in the area, evidence of the oil deposits that are so plentiful there today.[2]

Each year, Noah's obedience demonstrated God's <u>patience</u> with those who continued to rebel. Every board, every beam, and every bucket of pitch signaled God's intentions. There's nothing like one righteous man building a huge boat on dry land to send a message. During that time, he told those around him of God's coming judgment. But his comments fell on deaf ears. He only heard laughter and ridicule.

• • •

The Ark was exactly six times longer than it was wide. Today, modern shipbuilders use that same ratio because the engineering efficiencies are maximized. How amazing that when man's engineering skills were more primitive, God was already a master shipbuilder!

What Others are Saying:

Something to Ponder

☞ **GO TO:**

2 Peter 3:15 (patience)

Overcoming Struggles

☞ **GO TO:**

Matthew 24:45
(faithfulness)

Noah persisted building the Ark over 120 hot summers and cold winters. The only thing colder than the winter chill was the icy comments from those around him. In today's jargon, this would be a "hostile work environment." We may need Noah's <u>faithfulness</u> at times because when our lives reflect a relationship with God, we may hear critical comments. Our commitment to the Lord and the tasks he gives us will strengthen our resolve to work regardless of the loneliness.

THE BIG PICTURE 🔍

> **Genesis 7:1–24** At the right time, God directed Noah to take his family and enter the Ark, along with seven pairs of every clean animal and two pairs of every unclean animal. For the first time, rain fell on the earth. It lasted until the earth was completely flooded, and everyone on the earth died—except for Noah's family.

Rain? What's Rain?

Except for one man and his family, the entire world was in open rebellion against God. God's creation was now so corrupt, he was morally required to deal with those in rebellion. "*When the wicked thrive, so does sin, but the righteous will see their downfall*" (Proverbs 29:16).

What Others are Saying:

Something to Ponder

WARNING ▶

☞ **GO TO:**

Proverbs 6:16 (hatred)

Herschel H. Hobbs: Whatever may be one's attitude toward the Bible, it is evident that the fact of a deluge is written deeply in the mind of the human race. Approximately one hundred stories of a great flood may be found in various parts of the globe.[3]

Like a contagious disease, sin was spreading. More sinners emboldened more men toward more sin. Justice required action so God sent his judgment upon the earth. He would start anew by building the population from Noah's family.

There are times when we also are required to express our opinion of sin in this world. It takes a great deal of wisdom to know how and when to do it. But because God is a God of justice, he may want us to communicate his <u>hatred</u> of sin in this evil world.

Chronology of the Flood

Waiting in Ark	Noah enters Ark.	Genesis 7:7–9
	7 days later the rain begins falling.	Genesis 7:10–11
Water for 150 Days	40 days later the heavy rains stop.	Genesis 7:12
	110 days later waters recede and the Ark	
	runs aground on Mount Ararat.	Genesis 7:24; 8:4
Water receded in 150 days	74 days later mountain tops visible.	Genesis 8:5
	40 days later raven sent out, and dove sent out and returned.	Genesis 8:6–9
	7 days later dove sent out and returned with leaf.	Genesis 8:10
	7 days later dove sent out a third time and did not return.	Genesis 8:12
Earth dried in 70 days	Noah saw dry land.	Genesis 8:13
	Land is completely dry and Noah leaves Ark.	Genesis 8:14–19
	377 days were spent inside the Ark.	

THE BIG PICTURE 🔍

Genesis 8:1–9:19 God made the waters recede after awhile and Noah tested the depth of the water by sending out birds at different times. Eventually, the waters receded enough that Noah and his family could leave the Ark. On the fresh earth, Noah built an altar and God blessed Noah and his family. Plus, he established a covenant with Noah and his sons that he would never cause a similar flood to come upon the earth again.

covenant: a promise

☞ **GO TO:**

Hebrews 9:15 (covenant)

Man Of Worship, God Of Promise

The water was gone and the ground was dry, but Noah waited until God told him to leave the Ark. Noah entered the Ark in obedience, and he exited the same way. Once released from the confines of the ship, Noah made an altar and worshiped God. Noah blessed God with this act of worship. Then God blessed Noah, the second father of the human race, and made the first covenant with man. God promised never to destroy all of life again. He created a rainbow as a sign of that promise. Noah was told to be fruitful and multiply but was warned against killing men.

Robert H. Schuller: Don't trust the clouds—trust the sunshine. Don't set your compass by the flash of lightning—set it by the stars. Trust the sun—don't trust the shadows. Believe in your dreams—don't believe in your despairing thoughts. Have faith in your faith—and doubt your doubts. Trust in your hopes—never trust in your hurts. And you will move on eventually, effectively, inspiringly to faith's final phase: the cresting phase.[4]

What Others are Saying:

intrinsic: *belonging to
the real nature of a thing;
inherent*

transcendent: *separate,
beyond or apart from the
material*

KEY POINT

The rainbow tells us
God will never destroy
the people of the
earth again.

Even though God had killed the people of the earth, God explained to Noah that murder was wrong: *"and from each man, too, I will demand an accounting for the life of his fellow man. Whoever sheds the blood of man, by man shall his blood be shed; for in the image of God has God made man"* (Genesis 9:6). It's wrong because man was made in God's image, and we are valuable in ourselves.

Charles Darwin claimed we are evolved animals. He believed that since the creation never occurred, there wouldn't be a creator to have a claim on the created. Darwin argued that we only possess biologic value as a highly developed species. God doesn't look at us that way. Unlike animals, man has the capacity for morality, reason, and worship because we are made in God's image. Because of what God has done, we are more than physical beings. We possess **intrinsic** and **transcendent** value.

Job
. . . Gaining a Godly Perspective of Suffering

THE BIG PICTURE 🔍

> **Job 1:1–22** Job was a man who lived in the land of Uz and was considered blameless and a worshiper of Jehovah God. He had family and worldly blessings. Satan appeared before God in his throne room and accused Job of impure motives for following God. To prove Job's purity, God gave Satan permission to attack.

Round One: Rumblings In The Throne Room

Job was a rich man who feared and served God. He had a loving wife and seven sons and three daughters, who regularly met together to have fun. Job prayed for them and offered sacrifices on their behalf.

Satan appeared before God's throne to accuse God's followers. God pointed out Job as one of his loyal servants, saying, *"Have you considered my servant Job? There is no one on earth like him; he is blameless and upright, a man who fears God and shuns evil"* (Job 1:8). Satan accused Job of only serving God because God had blessed him. God gave Satan permission to remove Job's possessions, so Satan caused everything he owned to be destroyed. Even his children were killed as they feasted together. Job still stayed loyal—even as he grieved deeply. At the end of round one Satan was knocked down, but Job was still standing.

Oswald Chambers: In the case of Job, Satan asked permission to play havoc with his possessions and God gave him permission, and every possession Job had, even to his bodily health, went. But Job proved that a man would remain true to his love of God though all his possessions went to rack and ruin.[5]

What Others are Saying:

From Job's story, we learn:

- God knows everything about the people on the earth.
- Satan has access to God.
- Satan is looking for ways to accuse us and for the ways we fail.
- God put limits on what Satan can do to God's servants.
- It is possible to grieve deeply and yet not sin through blaming God.

Something to Ponder

Satan loves to find something in God's children that he can <u>accuse</u> us about before God. Even if there is nothing, Satan will scheme so that there can be something. That's why Jesus called him the "<u>father</u> of lies."

Remember This . . .

Overcoming Struggles

☞ **GO TO:**

Revelation 12:10 (accuse)

John 8:44 (father)

John 11:35 (wept)

![warning icon] **BUILD YOUR SPIRIT:** In the oriental custom of grieving, Job tore his robe, shaved his head, and fell to the ground. He also worshiped God, saying, "*Naked I came from my mother's womb, and naked I will depart. The Lord gave and the Lord has taken away; may the name of the Lord be praised*" (Job 1:21). Although some people think that Christians shouldn't grieve because they will see their dead again, it is possible to grieve and still trust God. God allows us to express our emotions even as we continue to believe God knows what he's doing in our lives.

At times of difficulty or grief, we can ask "Why?" without being unrighteous. The account of Job's grief said, "*In all this, Job did not sin by charging God with wrongdoing*" (Job 1:22). Job faced his deep loss but he didn't believe God had made a mistake. Even Jesus grieved over Lazarus' death and <u>wept</u>.

> **Job 2:1–10** Satan again stood before God. This time, he alleged Job stayed true to God only because Job's health hadn't been touched. God broadened his permission so that Satan could bring disease upon Job. But even with great painful sores on his body, Job still trusted God's will. Unfortunately, Job's wife didn't share his faith and wanted him to curse God. He refused.

Round Two: Sickness Will Break Him

In round one, Job's heart was broken. Now his body is broken with painful sores. But we quickly see why Job's wife didn't die with the children. Her loss couldn't have been more painful than her reckless comment to Job. *"His wife said to him, 'Are you still holding on to your integrity? Curse God and die!'"* (Job 2:9). Her faith was shattered and she held God responsible. She wanted someone to blame, and she wanted Job to join her in accusing God. Even Job's wife recognized he was still standing at the end of round two.

In the story of Job, everyone is accusing and blaming everyone else, except God and Job. That's how Satan's <u>schemes</u> work. He wants to sow seeds of discord and faultfinding. He uses trials and difficulties to make us think God isn't treating us right. Then if we manage not to blame God, we blame others.

Blaming others—or God—is a warning sign of spiritual heart disease. Blame springs from a heart that believes, "I deserve better. I know what is best for my life. I want it my way." That's like standing before God and wagging your finger in his face. But the same God who <u>loved</u> you enough to <u>send</u> his Son to die for your sin is the same God who allows struggles in your life but also provides the Holy Spirit to fill and <u>empower</u> you to cope with it all.

Remember This . . .

☞ **GO TO:**

Ephesians 6:11 (schemes)

WARNING

☞ **GO TO:**

Jeremiah 31:3 (loved)

John 3:16 (send)

Ephesians 3:16 (empower)

BUILD YOUR SPIRIT: Many people approach their relationship with God with the expectation things will always get better. But Job had the right attitude, even though his wife didn't. He replied, *"'You are talking like a foolish woman. Shall we accept good from God, and not trouble?' In all this, Job did not sin in what he said"* (Job 2:10). Job proved his heart was grateful to Jehovah God at all times, and he honored God through trusting him. We can do the same thing if we truly understand that in this world we will always have <u>problems</u>. It's only in heaven that we won't.

When most couples marry, the statement "for better or worse" is often repeated in their vows. There is an expectation that marriages will experience good and bad times. Evidently Job and his wife didn't have that phrase in their wedding vows because Job's wife wasn't prepared for this onslaught on their family. She was overwhelmed by grief. Job stayed true and was a spiritual leader in his family.

☞ **GO TO:**

John 16:33 (problems)

Grow Your Family

THE BIG PICTURE 🔍

> **Job 2:11–31:40** Three of Job's friends came to comfort Job in his deep affliction. But they aren't much help because they tried to convince Job he was being attacked because of some sin in his life. Job argued back saying he didn't have any hidden sin. Their conversation went back and forth but Job remained unconvinced of their perspective about suffering.

Round Three: But You *Must* Have Sin In Your Life!

Finally three friends joined Job in his battle: Eliphaz, Bildad, and Zophar. When they saw Job's deep grief, they could only sit with him in silence. Their mere presence must have been refreshing, like a boxer's corner attendants. Job finally broke the silence and complained about his situation, even saying he wanted to die. That opened the door. The blame game was about to raise its ugly head again. Job was facing the greatest battle of his life, and his friends were cheering against him! Job was now reeling in the ring. The crowd had turned against him, but he lasted another round.

Charles Colson: Job lost his home, his family (except for a nagging wife), his health, even his hope. The advice of friends was no help. No matter where he turned, he could find no answers to his plight . . . though it appeared God had abandoned him, Job clung to the assurance that God is who He is.[6]

At God's throne, Satan accused Job of being too innocent. Now Job's friends were accusing him of being guilty. The man couldn't win. But Job was convinced he had no sin he had not already confessed and that suffering can also happen to the godly. But the three men believed the innocent did not suffer.

What Others are Saying:

Something to Ponder

Eliphaz, Bildad, and Zophar were like accusers who:

- Give pat answers without compassion
- Don't ask, they tell
- Assume a person hasn't sought God's viewpoint
- Assume a person's theology is wrong without examining their own
- Misunderstand and twist what is said
- Believe it's impossible for a man to be acceptable in God's eyes
- Don't listen

With these men as his "friends," Job didn't need enemies!

In the book of Proverbs, a wise communicator is described as:

- Honest (4:24)
- Able to accept commands (10:8)
- Understanding (10:13)
- Using few words (10:19)
- Encouraging (12:25)
- Giving input at the appropriate time (15:23)

Ephesians 4:15 tells us to speak the truth in love. Sometimes truth is better left unsaid if it can't be done in love.

KEY POINT

True friends will listen more than talk.

☞ **GO TO:**

1 Samuel 23:21
(compassion)

Proverbs 11:12
(listening)

LEADERSHIP PRINCIPLE—Eliphaz, Bildad, and Zophar may have thought they were leading Job toward righteousness, but their leadership skills were lacking. Instead of leading with <u>compassion</u> and <u>listening</u>, they tried to force their opinions upon a hurting man. If we want to be effective in the lives of those who hurt, we must resist the temptation to "fix" the problem—especially if we don't truly understand the problem.

THE BIG PICTURE 🔍

Job 32–37 After Job and his friends finished with all their great theological discussions, another friend, Elihu, began to talk. He had heard what they all said but hadn't been introduced into the story yet. Elihu shared with them a more balanced perspective: that suffering wasn't always a punishment for sin.

Round Four: A Fresh Idea

Elihu was younger and had refrained from speaking, out of respect for his four older friends. But finally, he couldn't contain himself any longer. He believed suffering wasn't always a punishment for sin. Instead, God in his goodness uses it to draw people closer to himself—whether there is sin in a person's life or not. He said, *"God does all these things to a man—twice, even three times"* (Job 33:29). Elihu told Job the suffering wouldn't stop until he realized his arrogant defense of his innocence. Although Elihu's speech didn't attack as ferociously as the other three friends, he still wrongly assumed that suffering was always connected in some way to sin.

What Others are Saying:

Jessie Penn-Lewis: Elihu . . . perceived as he listened, that Job was becoming more and more concerned about clearing his own character, rather than justifying the love and wisdom of God in laying His hand upon him.[7]

Elihu portrayed God as:

- Never doing wrong (34:10)
- Seeing all of man's steps (34:21)
- Mighty and understanding (36:5)
- Exalted and a great teacher (36:22)

Something to Ponder

Whether a person is suffering because of sin or not, God still wants to help solve problems, deliver from sin, and correct weaknesses. Jesus <u>identified</u> the purpose of one man's suffering as an opportunity for God to be glorified. That's always the purpose of any of our struggles—whether it's a result of sin or not.

Overcoming Struggles

THE BIG PICTURE 🔍

> **Job 38–41** Without warning, God himself intervened into the discussion. We aren't told how he communicated or if he appeared in visual form, but a "whirlwind" was mentioned. He ignored the four friends standing nearby and questioned Job in order to show that he was sovereign over everything, even suffering in the world.

☞ **GO TO:**

John 9:3 (identified)

KEY POINT

The purpose of suffering is for God to be glorified.

Round Five: Job's Day In Court

Job was trying to sort out the issues of suffering when God came to him to demonstrate his love for Job. As God revealed his own greatness and sovereign authority over all the earth, Job lost all desire to proclaim his own innocence.

What Others are Saying:

Max Lucado: To recognize God as Lord is to acknowledge that he is sovereign and supreme in the universe.[8]

God asked Job to consider the following questions:

- Where were you when I created the universe?
- Did you help me create the morning?
- Have you walked in the depths of the ocean?
- Do you know when mountain goats give birth?
- Who takes care of an ostrich egg when its mother leaves it abandoned?

Something to Ponder

How would you have answered those questions? Job said, *"I am unworthy—how can I reply to you? I put my hand over my mouth. I spoke once, but I have no answer— twice, but I will say no more"* (Job 40:4–5). That would be a good thing for us to keep on the tip of our tongues.

God never did directly address the issues that Job and his friends had covered. It's as if God was saying all that wasn't important. What was important was that they knew he was sovereign and in control of everything. He communicated that his ways are <u>beyond</u> human comprehension. Even if he explained his actions, people wouldn't understand.

Remember This . . .

☞ **GO TO:**

Isaiah 55:8 (beyond)

⬛ WARNING ▶

If we try to figure out God and his way of thinking, we will only become frustrated. God knows the big picture and we can only see one small puzzle piece. When he makes decisions or answers our prayers in a certain way, he is basing it on everything he knows, not on the little we know. How much better to trust that he knows best.

Job 42:1–17 Job gave a final answer to God's revelation by affirming his belief that God could do anything he wanted and always knew the right thing to do. God then rebuked the original three friends for not speaking of him the way Job had. He commanded them to allow Job to pray for them so they wouldn't be punished. God then restored Job's fortunes and allowed him and his wife to have children again.

Vindication!

Although God didn't answer Job's concerns directly, Job had the satisfaction of having a direct conversation with him, which is what Job asked for in the first place. He cried out, "*Oh, that I had someone to hear me! I sign now my defense—let the Almighty answer me; let my accuser put his indictment in writing*" (Job 31:35). In the end, he was satisfied.

Larry Richards: The book of Job does not tell us why God allows good people to suffer. It does remind us that people of faith respond to suffering differently than those without faith.[9]

What Others are Saying:

Some people think that the story of Job is a fable, but James, the brother of Jesus, referred to Job's experience in the book he wrote about the Christian life. He wrote, "*As you know, we consider blessed those who have persevered. You have heard of Job's perseverance and have seen what the Lord finally brought about. The Lord is full of compassion and mercy*" (James 5:11). That would seem to be a confirmation of Job's story actually happening.

Something to Ponder

God never rebuked the comments of Elihu. He never even referred to what Elihu said. We can most likely assume, therefore, that God thought Elihu's ideas were acceptable and truthful, otherwise, he would have rebuked Elihu along with Job's other friends.

Remember This . . .

Just like Job, when we are suffering, we want to know God hasn't forgotten us or forsaken us. We want to know he's aware of our pain. Even if we don't learn why we are suffering, if we know he cares, that can be enough.

Overcoming Struggles

Study Questions

1. What were the dimensions of the Ark God instructed Noah to build?
2. After the flood, what did God's creation of the rainbow represent?
3. How did God control what happened to Job?
4. How did Job keep from blaming God?

CHAPTER WRAP-UP

- Noah and his family were the only people on earth whom God considered righteous. God chose Noah to build an Ark and save himself, his family, and the animals of the earth for the coming flood. (Genesis 6:5–12)

- Following God's instructions, Noah faithfully built an Ark for 120 years, even though the people around him criticized. When God sent the flood over all the earth, everyone and everything was destroyed, except the people and animals in the Ark. (Genesis 6:13–7:24)

- After the flood receded, everyone left the Ark. Noah again showed his faith in God by building an altar. God created the first-ever rainbow to symbolize his promise that he would never again destroy the earth by flood. (Genesis 8:1–9:19)

- Job was another righteous man who believed God couldn't do anything wrong. Even when Satan orchestrated the murder of Job's ten children and the destruction of everything he owned, Job still trusted God. (Job 1:1–22)

- When Satan saw that Job kept his allegiance to God, Satan broadened his attack (with God's permission) to include physical illness that took Job to the edge of death. Yet Job still didn't blame God for doing anything wrong. (Job 2:1–10)

- Four friends of Job tried to convince him he was suffering because he had sinned. Job maintained his innocence. At last, in answer to Job's cry, God responded by pointing to his own majestic sovereignty. Job was vindicated and richly rewarded for his steadfast faith. (Job 2:11–31:40)

9 MEN OF POWER: LESSONS IN MIGHT AND MISSTEPS

Let's Get Started

Although many people in the Bible had God's power, there are three men in particular who showed God's strength in remarkable ways. Samson was physically powerful but spiritually weak. Elijah had great power, calling down fire from heaven in a tremendous display of God's glory; but a queen intimidated him. Elisha, whom Elijah mentored, performed even more miracles than Elijah did.

All three of these men were people just like you and me. And just as God wanted to glorify himself through them, he wants to glorify himself through us. They weren't perfect and neither are we. If God can use them, he can use us. Let's see what we can learn from them.

Samson

. . . a Man of Great Physical Power

> **Judges 13:24–25** The woman gave birth to a boy and named him Samson. He grew and the Lord blessed him, and the Spirit of the Lord began to stir him while he was in Mahaneh Dan, between Zorah and Eshtaol.

Blessed And Stirred

An angel foretold Samson's birth, and said to his parents, *"No razor may be used on his head, because the boy is to be a Nazirite, set apart to God from birth, and he will begin the deliverance of Israel from the hands of the Philistine"* (Judges 13:5).

GO TO:

Numbers 6:2–7 (rules)

Numbers 6:19
(ceremony)

A Nazirite had to follow these <u>rules</u>:

- He had to abstain from wine and other fermented drink.
- He could not drink vinegar made from wine or from other fermented drink.
- He could not drink grape juice or eat grapes or raisins.
- He could not eat anything that came from the grapevine, not even the seeds or skins.
- No razor could be used on his head.
- He had to remain holy until the period of his separation to the Lord was over.
- He could not go near a dead body, not even that of his parents or relatives.

Most people who made such vows went through a <u>ceremony</u> of sacrificing their hair to the Lord. But Samson was born for a special work.

judges: presiding officers over Hebrew affairs

Israel was entering the end of a historical time when **judges** ruled the land (see illustration, page 123). The Hebrews were again under the thumb of the Philistines. Samson was one of the last judges and served Israel for twenty years. Unfortunately, Samson wasn't prepared for the crisis the Hebrews faced. He misused his gifts and the power the Holy Spirit gave him.

What Others are Saying:

Michael Wilcock: The Nazirite would say a definite no to certain perfectly natural things in order to show how definite was . . . his dedication of himself to God.[1]

BUILD YOUR SPIRIT: Although no one takes a Nazirite vow these days, we can do something with the same spiritual significance by **fasting** for a period of time from food or activity. The purpose is to develop spiritual muscles.

fasting: going without something desirable

GO TO:

Acts 14:23 (fasting)

Genesis 38:12 (Timnah)

Judges 14:1–4 Samson went down to <u>Timnah</u> and saw there a young Philistine woman. When he returned, he said to his father and mother, "I have seen a Philistine woman in Timnah; now get her for me as my wife." His father and mother replied, "Isn't there an acceptable woman among your relatives or among all our people? Must you go to the uncircumcised Philistines to get a wife?" But Samson said to his father, "Get her for me.

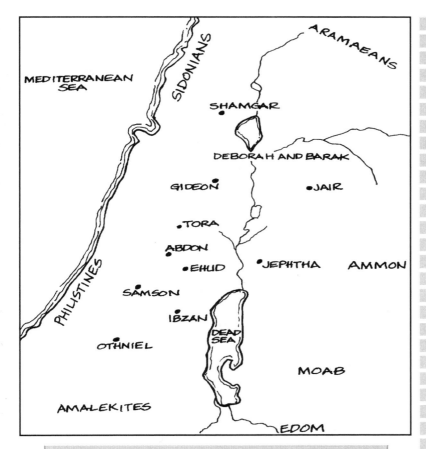

Period of the Judges

The Israelites often suffered oppression from outside clans, such as the Philistines. The judges were unofficial leaders who stepped in to deliver various groups of Israelites from the foreign oppressors. Often, after the judge brought military victory, he or she would also rule. This map shows the seats of the judges and the enemies of Israel.

KEY POINT

When we sacrifice, we develop our spiritual muscles.

She's the right one for me." (His parents did not know that this was from the Lord, who was seeking an occasion to confront the Philistines; for at that time they were ruling over Israel.)

I Want What I Want

Samson's appetite for pleasure overcame his devotion to God. Imagine a Nazirite wanting to marry a Philistine woman who worshiped the god Dagon (see illustration, this page). Samson repeated this desire to compromise God's rules until he paid for his excesses with his life.

Dagon

Known as the father of the god Baal, Dagon was associated with agriculture and the life-giving powers of water. He was the national god of the Philistines.

Dr. Tony Evans: Be clear on who you are. Present yourself as a slave of righteousness, not a slave of sin. You owe sin absolutely nothing. You are going to sin, but don't be a slave to sin. Don't let sin control you. Samson was a great man of God, but he became a slave to lust.[2]

Something to Ponder

Although God cannot be in the presence of evil, he uses it for his purposes. It seems that God allowed Samson to follow foolishness, intending to bring good from Samson's unrighteous conduct.

Grow Your Family

Since God doesn't want his children connected with unbelievers in marriage or business, we must teach our children that marrying or partnering with those who don't love and obey God will only bring great difficulty into their lives. "Do not be yoked together with unbelievers. For what do righteousness and wickedness have in common? Or what fellowship can light have with darkness? What harmony is there between Christ and **Belial**? What does a believer have in common with an unbeliever?" *(2 Corinthians 6:14–15).*

Belial: *name of a false god*

> **Judges 14:5–9** Samson went down to Timnah together with his father and mother. As they approached the vineyards of Timnah, suddenly a young lion came roaring toward him. The Spirit of the Lord came upon him in power so that he tore the lion apart with his bare hands as he might have torn a young goat. But he told neither his father nor his mother what he had done. Then he went down and talked with the woman, and he liked her. Some time later, when he went back to marry her, he turned aside to look at the lion's carcass. In it was a swarm of bees and some honey, which he scooped out with his hands and ate as he went along. When he rejoined his parents, he gave them some, and they too ate it. But he did not tell them that he had taken the honey from the lion's carcass.

Remember? No Contact With Dead Bodies?

God showed Samson what he could do with the Spirit of the Lord empowering him. As a Nazirite, he wasn't supposed to touch any dead thing. He violated his vows by returning to the carcass and taking the honey.

Satan is also called a roaring lion in the Bible. *"Your enemy the devil prowls around like a roaring lion looking for someone to devour. Resist him, standing firm in the faith, because you know that your brothers throughout the world are undergoing the same kind of sufferings"* (1 Peter 5:8–9). As Samson should have avoided the unclean lion carcass, we should avoid Satan's unclean influence in our hearts.

Remember This . . .

The Lord Jesus conquered Satan on the cross and <u>spiritual death</u> was eliminated. Like Samson, we can find sweetness in life from the victory of knowing Satan and his evil plans don't have to control us. But even though that fatal attraction is dead, we still must <u>choose</u> to live in God's power.

Overcoming Struggles

THE BIG PICTURE 🔍

> **Judges 14:10–20** For Samson's wedding feast, he bet his companions they couldn't figure out his riddle in seven days. When they couldn't, they bullied Samson's new wife into getting them the answer. When they answered Samson's riddle, he realized how they had figured it out. Angered, he killed some Philistines and took their clothing to pay off the bet.

☞ **GO TO:**

1 Corinthians 15:55–57 (spiritual death)

Romans 6:12 (choose)

KEY POINT

Even though Satan is a roaring lion, he's toothless.

Can't You Keep A Secret?

Samson's new wife deceived him because she favored her Philistine guests and also feared for her life. Samson killed those who turned his wife against him. Samson then abandoned his wife and ran to his parents' home.

This experience should have been a warning to Samson of his wrong choice in a wife, but he seemed oblivious to how he had brought this on himself. *"A man's own folly ruins his life, yet his heart rages against the Lord"* (Proverbs 19:3). His anger may indicate that he felt guilty but wasn't willing to face his own poor choices.

Something to Ponder

Samson increased his exposure to deception by marrying an unbeliever. When we love someone, we don't want to truthfully face how she is influencing us. Since his wife didn't care about spiritual things, she couldn't give help his spiritual perspective.

Remember This . . .

Overcoming Struggles

Anger is a deceptive emotion that tries to make others seem like the cause of our problems. There is also a behavior called "displacement" where we blame something or someone for our anger, but the cause is really something else. Ask yourself, "What am I really angry about?" Then you can deal with the real issue.

Grow Your Family

One of the advantages of marrying a Christian wife is to have her godly perspective to complement and add to your own. Two heads definitely are better than one, but that extra head should be based on the <u>mind of Christ</u>.

THE BIG PICTURE

Judges 15:1–8 When Samson heard his father-in-law had given his wife to someone else in marriage, Samson took out his anger on all the Philistines by tying burning torches to foxes and sending them through the grain fields to burn the Philistine crops.

I'll Teach You A Lesson

Setting the grain fields afire was a great threat to the Philistines because those fields provided the food for the next year. Ironically, instead of threatening Samson directly, the Philistines threatened Samson's wife, saying they would burn her and her father's house. She betrayed her husband again, and the very thing that she feared came upon her as she and her father's house were burned.

Samson's revenge didn't get his wife back. It just got him more troubles. We don't know why, but Samson had a hard time thinking clearly, which seems amazing considering he was a judge over Israel for twenty years. We don't hear about any of the good things that he did as a judge—if he did anything good. Evidently, God wants us to learn from the wrong choices Samson made.

GO TO:

1 Corinthians 2:16 (mind of Christ)

What Others are Saying:

Charles R. Swindoll: You'll find out what Samson discovered—focusing on the sensual side of life will bring one anxiety, one heartache, after another. . . . The revenge he took against the Philistines incited them to an intense hatred in return.[3]

126   GOD'S WORD FOR THE BIBLICALLY-INEPT

Revenge is never God's plan for us. He wants us to turn the other cheek if slapped. He is the one who is in charge of giving punishments and revenge.

WARNING

BUILD YOUR SPIRIT: We aren't even supposed to fret about the deeds or activities of the unrighteous. *"Do not fret because of evil men or be envious of those who do wrong; for like the grass they will soon wither, like green plants they will soon die away"* (Psalm 37:1–2). However, God does want us to fight the influence of evil by doing <u>good</u>.

☞ **GO TO:**

Romans 12:19 (revenge)

Romans 12:21 (good)

> **Judges 15:9–20** The Philistines took revenge on Samson by advancing on the men of Judah. Outnumbered and frightened, the men of Judah talked Samson into surrendering himself to the angry Philistines. As Samson was about to be handed over, God's power came upon him and he broke free and killed one thousand men.

I Did It My Way

Samson killed one thousand men with a club made of bone. The battle wasn't won because of the weapon or the man swinging it. It was because the Spirit of God moved the arm. Unfortunately, the man at the end of the arm took the credit. Then Samson said, *"With a donkey's jawbone I have made donkeys of them. With a donkey's jawbone I have killed a thousand men"* (Judges 15:16).

Samson believed his own press. Only later did he credit the Lord's help. The theme of his life seems to be found in verse 11: *"as they did to me, I'll do to them."*

Michael Wilcock: For the first time, he found himself in a situation he could not cope with. He asked for God's help instead of taking it for granted, and had a prayer answered. These remarkable events registered even with simple Samson.[4]

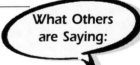
What Others are Saying:

Samson is mentioned in the Hall of Faith in Hebrews 11:32. Only the grace of God can explain how a man of such strength could be overshadowed by his moral weakness and then be included in a list of godly men and women.

Something to Ponder

☞ **GO TO:**

1 Corinthians 1:31 (boast)

2 Timothy 4:8 (crowns)

Revelation 4:10 (lay)

Proverbs 27:15–16 (nagging)

We must be very careful to not take credit or boast about that which God does. One day we will receive crowns in heaven with gems marking the things we did for God. But we won't keep them. We'll lay them in honor before God's throne—because he was the source of them.

THE BIG PICTURE 🔍

> **Judges 16:1–22** Samson lusted again, this time for Delilah. The Philistines paid her to find out the secret of his strength. After nagging him for a long while, Delilah finally got the truth: the source was his long hair. The Philistines attacked him, cut his hair, and were able to take him into bondage because he no longer had God's power.

Another Nagging Woman Breaks Him!

Samson's lust for women led him to Gaza so he could visit a prostitute. During this visit he escaped from some Philistines who had plotted to kill him. His third encounter with a Philistine woman would be different. Unrestrained lust poisoned all his judgment as he surrendered to Delilah. Samson's desire for "strange" women blinded him. When his seven braids were cut, he betrayed his sacred vow to Jehovah God.

What Others are Saying:

John Jewell: When the Philistines cut Samson's hair they took him, bound him, blinded him, danced around him, and made scorn and games of him. We are like Samson. The strength of our hair is the knowledge of the will of God. It is contained in our heads, the highest and principal part of us. If it is shorn off, if we are kept from hearing, reading, and understanding the Bible, then we will succumb to superstition.[5]

Remember This . . .

Nagging goes all the way back in history. Samson's first wife nagged him and so did Delilah. *"With such nagging she prodded him day after day until he was tired to death"* (Judges 16:16). Obviously, Satan knew the chink in Samson's armor, and he worked at it persistently through the ungodly women Samson chose. If Samson had picked more wisely, maybe he wouldn't have had to deal with so much destructive nagging.

Lust is like a whirlpool. The excitement of the forbidden spins you faster, filling your emotions with excitement. But the faster you spin, the deeper you plunge. When that whirlwind spits you out, there is no escape from the shame, loss of reputation, and suffering. The anguish is always greater than the <u>pleasures</u> of the sin.

Satan knows the chink in your armor. That's why you should always wear the <u>armor</u> of God. It gives us all the protection and power we need to fight against evil forces.

If your wife tends to nag you, could it be because you don't respond? Women often feel helpless in trying to get their husbands to meet their needs. As a result, anger feeds their relentless asking. You can turn that around by being responsive to her requests and desires.

THE BIG PICTURE 🔍

> **Judges 16:23–31** While Samson was in the custody of the Philistines, they gouged out his eyes. But eventually, his hair grew back and his strength increased. When given the opportunity, in his last moments, he called upon God for help. He caused the death of three thousand Philistines, but it cost his own life, too.

☞ **GO TO:**

Titus 3:3 (pleasures)

Ephesians 6:11 (armor)

From Judge To Prisoner

As a prisoner Samson was strapped into a harness like an ox, grinding wheat in a Philistine mill. After his eyes were gouged out, the darkness deepened his relationship with God. But his earlier choices had ended his chance to deliver Israel from the Philistines. The strongest man in the world ended up one of the most pitiful weaklings in biblical history. He was the laughingstock of his enemies and a warning to all of us.

Oswald Chambers: The spirit of obedience gives more joy to God than anything else on earth. By our obedience, we show that we love Him. The best measure of a spiritual life is not its ecstasies, but its obedience.[6]

What Others are Saying:

Most troubling was Samson's final prayer. Instead of seeking power to avenge the name of God, he asks God for strength so that he could take revenge for the loss of his eyes. Samson missed God's best for him and the Israelites.

Remember This . . .

☞ GO TO:

Genesis 31:21 (Gilead)

1 Kings 12:19 (revolted)

Do you sense God has a claim on your life? Does this claim have some goal? Or, are you tuning out God's plan and flirting around the edges of some whirlpool that threatens to pull you in? All of us who know God are called to obey him and serve him. Our choices can fill our lives with regret or fill our lives with fulfilling service. Which do you choose?

Elijah

. . . from Loner to Mentor

> **1 Kings 17:1** Now Elijah the Tishbite, from Tishbe in Gilead, said to Ahab, "As the Lord, the God of Israel, lives, whom I serve, there will be neither dew nor rain in the next few years except at my word."

New Prophet Confronts King

After the reigns of Saul, David, and Solomon, the ten northern tribes of Israel <u>revolted</u> against the reign of David's throne. Jeroboam, the first king of the northern tribes, posted two calf images near the borders for his people to worship. After he died, six more kings came to power over the course of forty years. None of them did anything to return the people to the Lord.

King Ahab then came to power. Ahab married a woman from a nearby kingdom. Her name was Jezebel and she was a committed worshiper of Baal, the foreign god (see illustration, page 133). Once she felt secure in her position as queen, it became clear she was the real power behind the throne. She influenced Ahab to set up an altar for Baal in Samaria, the capital of Israel. Then she began killing the prophets of Jehovah to rid the land of any godly influences. It was time for an extraordinary man to enter the picture. His name was Elijah.

What Others are Saying:

J. Sidlow Baxter: Here is the man who bearded the beast in its very lair, the man who strode into the king's audience-chamber and denounced the king to his face, in the name of Jehovah. Here is the Martin Luther of old-time Israel.[7]

Imagine walking into the palace and uttering God's judgment to the king. The likelihood of surviving such an event was remote. Through his act, Elijah revealed his enormous <u>courage</u>. Courage is always rooted in three things: **purpose**, **justice**, and **duty**. Elijah possessed all three.

1. Purpose: As God's prophet, Elijah possessed focused purpose. Just like a police officer, fireman, or soldier is motivated by his calling, Elijah moved toward trouble with confidence. His **authority** came from his relationship with God and his calling compelled him to act.
2. Justice: Elijah also possessed a divine sense of justice. As one who knew God and his commands, it was clear to Elijah that the Kingdom of Israel's <u>idolatry</u> was breaking God's heart. Elijah's initial statement demonstrated how deeply rooted he was in the Law.
3. Duty: Elijah acted from duty. He was a prophet of God! It was his role and job to stand for God's righteousness. He hurled a challenge in Ahab's face because God sent him there. In a sense, Elijah was just doing his job.

BUILD YOUR SPIRIT: It is God's Word, the Bible, that strengthens us and gives us the same kind of courage that Elijah possessed. God told Joshua, *"Do not let this Book of the Law depart from your mouth; meditate on it day and night, so that you may be careful to do everything written in it. Then you will be prosperous and successful"* (Joshua 1:8). The more we study the Bible, the more our spiritual inner life is strengthened.

THE BIG PICTURE

1 Kings 17:2–18 After Elijah made his powerful pronouncement to Ahab, the Lord told Elijah to leave Samaria. Elijah obeyed and stayed in a cave where ravens brought bread and meat for him to eat every morning and evening. Elijah drank water from a nearby brook. When the brook dried up, God sent him to a widow's house where God miraculously reproduced food for their provision.

On-The-Job Training

After Elijah delivered God's judgment to Ahab in Beersheba, God told Elijah to flee to the Kerith Ravine, east of the Jordan River,

Something to Ponder

☞ **GO TO:**

Matthew 14:27 (courage)

Ephesians 2:10 (purpose)

Leviticus 19:15 (justice)

1 Kings 14:9 (idolatry)

purpose: *reason for living*

justice: *fairness*

duty: *obligation*

authority: *command*

KEY POINT

God's Scriptures teach us to recoil at injustice.

This map shows where major events occurred in Elijah's life. The events are numbered chronologically.

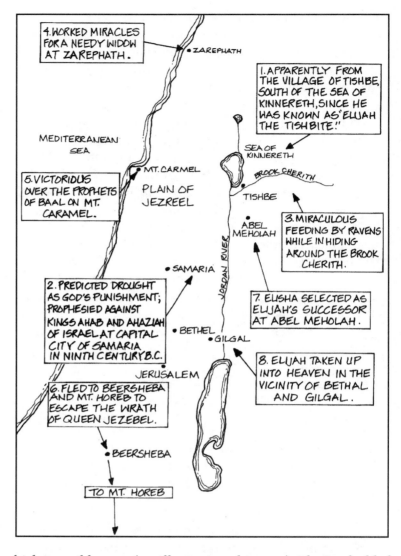

4. WORKED MIRACLES FOR A NEEDY WIDOW AT ZAREPHATH.

• ZAREPHATH

1. APPARENTLY FROM THE VILLAGE OF TISHBE, SOUTH OF THE SEA OF KINNERETH, SINCE HE HAS KNOWN AS 'ELIJAH THE TISHBITE.'

MEDITERRANEAN SEA

SEA OF KINNERETH

MT. CARMEL

BROOK CHERITH

5. VICTORIOUS OVER THE PROPHETS OF BAAL ON MT. CARAMEL.

PLAIN OF JEZREEL

TISHBE

ABEL MEHOLAH

3. MIRACULOUS FEEDING BY RAVENS WHILE IN HIDING AROUND THE BROOK CHERITH.

• SAMARIA

JORDAN RIVER

2. PREDICTED DROUGHT AS GOD'S PUNISHMENT; PROPHESIED AGAINST KINGS AHAB AND AHAZIAH OF ISRAEL AT CAPITAL CITY OF SAMARIA IN NINTH CENTURY B.C.

7. ELISHA SELECTED AS ELIJAH'S SUCCESSOR AT ABEL MEHOLAH.

• BETHEL
• GILGAL

JERUSALEM

8. ELIJAH TAKEN UP INTO HEAVEN IN THE VICINITY OF BETHAL AND GILGAL.

6. FLED TO BEERSHEBA AND MT. HOREB TO ESCAPE THE WRATH OF QUEEN JEZEBEL.

• BEERSHEBA

TO MT. HOREB

drought: land without rain

which is a wilderness (see illustration, this page). The Lord added, *"You will drink from the brook, and I have ordered the ravens to feed you there"* (1 Kings 17:4). But the brook slowed to a trickle as the **drought** impacted the countryside. God was protecting Elijah from Ahab and teaching the prophet to depend on his Lord.

When the brook dried up, God told Elijah to go eighty miles to the west coast, to a town called Zarephath (see illustration, this page). There he would meet a widow who would provide for him. Just as God had said, Elijah found her, a Gentile believer who was about to die from starvation. She responded to Elijah's command to feed him, by wondering out loud how she could provide enough

Baal

Baal was a weather god associated with thunderstorms and fertility. The Israelites fell into and out of Baal worship throughout their history because Baal's influence was strong in foreign tribes.

for Elijah, herself, and her son. Elijah told her to trust God. She obeyed Elijah's request for food and served him first. God honored her faith and obedience. From that day on, there was always enough food to feed them.

Howard Hendricks: My heart leaps at these words because they are in such contrast to my own experience. If I had been in Elijah's shoes, I suspect I might have gotten into an argument with God. I would have listed all the reasons why I was sure that he was making a mistake. . . . But that's not what Elijah did. He simply "did what the Lord had told him."[8]

What Others are Saying:

BUILD YOUR SPIRIT: If you are faced with a bitter life situation that seems to chase your spirit the way Ahab chased Elijah, you need to look closely at Elijah's life. God wants you to give up your self-dependency and <u>depend</u> upon him. If you are thirsty for relief and the only brook you have clung to is now slowing to a trickle, it is time to tap into a new river of life.

GO TO:

Psalm 62:7 (depend on God)

THE BIG PICTURE

1 Kings 18:1–39 The Lord directed Elijah to meet with Ahab on Mount Carmel and propose a test between Baal (see illustration, this page) and Israel's one true God, Jehovah. Ahab and his "team," the 450 priests of Baal, tried to **cajole** their impotent god to burn up their sacrifice. They couldn't make it happen.

cajole: coax

The Showdown

After three years of drought, God arranged for a showdown between Ahab's deity and Elijah's. The confrontation took place on Mount Carmel (see illustration, page 132) regarded as Baal's sacred place, where Ahab assembled 450 false prophets against Yahweh's lone prophet. Thousands of Israelites showed up for this contest like some sports event. Elijah challenged them to make up their minds: *"How long will you waver between two opinions? If the Lord is God, follow him; but if Baal is God, follow him"* (1 Kings 18:21). Elijah challenged the prophets of Baal to place a bull on their altar and call on the name of their god. Elijah would then do likewise. The god who answered by sending fire would prove he is the one true God.

The crowd really enjoyed watching what would happen. Elijah may have been part showman and worked the crowd. The priests called on Baal for six hours, and during that time Elijah trash-talked them with helpful suggestions, such as "Shout louder! Your god can't hear you. Gosh, maybe it's his nap time!" The prophets cut themselves in an effort to force Baal to answer their prayers. But nothing happened.

Then Elijah took his turn. He called the people to gather around. They closely watched as he set up <u>twelve stones</u> representing the twelve tribes of Israel, then dug a trench around this altar. After the bull was **slain** and laid on the wood, Elijah asked the crowd to drench the entire altar with water from four large containers. Once completed, Elijah told them to repeat the soaking two more times. The water ran down the altar and even filled the trench. The stage was set!

This kingdom had been worshiping both God and Baal for some time. Whenever our loyalties are split, there is a sense of uncertainty. The masses may have been ready for a change.

Sometimes as we try to overcome a sin in our lives, we need to risk like Elijah did. Risking for us might mean telling someone about our struggle and asking him to pray for us. God will honor that **vulnerability**. God says, *"Therefore confess your sins to each other and pray for each other so that you may be healed. The prayer of a righteous man is powerful and effective"* (James 5:16).

☞ **GO TO:**

Exodus 28:21 (twelve stones)

slain: killed

Remember This . . .

Overcoming Struggles

vulnerability: opening for possible hurt

> **1 Kings 18:36–37** At the **time** of the sacrifice, the prophet Elijah stepped forward and prayed, "O Lord, God of Abraham, Isaac, and Israel, let it be known to-day that you are God in Israel and that I am your servant and have done all these things at your command. Answer me, O Lord, answer me, so these people will know that you, O Lord, are God, and that you are turning their hearts back again."

time: *3:00 P.M.*

Elijah Prays

The crowds must have hushed as they waited. How could one man compete against 450 priests? After the priest's six-hour prayer marathon, many of those present were probably bewildered when Elijah merely prayed two sentences and stopped. What a contrast!

W. Phillip Keller: Just as the whole of the sacrifice, the wood, the altar, the soil upon which he now stood had been soaked, saturated, and literally submerged in water, so your own soul, spirit, and body have been submerged and saturated and soaked in the Word of the Lord. All was within the will of Jehovah God.[9]

The major difference between other world religions and Christianity is the focus upon the source of effort. With world religions, man must earn his relationship with the god he worships. But Christianity and a relationship with Jehovah is focused upon God's **grace** which provided a way to be **redeemed** through Jesus' sacrificial death. Elijah didn't use his own efforts to make anything happen. Instead he prayed and depended on God's power.

• • •

Elijah's prayer served two purposes: to establish himself in the eyes of others as an obedient servant of God and to get the Israelites to turn their hearts back to Jehovah God.

BUILD YOUR SPIRIT: When we see that God offers salvation as a <u>free gift</u>, not as something to be earned, we are encouraged. We know we can't ever be "good enough" to <u>deserve</u> God's love, therefore we can accept it as he offers it: unconditionally. Whereas people in other religions must always wonder whether they've performed well enough, Christians can know for sure.

What Others are Saying:

Something to Ponder

☞ **GO TO:**

Romans 3:24 (grace)

Galatians 3:13 (redeemed)

Ephesians 2:8–9 (free gift)

Titus 3:5 (deserve)

grace: *undeserved favor*

redeemed: *bought back*

> **1 Kings 18:38–19:8** Elijah victoriously called fire down from heaven on Mount Carmel and called for the killing of the prophets of Baal. The predicted rain arrived and ended the drought. Queen Jezebel threatened Elijah, and he fled to escape her wrath. He grew depressed and prayed for death.

Watch Out! Success Is A Trap!

After Elijah prayed, fire fell from heaven and consumed the sacrifice, the wood, the stones, the soil, and the water in the trench. The people cried out, *"The Lord he is God!"* (1 Kings 18:39). At Elijah's request, the crowd seized the prophets of Baal and killed them. When Jezebel heard of this, she was furious. She sent word to Elijah that he would die before the next day because of what he had done. Elijah, filled with fear, fled to Judea.

What Others are Saying:

Something to Ponder

☞ **GO TO:**

Job 4:14 (fear)

immobilize: *make motionless*

Remember This . . .

WARNING

Oswald Chambers: An average view of the Christian life is that it means deliverance from trouble. It is deliverance in trouble, which is very different.[10]

Elijah's depression shows that he was a man like us. It also revealed how <u>fear</u> can powerfully **immobilize** any of us, even when we serve God successfully. How could a threat from Jezebel have overwhelmed him after those mountaintop experiences? For three and one-half years, Elijah had trusted God completely for his very existence. Elijah even exhorted the widow, *"Do not be afraid"* (1 Kings 17:13). What was the difference this time? We are all more vulnerable after a great victory. It is so easy to become self-confident and self-assured after an experience like this.

In the middle of the Negev Desert, Elijah stopped and prayed, *"I have had enough, Lord. Take my life; I am no better than my ancestors"* (1 Kings 19:4). It was apparent Elijah was severely depressed. Mercifully, the Lord did not answer his prayer. At the end of his rope, Elijah fell asleep under a tree.

Satan watches for the times when we're successful and then uses our new confidence to make us proud. That pride makes us depend upon ourselves and sometimes even credit ourselves for what God did. After success, we must be careful to keep our eyes on God and acknowledge that he made it possible.

Some commentators believe Elijah was depressed because he had failed to end the worship of Baal. But others suggest it was caused by a sense of personal failure in his lack of trust in God when Jezebel threatened him. He might have mentally put himself down for his failure to believe God could deliver him. Although Elijah left Mount Carmel in victory, he never witnessed what God might have accomplished if he had stayed in Jezreel and faced Jezebel's threat head on.

LEADERSHIP  PRINCIPLE—Elijah caved in to the darkest paralyzing aspect of fear. It caused him to flee from his work and did not allow God to supernaturally intervene as he had in the past. Fear diminishes our ability to focus on what God has done through us as leaders and as believers in the past. Fear also clouds our concentration on God's power and causes us to focus on our own inability. The solution is to keep <u>focused</u> on God's powerful <u>abilities</u>.

> **1 Kings 19:9–21** God met with Elijah and gently allowed him to express his feelings of depression. Afterwards God met his physical needs with rest and nourishment and directed him to anoint two new kings and Elisha as his successor. Elijah obeyed and his depression lifted.

Solution For Depression

God directed Elijah to <u>Mt. Horeb</u> (see illustration, page 132), the same place he revealed himself many years earlier to Moses. There Elijah complained to God that he had been **zealous** for him and his kingdom. He rehearsed how the Israelites had rejected God's covenant and killed his prophets. He whined that he was the only one left, and his life was at risk.

God answered his complaints by showing him powerful winds, earthquakes, and fire. Then God spoke to Elijah in a gentle whisper. Elijah again rehearsed how he had been zealous for God and His kingdom. God graciously listened and then gave him three tasks: anoint two different kings and select Elisha as his successor. Then, God gently revealed that there were actually seven thousand faithful believers in Israel.

Elijah left the mountain and found Elisha in a field. He placed the prophet's robe around Elisha's shoulders. Elisha left his family and for ten years was **<u>mentored</u>** by Elijah.

Overcoming Struggles

KEY POINT
Success can make us vulnerable to failure. At those times, we should be more careful.

☞ **GO TO:**

Hebrews 12:2 (focused)

Jude 24 (abilities)

TBP-

zealous: *enthusiastic*

☞ **GO TO:**

Exodus 3:1 (Mt. Horeb)

1 Peter 5:5 (mentor)

mentored: *taught by an adviser*

Something to Ponder

Remember This . . .

☞ **GO TO:**

Psalm 103:13–14 (compassionate)

Proverbs 12:15 (relationships)

God wants to address our pity parties in the same way he did Elijah's. If we'll listen to his <u>compassionate</u> whisper, we'll be able to hear that we are not alone and that he wants to help us. The help may come as he gives us new tasks; or sometimes we need to get our attention off ourselves, so the help comes when God gives us someone to mentor or help.

The gentle whisper Elijah heard can symbolize the quiet inner guidance God uses to direct us. In this example, Elijah learned how to pass both God's authority and his own ministry to successors.

LEADERSHIP PRINCIPLE—When a man is in leadership, he may think he should be a loner. He may think that separating himself emotionally from others distinguishes him as a strong leader. But that may only open him to the possibility of depression and moral failure—or at the least, isolation. Mentoring others and developing healthy <u>relationships</u> with them can diminish the possibility of those destructive tendencies.

BUILD YOUR SPIRIT: When Elijah was depressed, God allowed him to express his feelings and work through his grief and disappointment. When you and I are depressed, we may think God will put us down for our feelings. Just as God dealt gently with this man who called fire down from heaven, he will deal gently with you and me. Elijah's story is an incredible picture of God's grace reaching out to a wounded man. In the same way, he desires to reach out to us when we are hurting.

God's solutions for depression:
- Trust God.
- Seek new purpose.
- Help others.
- Nourish the body.
- Express feelings candidly.

Overcoming Struggles

> **1 Kings 20:13–2 Kings 2:11** Ahab died and his son Ahaziah became king. Because Baal worship continued in the kingdom, Elijah prophesied the new king's death. Arrogantly, Ahaziah sent fifty soldiers to seize Elijah, but they were killed by fire falling from heaven. The king sent another fifty. They also were killed. The king sent fifty more soldiers, but this time their leader had the sense to plead for their lives. Elijah agreed to return with them. He once again told the king, "You will die." In time, Elijah was taken up into heaven without actually dying physically.

Last Steps For Elijah

During Elijah's sunset years we get a glimpse of a changed man. Once independent and a loner in the wilderness, Elijah became a man who embraced his fellow prophets and developed a deep friendship with Elisha. In his last years of life, Elijah touched the lives of many. He and his **protégé**, Elisha, visited the prophet training centers in the region. Just before Elijah was taken up by God, he parted the waters of the Jordan River and he and Elisha walked across. Soon after, Elijah was taken to heaven in a flaming chariot, leaving his position and ministry to Elisha.

protégé: disciple or student

Howard Hendricks: Elijah must have come to the end of his life with a profound sense of significance. It was not just that he had accomplished great things. He had, but more than that, he was leaving a legacy—the legacy of a man into whose life he had poured his own.[11]

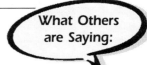

What Others are Saying:

In the New Testament Elijah is mentioned by <u>James</u>, the brother of Jesus, as an example of a man who believed in and practiced prayer. James refers to him as a man who is just like us. Considering the tremendous works that Elijah did, God evidently must want us to work similar works of faith. In a sense, we each can be just like Elijah because God <u>respects</u> any man's prayers of faith.

Something to Ponder

☞ **GO TO:**

James 5:17 (James)

Daniel 9:17 (respects)

LEADERSHIP 🦅 **PRINCIPLE**—Although some may think that operating alone marks the strength of a man, Elijah learned that God wants men to interact with others and even mentor those who will continue God's work. Some would argue the time he spent with Elisha was Elijah's most important work. Who better to prepare the next prophet of God?

The best mentoring that a man can do is to invest in the lives of his family. Although a career may seem very important and take much time, only the investment of love and attention to the members of a man's family will bring the same kind of success that Elijah had. God even wants a man to be willing to give his life for his family.

Grow Your Family

☞ **GO TO:**

Ephesians 5:25 (give)

KEY POINT

God wants us to invest in the lives of others.

☞ **GO TO:**

Numbers 13:5 (Shaphat)

Elisha
. . . the Miracle Man

> **1 Kings 19:19–21** So Elijah went from there and found Elisha son of Shaphat. He was plowing with twelve yoke of oxen, and he himself was driving the twelfth pair. Elijah went up to him and threw his cloak around him. Elisha then left his oxen and ran after Elijah. "Let me kiss my father and mother good-by," he said, "and then I will come with you." "Go back," Elijah replied. "What have I done to you?" So Elisha left him and went back. He took his yoke of oxen and slaughtered them. He burned the plowing equipment to cook the meat and gave it to the people, and they ate. Then he set out to follow Elijah and became his attendant.

Career Change

Elijah was known throughout the land as a mighty prophet of power. When challenged by Elijah to join in service to the Lord, Elisha jumped at the chance. He demonstrated total commitment by sacrificing his oxen—obviously, he didn't plan to resume plowing any day soon. There was nothing for him to return home to. For ten years, he walked with Elijah as a friend. Years spent as a servant, encourager, and companion prepared him for his new role as successor to the prophet Elijah.

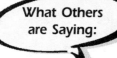
What Others are Saying:

Bruce H. Wilkinson and Larry Libby: Elisha's first ministry was simply to become Elijah's friend. To be a listening ear; to offer words of counsel. To just be there. He poured the refreshing water of encouragement over Elijah's heart as a close companion.[12]

We don't know what it meant for Elisha to have the prophet's mantle placed on his shoulder. It could have been a common action that prophets frequently used. Regardless, it's obvious that Elisha knew immediately what it meant. We also don't know if Elijah and Elisha had previous contact. We do know that Elijah had earlier been <u>instructed</u> by God to go and commission Elisha as his successor, but whether Elijah knew him previously, we don't know.

It might not be clear today that Elijah gave permission to Elisha to go and do the things he asked. But based on the language of that day, when Elijah said, "*What have I done to you?*" that was the same as saying, "Do as you please" or "What have I done to stop you?"

From the fact that Elisha was leading twelve yoke (pairs) of oxen, we know that he was a well-to-do farmer and had a lot to give up. Just as Elisha destroyed everything that could draw him back from serving God, so must we. Jesus warned that, *"No one who puts his hand to the plow and looks back is fit for service in the kingdom of God"* (Luke 9:62).

BUILD YOUR SPIRIT: The only way to grow spiritually is to be <u>convinced</u> that Jesus is God, and that he died for your sins. In addition, we must surrender to God's control and be committed to growing in his power. Although we won't do all these things perfectly, a half-hearted consideration of Jesus' claims will prevent us from becoming committed. We must count the <u>cost</u> and then surrender.

> **2 Kings 2:1–6** When the Lord was about to take Elijah up to heaven in a whirlwind, Elijah and Elisha were on their way from Gilgal [see illustration, page 132]. Elijah said to Elisha, "Stay here; the Lord has sent me to Bethel." But Elisha said, "As surely as the Lord lives and as you live, I will not leave you." So they went down to Bethel. The company of the prophets at Bethel came out to Elisha and asked, "Do you know that the Lord is going to take your master from you today?" "Yes, I know," Elisha replied, "but do not speak of it." Then Elijah said to him,

Something to Ponder

☞ **GO TO:**

1 Kings 19:16 (instructed)

Remember This . . .

WARNING

☞ **GO TO:**

Romans 4:24 (convinced)

Luke 14:28–33 (cost)

KEY POINT

Count the cost and then surrender to God.

> "Stay here, Elisha; the Lord has sent me to Jericho." And he replied, "As surely as the Lord lives and as you live, I will not leave you." So they went to Jericho. The company of the prophets at Jericho went up to Elisha and asked him, "Do you know that the Lord is going to take your master from you today?" "Yes, I know," he replied, "but do not speak of it." Then Elijah said to him, "Stay here; the Lord has sent me to the Jordan." And he replied, "As surely as the Lord lives and as you live, I will not leave you." So the two of them walked on.

I Know You're Going To Leave Me!

Elijah and Elisha both sensed that God would be taking Elijah up into heaven without experiencing death. We don't know how, but maybe God had communicated that to Elijah and then he had told others. When the other local prophets mentioned it to Elisha, he told them to be quiet. Maybe it was too painful for him to discuss.

What Others are Saying:

Remember This . . .

☞ **GO TO:**

Genesis 5:24 (Enoch)

Steve Farrar: If you . . . travel into the future, what would your legacy look like? Would there be a chain linking generation to generation with godly men who in turn produce more godly men?[13]

Elijah gave Elisha a challenge. He could choose to stay or he could choose to come with him and experience what God had in mind.

• • •

Only two people in the Bible never experienced death. One is Enoch and the other is Elijah. Even Jesus died, but then later was raised from the earth in his resurrected body. Obviously, this practice of taking people off the earth without them dying was not something God did often.

🚶 **BUILD YOUR SPIRIT:** Just as Elisha had to choose whether to continue traveling on in discomfort in order to receive the blessing and power of Elijah, we must choose to be inconvenienced in order to live a godly life. For some it will mean service in a foreign country. For others, it may be a financial sacrifice, or it could mean standing alone in a family to represent Christ. Being a Christian isn't always comfortable, but it does bring eternal benefits and blessings.

> **2 Kings 2:7–10** Fifty men of the company of the prophets went and stood at a distance, facing the place where Elijah and Elisha had stopped at the Jordan. Elijah took his cloak, rolled it up and struck the water with it. The water divided to the right and to the left, and the two of them crossed over on dry ground. When they had crossed, Elijah said to Elisha, "Tell me, what can I do for you before I am taken from you?" "Let me inherit a double portion of your spirit," Elisha replied. "You have asked a difficult thing," Elijah said, "yet if you see me when I am taken from you, it will be yours—otherwise not."

Give Me A Double Portion Of Power

Everyone was waiting to see this incredible sight. They lined up along the Jordan River like spectators at a soccer game. Elijah did one last miracle, showing again the power of his cloak—which Elisha could inherit if he watched at the right time. Ten years earlier, Elisha had given up everything to follow Elijah. At the end, the only thing he asked was Elijah's blessing, like the blessing a father would give a son.

Elisha was passionate about becoming a prophet of God. When he asked for a double portion, Elijah responded that his request was *"a hard thing."* Elijah must have known that only God could give a double portion.

<u>Solomon</u>, a past king of Israel, had an opportunity to ask God for anything he wanted. He chose wisdom. As a result, God also gave him riches and victory. Like Solomon, Elisha could have asked Elijah for something material, but he chose something spiritual.

Every Christian should have a passionate desire for spiritual things. When we know how much God <u>loves</u> us, we will want to read his loving words in the Bible. When we recognize how <u>wise</u> God is, we will want to pray to find out his perspective. When we concentrate on how he <u>knows</u> the best thing for us to do, we'll want to obey.

☞ **GO TO:**

1 Kings 3:9 (Solomon)

Psalm 146:8 (loves)

Romans 16:27 (wise)

1 John 3:20 (knows)

Something to Ponder

Remember This . . .

WARNING

 **BUILD YOUR SPIRIT:** There are many good reasons why we should be passionate about spiritual things. Not counted among them is the idea that following God will also bring us earthly gain. The Apostle Paul wrote, *"What is more, I consider everything a loss compared to the surpassing greatness of knowing Christ Jesus my Lord, for whose sake I have lost all things. I consider them **rubbish**, that I may gain Christ"* (Philippians 3:8).

> **2 Kings 2:11–14** As they were walking along and talking together, suddenly a chariot of fire and horses of fire appeared and separated the two of them, and Elijah went up to heaven in a whirlwind. Elisha saw this and cried out, "My father! My father! The chariots and horsemen of Israel!" And Elisha saw him no more. Then he took hold of his own clothes and tore them apart. He picked up the cloak that had fallen from Elijah and went back and stood on the bank of the Jordan. Then he took the cloak that had fallen from him and struck the water with it. "Where now is the Lord, the God of Elijah?" he asked. When he struck the water, it divided to the right and to the left, and he crossed over.

Wow! Whirlwind And Fire!

The whirlwind that Elisha saw was most likely the same kind of storm represented in the <u>pillar</u> of smoke and fire that accompanied the Israelites as they traveled through the wilderness. After Elijah was gone, Elisha picked up his cloak and called upon God to use him, like God had used Elijah.

Elisha called Elijah "father" and was so grieved by the loss of seeing Elijah transported into heaven that he ripped his own clothes. But it could also represent a shedding of his old life as a prophet-in-training. He was now a full-blown prophet and his new wardrobe was the prophet's mantle.

BUILD YOUR SPIRIT: In a sense, we each "rip off" our old sinful <u>clothing</u> when we accept Christ as Savior and surrender to his Lordship. Just as the stripping of Elisha's clothes could mean final surrender of everything that would prevent him from assuming the mantle and authority of Elijah, you

☞ **GO TO:**

Exodus 13:21 (pillar)

Remember This . . .

☞ **GO TO:**

Colossians 3:8 (clothing)

must also give up everything that prevents you from experiencing your full authority as Christians. Give up sin and selfishness, and instead, *"clothe yourselves with compassion, kindness, humility, gentleness and patience"* (Colossians 3:12).

> **2 Kings 2:15–18** The company of the prophets from Jericho who were watching, said, "The spirit of Elijah is resting on Elisha." And they went to meet him and bowed to the ground before him. "Look," they said, "we your servants have fifty able men. Let them go and look for your master. Perhaps the Spirit of the Lord has picked him up and set him down on some mountain or in some valley." "No," Elisha replied, "do not send them." But they persisted until he was too ashamed to refuse. So he said, "Send them." And they sent fifty men, who searched for three days but did not find him. When they returned to Elisha, who was staying in Jericho, he said to them, "Didn't I tell you not to go?"

Go Look If You Want To

Elisha wasn't surprised at his own power, for God had been preparing him for this very moment. But evidently, the other prophets weren't so sure. Elisha tried to dissuade them from searching for Elijah, but finally gave in. It appears Elisha still had some learning to do about not letting other people influence him. But regardless, he already had their respect, for they bowed down to him.

LEADERSHIP PRINCIPLE—As leaders, we must not be unduly influenced by the opinions of others. Although this is hard and something even Elisha had to learn, we will have more freedom to obey God and do the right thing when we aren't overly worried about what other people think.

THE BIG PICTURE

> **2 Kings 2:19–22; 4:1–6:13** God worked many miracles through Elisha. God's power became well known among the Israelites and his name spread throughout the world.

The Double Portion Has Come True

Elisha's passionate desire to glorify God and be used by him was rewarded. Even after he died, his bones did a miracle. When a dead person was thrown into Elisha's grave, the man came back to life.

Bruce H. Wilkinson and Larry Libby: Elisha never tried to imitate Elijah! It was not Elijah's mannerisms, style, or methods he had requested; it was Elijah's strength and spirit. Now, endowed with that strength, Elisha was free to utilize his own gifts—he was free to be himself.[14]

Dr. Tony Evans: God never meant for his blessings on your life and mine to produce pride. The more we are blessed, the more humble we should be. The more we have, the lower we should go. Pride says, "I pulled myself up by my own bootstraps." What God says is, "I gave you the boots! I put them on you."[15]

Remember This . . .

God never wants a person whom he uses to take credit for the things they do in God's power. In all things, God wants to be **<u>exalted</u>** and **magnified** in the eyes of others through the works we do for him.

☞ **GO TO:**

Philippians 1:20 (exalted)

It is a very serious offense in God's eyes for someone to take the glory that only God deserves. God is a jealous God and he is the source of everything good that happens on the earth. *"I am the Lord; that is my name! I will not give my glory to another or my praise to idols"* (Isaiah 42:8). If we attribute the good in our lives to something or someone other than God—even ourselves—then it becomes a "god." God cannot allow that to happen because only he deserves to be credited.

WARNING

exalted: *lifted up*

magnified: *made more apparent*

Nothing is too hard for God. His <u>power</u> makes everything that he desires possible. The disciples thought it was impossible for the <u>rich</u> to enter heaven, but Jesus said it was possible. The <u>virgin</u> Mary thought it was impossible for her to become pregnant, but the Holy Spirit made it possible. Everyone thought it was impossible for Jesus to be raised from the <u>dead</u>, but God made it possible. When we begin to feel hopeless or helpless about our situation or problem, we can remember that with God, all things are possible.

Overcoming Struggles

Summary of Miracles of Elisha and Their Meaning

Miracle	Meaning	Scripture
Jordan divided	Demonstrated the transfer of power from Elijah to Elisha.	2 Kings 2:14
Waters healed at Jericho	Demonstrated the Lord, not Baal, could heal the spiritual pollution of their soul.	2 Kings 2:21
Mocking youths torn by bears	Demonstrated the consequences of open disrespect for the Lord.	2 Kings 2:24
Water supplied	Deliverance from enemy.	2 Kings 3:16
Widow's oil multiplied	Faith rewarded with abundance.	2 Kings 4:5
Barren woman gave birth and her child raised from death	God's power was exhibited in answer to earnest prayer.	2 Kings 4:35
Poisoned stew rendered harmless	Represented the poison of false gods and how God could make them unable to influence his people.	2 Kings 4:41
Loaves multiplied	God could expand the resources dedicated to him.	2 Kings 4:43
Naaman healed	Proof of God's power even over leprosy.	2 Kings 5:10
Gehazi struck with leprosy	Gehazi had lied and God disciplined him.	2 Kings 5:27
Iron ax head caused to float	God could supernaturally provide for his servant's needs.	2 Kings 6:6
Syrians smitten	God protected his people.	2 Kings 6:18
Resurrection of a man	If God could bring a dead man back to life, then he could give victory to Israel.	2 Kings 13:21

Study Questions

1. What did Samson force his parents to get for him even though they objected?
2. How did Delilah finally force Samson to tell her the secret of his great physical strength?
3. What did Elijah do on Mount Carmel that brought glory to God?
4. What kind of solutions did God give Elijah for his depression?
5. When Elijah was about to be carried up into heaven, what did Elisha ask for from Elijah?
6. How did Elisha know he had received the double portion of power that he asked for from Elijah?

☞ **GO TO:**

Psalm 68:35 (power)

Matthew 19:26; Mark 10:27; Luke 18:27 (rich)

Luke 1:37 (virgin)

Acts 2:24 (dead)

- Samson was chosen by God to be a Nazirite but foolishly wanted a wife from the Philistine camp. Samson always seemed to want more, even more than God wanted for him. (Judges 14:1–4)

- Delilah eventually convinced Samson to tell her the secret source of his strength, and it caused him to be captured by the Philistines. Samson's divided loyalty brought an early death. (Judges 16:1–22)

- Elijah was a powerful prophet of God who defeated the priests of Baal by calling down fire from heaven. (1 Kings 18:1–39)

- After that successful display, Elijah was threatened by Queen Jezebel and he ran away, fearful and depressed. But God brought him the help he needed through Elisha and a new mission. (1 Kings 19:9–21)

- Elisha was Elijah's fully committed assistant. When Elijah was about to go up into heaven, Elisha asked him for a double portion of power. (2 Kings 2:7–10)

- Elisha did even more miracles than Elijah and was a powerful representative for God among the people. (2 Kings 2:19–22; 4:1–6:13)

10 MEN OF WISDOM: LESSONS IN OBEYING GOD'S WORD

CHAPTER HIGHLIGHTS

- Samuel's Long, Glorious Service
- Solomon's Challenge: Reign Wisely
- Ezra Valued the Scriptures
- Nehemiah Fought Great Opposition

Let's Get Started

Wisdom is something we all want. But it can be elusive. We think we've finally gained some; then an unfamiliar situation arises, and we're clueless as to how to handle it. But God wants to give us wisdom—a wisdom that he defines as *"first of all pure; then peace-loving, considerate, submissive, full of mercy and good fruit, impartial and sincere"* (James 3:17).

Many men of the Bible had that kind of wisdom, but four men stand out. The first, Samuel, was a prophet, intercessor, priest, and judge, who was God's man at a turning point in Israel's history. As the last judge of Israel, Samuel oversaw their transition from a tribal people into a monarchy.

The second, Solomon, king of Israel, had supernatural wisdom, but that didn't always help him have a heart for God. The third and fourth, Ezra and Nehemiah, were both exiled Jews who called upon God and his Law to empower them to take courageous steps to build the people of Jerusalem.

Want wisdom? Me too. Let's see what rubs off when we hang out with wise guys.

☞ **GO TO:**

James 1:5 (wisdom)

Samuel

. . . Prophet of Integrity

THE BIG PICTURE

> **1 Samuel 1–3** Hannah was barren. She vowed that if she became pregnant, she would dedicate her child to serve in the temple. God answered her prayers, and she gave her son, Samuel, over to Eli, the temple priest, to be raised in the service of the Lord. As a youngster, Samuel learned to hear God's voice. God told him Eli's sons would be judged because they were wicked.

Are You Speaking To Me?

panoramic: high-level; overall

We only get a **panoramic** view of Samuel's life. His mother Hannah prayed for a child and, out of gratitude, she dedicated the child to serving the Lord. When Samuel turned three, Hannah took him to the tabernacle and gave him to Eli, the high priest. Eli proved a poor father with his own sons, but his father/mentor role with Samuel was successful.

Something to Ponder

When Samuel heard God's voice, he didn't know who was speaking. He thought it was Eli. Eli told Samuel to respond, *"Speak, Lord, for your servant is listening"* (1 Samuel 3:9). When Samuel heard God's message of judgment for Eli and his family, he was afraid to tell Eli. Finally, at Eli's urging, he did.

What Others are Saying:

Bruce H. Wilkinson and Larry Libby: When the Lord saw that Samuel could be trusted with even a heartbreaking task like this, he did not hesitate to place more and more authority into Samuel's hands. He began to use the young man as his spokesman to a whole generation.[1]

Remember This . . .

God's words to prophets or anyone during this point in Israel's history were very rare. No wonder both Eli and Samuel didn't recognize God's voice. For centuries, there hadn't been anyone God could trust with his message.

WARNING

We should be careful about claiming that we hear God's voice. In 1 Samuel 3:19 it says, *"The Lord was with Samuel as he grew up, and he let none of his words fall to the ground."* In other words, everything he prophesied was fulfilled.

BUILD YOUR SPIRIT: When we ask God to speak to us, we must be willing to obey. To ask God to speak to us with no intention of obeying is called "testing God," an arrogant and dangerous practice.

> **1 Samuel 7:3–6** And Samuel said to the whole house of Israel, "If you are returning to the Lord with all your hearts, then rid yourselves of the foreign gods and the Ashtoreths and commit yourselves to the Lord and serve him only, and he will deliver you out of the hand of the Philistines." So the Israelites put away their Baals and Ashtoreths [see illustration, page 133], and served the Lord only. Then Samuel said, "Assemble all Israel at Mizpah and I will intercede with the Lord for you." When they had assembled at Mizpah, they drew water and poured it out before the Lord. On that day they fasted and there they confessed, "We have sinned against the Lord." And Samuel was leader of Israel at Mizpah.

First Public Ministry

All of Israel was in sorrow because the Lord had seemingly abandoned them. But they had wandered away from God and were worshiping idols. In a large public meeting, Samuel challenged the country to destroy their Ashtoreth poles and commit themselves to the real God. During this time of prayer and sacrifice, many Israelis must have turned back to the Lord, since they asked Samuel to seek God's intervention.

F. B. Meyer: The power of Samuel's prayers was already known throughout the land, like those of John Knox in the days of Queen Mary. The people had come to believe in them. If only Samuel would pray, they might count on deliverance. They knew that he had prayed; they now entreated that he would not cease.[2]

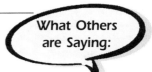

What Others are Saying:

Something to Ponder

Over and over again in the history of Israel, during times of prosperity they turned away from God. He would then allow them to be conquered by their enemies. This difficulty made them seek God's help. God would then rescue them. During times of peace and prosperity, they would turn away from God again. And so the cycle continued.

LEADERSHIP  **PRINCIPLE**—As leaders, we need to be sensitive to the spirit of the people we have responsibility over. If they are resistant, then we must be cautious about trying to lead them to new areas of growth or challenge. But if they are willing, we can jump forward with power.

Just as God responded every time the Israelites called for help, he will never fail to respond to our pleas in the midst of our struggles. Even if we have tried unsuccessfully over and over again to defeat a sin in our lives, he wants to help us.

THE BIG PICTURE

1 Samuel 8–10 In his old age, Samuel retired and appointed his sons as judges in his place. But they didn't have a heart for God as Samuel did. The Israelites recognized that and complained. They wanted a king. After Samuel prayed about their request, he warned them about the disadvantages of having a king. Then, at God's direction, he anointed Saul as Israel's first king.

It's Retirement Time But He's Busy Choosing A King

Samuel's sons actually used their leadership positions for their own financial advantage. They took bribes and ruled unfairly. When the people experienced injustice, they thought a king would make them happy. Samuel was grieved the nation wanted a king. After all, the Lord, who had delivered them from Egypt, was their real king.

Samuel never experienced a close relationship with his real father. Although Samuel grew in great stature, his sons, like Eli's sons, brought shame upon the nation when placed into leadership. Evidently, Samuel was unable to lead his sons into a close relationship with God like he had. Maybe that was because he didn't have a close relationship with his own father.

Steve Farrar: There is a balance between firmness and tenderness that good fathers constantly try to achieve. Most of us tend to err on one side or the other. But we must strive to maintain that balance for the sake of our children. Don't get discouraged in your attempts to find the balance. Hang in there. . . . We find balance by losing it.[3]

Something to Ponder

What Others are Saying:

Overcoming Struggles

The request for a king by the Israelites was not improper. God had <u>promised</u> them such a leader, but they refused to wait for God's perfect timing. They wanted to be ruled by kings like the rest of the world.

The Israelites would suffer from having a king but they wanted what they wanted! We suffer, too, when we demand something that God doesn't want to give us or we grab it before the proper timing. Sometimes he allows us to have what we demand and then we're sorry. Experiencing the consequence of our hastiness makes us more willing to wait for God the next time.

BUILD YOUR SPIRIT: Just as Israel wanted to be like the nations around them who had kings, we can fall into the wrong idea that what others have will bring us contentment and satisfaction. But whatever it is you want, unless God wants it for you, it will never satisfy.

THE BIG PICTURE 🔍

1 Samuel 12:1–25 Samuel gave a challenge and a sermon to the people of Israel. He reminded them of his own integrity and of their sin in asking for a king. They responded by asking for forgiveness, and he assured them God would not abandon them.

A Little Pep Talk

Samuel gave a parting shot in this speech as he confirmed Saul as the new and first Israelite king. He:

- Asked them to come up with any example of how he had been dishonest or ungodly (verses 1–3)
- Reviewed God's faithfulness in the past throughout the history of Israel (verses 6–12)
- Confirmed Saul as king and commanded both him and them to follow God's commandments (verses 13–14)
- Told them that if they followed God's commands, they would experience success, but if not they would be judged (verses 15–16)
- Called thunder and rain down upon everyone because they had sinned in seeking a king before God's time (verses 17–18)

Remember This . . .

WARNING

☞ **GO TO:**

Deuteronomy 17:14–20; Genesis 17:6 (promised)

KEY POINT

Wait for God's perfect timing.

What Others are Saying:

F. B. Meyer: It was a great opportunity to show them where they had gone wrong, and a man whose own hands are clean is permitted to be the sincere critic of others' misdoing. See to it that your own eye is single, and that the beam is extracted from it before you **essay** to remove the **mote** from your brother's eye.[4]

Something to Ponder

The forcefulness of his words and the sudden thunderstorm got everyone's attention. They confessed their sins, asking Samuel to pray that they wouldn't die. He did and then encouraged them to serve and fear God. Samuel had been effective!

☞ **GO TO:**

Matthew 7:4 (mote)

1 Thessalonians 1:2 (pray)

essay: make effort

mote: speck

LEADERSHIP PRINCIPLE—Samuel said, "*As for me, far be it from me that I should sin against the Lord by failing to pray for you. And I will teach you the way that is good and right*" (1 Samuel 12:23). If we are leading people, especially in an area of ministry, then it is sin for us to not pray for them.

> **1 Samuel 13, 15–16** Samuel continued to be a courageous judge by confronting Saul's sin of offering a sacrifice he wasn't authorized to present. Then Saul disobeyed a second command of God and rationalized his behavior. Even when Saul asked for forgiveness, Samuel told him God had removed his kingly position from him. Saul's removal grieved Samuel deeply. God sent Samuel to anoint the future king, a young shepherd named David. Samuel died and everyone mourned for him.

I Told You So!

Samuel must have felt like saying to the Israelites, "I told you this king idea wouldn't work!" Saul's disobedience grieved him and it took a lot of courage to confront Saul.

When Samuel anointed David as the king who would replace Saul, he must have been relieved and thrilled to know that God had chosen a man after God's own heart. Samuel is listed in the Hall of Faith.

☞ **GO TO:**

Hebrews 11:32 (Hall of Faith)

Something to Ponder

Samuel's courage is more than we might think because a king had the power to kill anyone, even a favored prophet of the people. Also, Saul had proven himself mentally and emotionally unstable by throwing spears at people who made him unhappy.

Samuel demonstrated his heart for God by being grieved about the same things that grieved God. He was deeply saddened that the king of Israel didn't make righteous choices.

LEADERSHIP  PRINCIPLE—There will be times when we will be grieved over someone's sin and we must confront them. Just as God gave Samuel the <u>courage</u> he needed, he will give us the courage to do the right thing.

Remember This . . .

☞ **GO TO:**

Acts 23:11 (courage)

Solomon

. . . Wise Mind, Empty Heart

THE BIG PICTURE 🔍

> **1 Kings 1** Twenty-year-old Solomon had a rocky start to his reign as king over all of Israel and Judah. As his father, David, was about to die, Solomon's half-brother, Adonijah, set himself up as king, even though David had previously determined that Solomon would take the throne. Solomon's mother, Bathsheba, and Nathan the prophet, intervened and pressed David to publicly declare Solomon as the king.

A Rocky Start

King David was near death when his son Adonijah declared himself king, made sacrifices, and started a big celebration. He enlisted the support of Joab, David's ruthless army commander, and Abiathar the high priest. Surprisingly, the destined king, Solomon, was absent from this drama.

Adonijah's bid for the throne was dangerous for Solomon. If David delayed in declaring Solomon king and Adonijah was successful, Solomon and all his friends would be treated as traitors and most likely be killed. This was the common practice of all new kings, so that no one would rise up and threaten their position and authority.

But David made it clear that Solomon was to be appointed king, and the near **coup** by Adonijah was stopped. Later, when Solomon held his rightful position as the king, he handled these acts of rebellion decisively.

When the coup was halted, Adonijah knew his life was in danger, so he pleaded for mercy from Solomon. Solomon gave it to him, promising that he wouldn't kill him. This first act of mercy in his reign would become a common practice of Solomon's.

coup: *rebellion to overthrow a head of state or government*

Something to Ponder

GO TO:

Jude 1:22–23 (Mercy)

BUILD YOUR SPIRIT: Solomon's mercy is a trait that we all need to develop. <u>Mercy</u> is that response that recognizes someone doesn't deserve love but we choose to give it anyway. It's very similar to grace. Mercy and grace are the opposites of bitterness and resentment. Mercy and grace are healthy responses. Bitterness and resentment only poison and destroy our contentment and joy.

THE BIG PICTURE

> **1 Kings 2** Before David died, he instructed Solomon to execute all of his enemies. Adonijah, his half-brother, asked Bathsheba to intercede on his behalf so he could marry Abishag, a concubine of David. Solomon rightly saw this action as laying a foundation for a future attempt to take the throne. Since Adonijah had responded to mercy by making another attempt to usurp the throne, Solomon had him executed. Two others were killed and Abiathar the priest was fired from his position.

Revenge: A Horrible But Necessary Way To Start

Although David was the warrior and Solomon a man of peace, he began his reign by:

- Executing Adonijah for covertly seeking the throne
- Deposing Abiathar from the high priesthood for siding with Adonijah
- Executing Joab for treason and murder
- Imprisoning then executing Shimei for cursing David and transgressing house arrest

What Others are Saying:

Thomas L. Constable: In all Solomon's dealings with his political enemies—men who conspired against the will of God during David's reign—the young king's mercy and wisdom stand out. Because of his wise handling of these threats to the throne the kingdom was then firmly established in Solomon's hands.[5]

Something to Ponder

Solomon needed to establish his kingdom with authority. David's reluctance to hold others accountable worked for him, but threatened the stability of Solomon's reign. Solomon paid the consequences of his father's weaknesses and had to execute a lot of people to solidify his authority.

Solomon had said he wouldn't kill Adonijah but that promise was based on Adonijah's commitment to not threaten his throne. Adonijah blew that commitment when he asked Bathsheba to intervene with Solomon so that he could marry one of David's concubines, for marrying one of the king's wives or concubines was essentially a claim to the throne. The people would feel justified in supporting Adonijah, who, as an older son of David, should have the first rights to the throne. Solomon recognized Adonijah's clever ruse and nipped it in the bud.

Remember This . . .

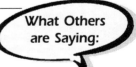

BUILD YOUR SPIRIT: Just as Solomon needed to put his kingdom in order, as Christians we need to put to death all those things that could damage or diminish the reign of Christ in our hearts. These can be things like worry, fear, anger, distrust, or believing wrong ideas about God.

THE BIG PICTURE

1 Kings 3 Solomon began his reign by marrying a daughter of Pharaoh, and, although he loved God, he sacrificed and burned incense to the local gods. Then God revealed himself in a dream, and asked what Solomon wanted. Solomon requested wisdom to reign. Because Solomon asked for such a selfless thing, God promised him wisdom along with riches and honor. His newly-given wisdom was quickly revealed when he wisely solved the problem of two women who claimed the same baby.

A Noteworthy Request

Too bad Solomon didn't ask for wisdom before he married the Pharaoh's daughter. This was a political marriage and secured his southwest border. She would be the first of many women who would introduce idolatry to his realm.

James I. Packer: What makes life worthwhile is having a big enough objective, something which catches our imagination and lays hold of our allegiance; and this the Christian has, in a way that no other man has. For what higher, more exalted, and more compelling goal can there be than to know God?[6]

What Others are Saying:

Solomon pleased the Lord when he asked for wisdom. He was twenty years old when he became king and he knew he was in over his head. Under Solomon's reign, Israel prospered more than at any other time.

However, a bad seed was imbedded in Solomon's request for wisdom. His prayer looked good but it was self-centered. He wanted wisdom to rule men. If David had been given the same choice, he likely would have asked for the ability to serve God more completely. David's cry would have been, "More of you, God." Solomon's cry was, "More wisdom for me." Look at Psalm 72, which was written by Solomon. The focus and attention was clearly toward the king.

BUILD YOUR SPIRIT: Solomon should have requested better knowledge of God. You would think wisdom would lead us to get to know God better. But if our motives are rooted in feeding our egos and needs, there is little room left for godly wisdom. We should model our requests after Paul's petition: "*I keep asking that the God of our Lord Jesus Christ, the glorious Father, may give you the Spirit of wisdom and revelation, so that you may know him better*" (Ephesians 1:17).

THE BIG PICTURE

1 Kings 4 Solomon's wisdom also was revealed in his administration skills. He was a capable delegator, pulling together a talented group of managers to help him rule. Although his kingdom was vast, it enjoyed prosperity and joy [see illustration, page 159].

No End To The Riches

To illustrate the scope of Solomon's riches and wisdom, the biblical record listed many facts about Solomon's reign.

His Land

- The people in his land were numerous and enjoyed great prosperity (1 Kings 4:20).
- The property stretched from the Euphrates River to the land of the Philistines and to the border of Egypt (1 Kings 4:21).
- The kingdoms within those areas paid taxes to support Solomon's grand kingdom (1 Kings 4:21).
- There was no fighting within his border (1 Kings 4:24).
- Every person felt safe (1 Kings 4:25).

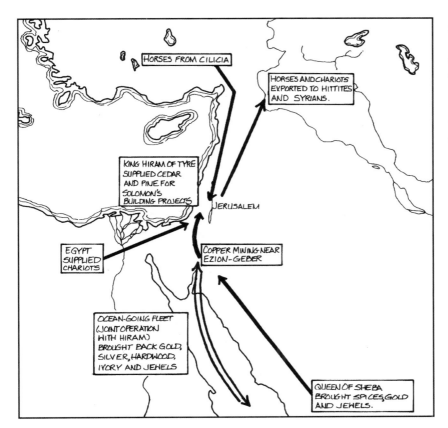

King Solomon's Trade

The central location of Solomon's kingdom allowed him to control the trade routes throughout the region. His wisdom and wealth brought great prosperity to Israel.

(Map labels:)
HORSES FROM CILICIA

HORSES AND CHARIOTS EXPORTED TO HITTITES AND SYRIANS.

KING HIRAM OF TYRE SUPPLIED CEDAR AND PINE FOR SOLOMON'S BUILDING PROJECTS

JERUSALEM

EGYPT SUPPLIED CHARIOTS

COPPER MINING NEAR EZION-GEBER

OCEAN-GOING FLEET (JOINT OPERATION WITH HIRAM) BROUGHT BACK GOLD, SILVER, HARDWOOD, IVORY AND JEWELS

QUEEN OF SHEBA BROUGHT SPICES, GOLD AND JEWELS.

His Palace

In one day, Solomon's household and visitors consumed:

- 185 bushels of fine flour
- 375 bushes of meal
- 10 fat oxen
- 20 pasture-fed oxen
- 100 sheep
- Numerous deer, gazelles, roebucks, and fattened fowl (1 Kings 4:22–23)

His Support Staff

At Solomon's disposal were:

- 40,000 stalls of horses for his chariots
- 12,000 horsemen
- Numerous helpers to provide for King Solomon, his guests, the banquet tables, and the **livery**

livery: stable of horses

Solomon's Accomplishments

Solomon was considered wiser than any person born up to that day. From his great mind, he produced:

- 3,000 proverbs (most of which are recorded in the biblical book, the Proverbs)
- 1,005 songs (of which one is Psalm 72)
- Knowledge about a variety of trees, animals, insects, and fish
- A new system of government that worked
- The Temple
- Peace and prosperity (1 Kings 4:20)

THE BIG PICTURE

> **1 Kings 5–7** Solomon used the best possible materials to build the Temple, a house for God [see illustration, page 161]. He sent far away for the building materials and then put the most talented craftsmen in charge of building it. It was dedicated seven years after it was begun. He also built his own home after that. Both the temple and his home were elaborately furnished.

Two Incredible Building Projects

The skilled craftsmen needed to complete this task were allowed two months off for every month of work. With three shifts rotating, it took seven years to build the temple. Some commentators believe this work schedule demonstrated Solomon's concern for these employees and their family life.

But the focus on opulence and wealth foreshadowed the nation's decline. Style became more important than substance. Solomon began to depend upon the things around him rather than a vibrant relationship with the Lord.

Here are some basic facts about these buildings:

- The Temple was 2,700 square feet.
- The Temple was built of white limestone, cedar, and a gold exterior.
- The cedars used from the mountains of Lebanon were very old trees with hard, beautiful wood. They resisted decay and insect infestation.
- Solomon's house was 11,250 square feet and took thirteen years to build.

Something to Ponder

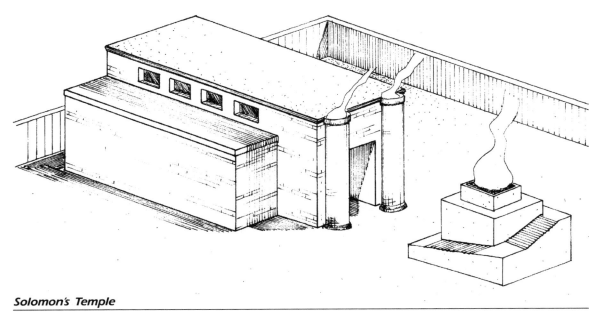

Solomon's Temple

Solomon lavished tons of gold on the magnificent Temple he built to honor God. At today's prices, it would be worth five billion dollars.

King David had wanted to build the Temple for his God, but God wouldn't <u>allow</u> him to do it because he was a man of war. Instead, God told him through the prophet Nathan that his son would do it.

BUILD YOUR SPIRIT: Just as Solomon made sure that the very best materials were used to build the house of God, we should give our very best to God. He gave us his very best: his sinless son, Jesus Christ, for the sins of the world.

THE BIG PICTURE 🔍

> **1 Kings 8** To celebrate the finishing of the Temple and to invite God to reside there, Solomon arranged for the Ark of the Covenant, along with the other items from the Lord's tent, to be installed. God's presence filled the Temple and Solomon gave a sermon and a prayer. All the Israelites attending rejoiced.

Remember This . . .

☞ **GO TO:**

2 Samuel 7:13 (allow)

Opening Day

In Solomon's sermon to the Israelites, he:

- Blessed the Israelites
- Blessed God
- Credited God for fulfilling his promise that David's son would build the Temple

In Solomon's prayer, he:

- Praised God for his faithfulness and loving-kindness (verses 23–26)
- Stressed that God can't be contained by a building but that God had chosen to reside in the Temple (verses 27–30)
- Revealed the purposes of the Temple for gaining forgiveness (verses 31–40)
- Responded to the call of the foreigner (verses 41–43)
- Sought victory in battle (verses 44–45) and deliverance from captivity (verses 46–53)

Something to Ponder

Solomon's blessing of the people certainly gives us a glimpse of a man who sought God. He said, *"May he turn our hearts to him, to walk in all his ways and to keep the commands, decrees and regulations he gave our fathers. . . . But your hearts must be fully committed to the Lord our God, to live by his decrees and obey his commands, as at this time"* (1 Kings 8:58, 61). It seems as if the many <u>women</u> he married from heathen backgrounds gradually turned his heart away from God.

☞ **GO TO:**

1 Kings 11:14 (women)

Remember This . . .

For fourteen days, all the people rejoiced. They had concentrated on God's goodness and that fueled their joy.

BUILD YOUR SPIRIT: God wants us to have times of celebration and to have a time of rest on the Sabbath. We need rest and rejoicing to combat the stress of living.

THE BIG PICTURE 🔍

> **Proverbs 1–31** During Solomon's reign, he was a prolific writer and wrote three thousand proverbs. Only eight hundred of them are compiled in the book of Proverbs. They cover many aspects of daily life. Their purpose is to help men develop wisdom that will honor God.

Solomon Spills His Wisdom

Topic	Selected Proverbs
Adultery	5:1–6 / 6:24–32 / 7:6–27 / 22:14 / 23:26–28 / 29:1 / 30:7
Alcohol	20:1 / 23:20, 21, 29–35 / 31:4–7
Crime	6:30–31 / 10:9–16 / 13:11 / 15:6, 27 / 16:8, 19 / 17:15, 23
Discipline	3:11–12 / 5:12–14 / 9:7–10 / 13:18, 24 / 19:18 / 22:15 / 27:5
Friendship	12:26 / 13:20 / 16:28 / 17:17 / 18:1, 24 / 19:17 / 22:10
Gossip	11:13 / 16:28 / 18:8 / 20:19 / 26:22
Government	8:15–16 / 14:28, 34–35 / 16:12–15 / 18:17 / 24:24–25 / 25:5
Laziness	6:9–11 / 12:24–27 / 13:4 / 15:19 / 19:15 / 20:4, 20 / 24:30–34
Lies	6:16, 17 / 12:17–19, 22 / 14:5, 24 / 17:4, 20 / 24:28–29 / 30:8
Love	10:12 / 15:17 / 16:6 / 17:9, 17 / 19:22 / 20:6
Neighbors	3:29, 30 / 6:16–19 / 11:9 / 14:20, 21 / 26:17–20 / 29:5
Parent/child	6:20–23 / 10:1 / 15:20 / 17:6, 21, 25 / 22:6 / 23:13–14, 22, 24
The Poor	13:8, 18, 23 / 14:20, 31 / 17:5 / 19:1, 4, 7, 17, 22 / 30:11–14
Pride	6:16–17 / 8:13 / 11:2 / 15:25 / 18:5, 18 / 18:12 / 25:6–7
Temper	14:17, 29 / 15:1, 18 / 16:32 / 19:19 / 22:24–25 / 29:11, 22
Wealth	10:2, 4, 15, 22 / 11:4, 28 / 13:8, 21–22 / 14:24 / 20:21 / 23:4–8
Work	12:11, 14, 24, 27 / 14:23 / 16:26 / 18:9 / 22:29 / 27:18, 23–27

If everyone followed the wise advice of Solomon's proverbs, we would all be much happier and have more fulfilling relationships. He covers just about every possible topic and offers a balanced view of life with God's perspective in mind.

Something to Ponder

THE BIG PICTURE 🔍

> **1 Kings 9–11:8** God again appeared to Solomon and warned him to be careful to follow God's commandments. Unfortunately, shortly after, Solomon began a spiritual decline. He sold some Israelite cities, enslaved other nationalities, multiplied his wealth, gathered more horses, married foreign wives, and worshiped idols.

Great Knowledge, Little Responsibility

Solomon had no limit to his wisdom and no limit to his desire for pleasure and power. Administratively, his skills were the greatest in the world. But at times, he lacked character, especially in the realm of lust. Character does count. Solomon's control over his appetite for women was non-existent. He allowed himself to experience just about anything he wanted. Because he was so rich, nothing was withheld from him.

☞ **GO TO:**

Deuteronomy 17:20
(pride)

*Remember
This . . .*

WARNING ➤

KEY POINT

Nothing satisfies in
this world, except
God.

☞ **GO TO:**

Philippians 3:7–8 (best)

Bruce H. Wilkinson and Larry Libby: God had said that the king of Israel was not to rule in such a way that his head would become lifted in <u>pride</u> over his countrymen. But Solomon fashioned for himself a gigantic throne of gold and ivory, adorned with twelve carved lions on its ascending steps.[7]

When God first gave the instructions for the future kings of Israel, he specifically said, *"The king, moreover, must not acquire great numbers of horses for himself or make the people return to Egypt to get more of them, for the Lord has told you, 'You are not to go back that way again.' He must not take many wives, or his heart will be led astray. He must not accumulate large amounts of silver and gold"* (Deuteronomy 17:16–17). Solomon broke all those rules. No wonder his heart turned away—God said it would.

We may think that God is being mean when he withholds certain things from us, especially things that we think will benefit us, but he knows what will draw our hearts away from him. He knows that being close to him is the <u>best</u> thing that could possibly happen to us. Nothing should draw us away from that.

THE BIG PICTURE 🔎

Ecclesiastes 1–12 In the ebb of Solomon's life, he penned a book of the Bible that revealed his deep disillusionment about life. In these writings, he philosophically examined the fruitlessness and futility of what most people think will bring them happiness and contentment: wisdom, pleasure, accomplishments, and work. He concluded after living almost sixty years that none of those things can satisfy. Only God can.

It Is All Worthless

Wisdom filled Solomon's life as a gift from God in answer to prayer. Songs flowed from his heart. His government worked like a clock. Everything about his kingdom and throne seemed in order. But in Ecclesiastes, Solomon said everything he had done was meaningless. His life ended in vanity, idolatry, sensuality, emptiness, and despair. He came to believe, *"All his days his work is pain and grief; even at night his mind does not rest. This too is meaningless. A man can do nothing better than to eat and drink and find satisfaction in his work"* (Ecclesiastes 2:23–24).

Ray Stedman: Here is the true message of this book. Enjoyment is a gift of God. There is nothing in possession, in material goods, in money, there is nothing in man himself that can enable him to keep enjoying the things he does. But it is possible to have enjoyment all your life if you take it from the hand of God. It is given to those who please God.[8]

Contrast David's experience: *"To the Lord I cry aloud, and he answers me from his holy hill. I lie down and sleep; I wake again, because the Lord sustains me"* (Psalm 3:4–5). Both men experienced power, wealth, many wives, and great failures. One had a heart for God and the other had a heart that broke from emptiness.

Something to Ponder

BUILD YOUR SPIRIT: The world says get more and be more, go for the gusto, do your own thing, and do it your way. But none of that will bring lasting satisfaction. Only a heart obeying God and seeking rewards in heaven will have the <u>contentment</u> that God desires for us.

THE BIG PICTURE

☞ **GO TO:**

1 Timothy 6:6 (contentment)

---

1 Kings 11:9–43 Because Solomon had turned away from God's commandments, God rebuked him. He declared that the kingdom would be removed from Solomon's descendants. In the last years of his reign, enemies attacked Israel from the outside and Israelites rebelled against him. Even though Solomon tried to fight these dissensions, he couldn't prevent God's prediction from coming true. Solomon died after reigning forty years.

KEY POINT

Wisdom keeps us doing things right, but passion for God makes sure we do the right things.

The Ladder Of Success Was Against The Wrong Wall

Though he was the famous builder of a grandiose temple and palace, and the richest man in the world, Solomon alienated his own people because he burdened them with excessive taxes and work. Leaders of other countries admired his wealth and wisdom but all this pride was poison to his own people. He turned his back on a living relationship with God and sought everything this world could give. Unspeakable riches, seven hundred wives, three hundred concubines, and one prideful heart destined his reign for failure. There was never enough.

Patrick M. Morley: The culture we live in values possession and accomplishment higher than people and relationships. . . . Instead of encouraging and nurturing family and relationship values, our culture suggests professional achievement and financial success are the measure of a man.[9]

This world's search for information and knowledge will lead to the same emptiness Solomon found, unless it is guided by a heart filled with a passion for God. Unless this is the foundation, wisdom and knowledge become empty distractions.

Solomon had little spiritual power because he didn't practice what he preached. He sought platitudes and shortcuts to success. His generation became idolaters and lived in immorality.

Solomon's short sermons, called proverbs, offered practical instruction on life, money, marriage, children, and on how to be blessed and behave. But his life demonstrated a spiritual weakness. Seek wisdom for your mind but apply it to your heart.

Ezra

. . . Man of the Law

THE BIG PICTURE

Ezra 7 Way back when God made his covenant with the Israelites through Moses, He explained to them the blessings that they would receive if they obeyed the law, and the curses they would experience if they disobeyed. They disobeyed, early, long, and often. One of the covenant curses was that God would allow the Jews to return to captivity, and the curse was fulfilled during the prophet Jeremiah's lifetime. When the Israelites had been captives in Babylon for 70 years, God felt they had learned their lesson. He began allowing them to return to Judea.

The second Jewish group to return to Jerusalem was led by Ezra in 457 B.C. Previously, Zerubbabel had taken a group of exiled Israelites back to Jerusalem eighty years earlier (538–515 B.C.). That is what was chronicled in the first six chapters of the book of Ezra. The Persian King Cyrus sent that first group. Ezra was allowed to return with his group by King Artaxerxes of the Persian Empire [see illustration, page 167].

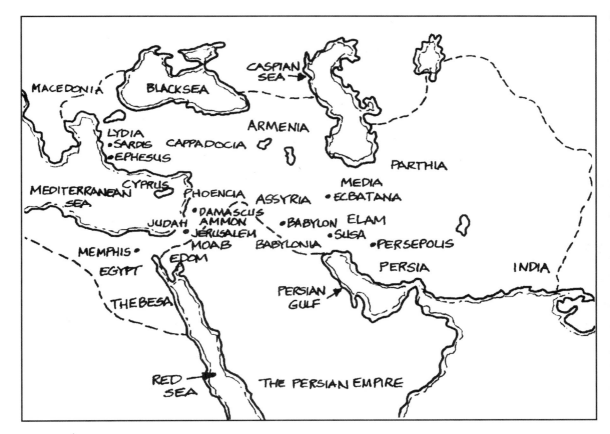

Persian Empire

The Persian Empire dominated the ancient world at the time of Ezra.

Talk About Being Empowered For A Job!

The king gave Ezra power to return to Jerusalem through a decree that supported any Jew's decision to return to Jerusalem. Artaxerxes even gave Ezra the utensils that had been stolen previously from Solomon's Temple, and money for his return. This was a tremendous boost to the Jew's desire to rebuild the flattened Temple (see illustration, page 168).

F. Charles Fensham: It seems as if Ezra was sent to an inspection to see if the law of God was still being kept. For the Persian king . . . it was a necessity that peace should prevail in Judah.[10]

KEY POINT

Nothing stops God from what he wants to do.

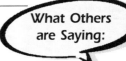
What Others are Saying:

Something to Ponder

GO TO:

Isaiah 44:28–45:1
(Isaiah)

Remember This . . .

☞ **GO TO:**

Proverbs 21:1 (kings)

Time Line

The Captivity and Return of the Jews.

During the era that Ezra wrote about, other religious leaders in the world were living: Buddha in India, Confucius in China, and Socrates in Greece. Those men didn't seek the Jewish Jehovah God. But for any who would seek him, the Hebrew God revealed himself through the fulfillment of a prophecy made by <u>Isaiah</u>. Isaiah had predicted two hundred years before it happened that a king would allow the exiled Jews to return to their homeland. He named the king specifically: Cyrus. Only a real God could have made such a stunning prediction and controlled the circumstances to make it happen.

This king, Artaxerxes, is not the same king mentioned in the Biblical book of Esther. It was his son. The name, Artaxerxes or Xerxes, was not only a formal name but a title meaning "king."

BUILD YOUR SPIRIT: God gave Ezra favor with the king because God wanted Ezra to fulfill his mission. *"The king had granted him everything he asked, for the hand of the Lord his God was on him"* (Ezra 7:6). Whenever God wants something done, it will get done. God has the power to create and control. He influences even <u>kings</u> and nations. If God wants you to do something, don't worry; he can make it happen.

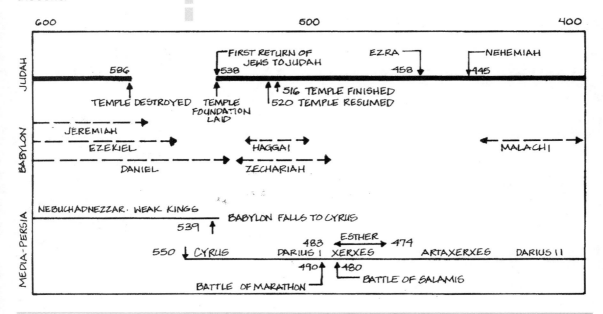

Ezra was a **scribe** and the king recognized the <u>wisdom</u> that God had given him. When we apply what we learn in the Bible to our lives, then others will see the impact that God has on us. The Bible is a <u>source</u> of teaching, **reproof**, correction, and training in righteousness.

THE BIG PICTURE 🔍

> **Ezra 8** Ezra listed the names of the people who signed up to go back to Jerusalem. With women and children, the group most likely numbered four to five thousand. This group was much smaller than the group that had returned with Zerubbabel, who took back nearly fifty thousand.

A Smaller Group That's Missing Someone

As Ezra assembled the returnees, he recognized that no one from the tribe of Levi was there. The Levites were the priests and were responsible to <u>teach</u> the Law and <u>serve</u> in the Temple. Ezra sent some of the leaders to go recruit Levites with a specially prepared message. It worked. Thirty-eight Levites joined them, along with 220 temple servants.

Then Ezra proclaimed a fast, asking for God's help and protection, especially since he had turned down military protection from the government. After a four-month trip, Ezra and the group arrived safely in Jerusalem.

Maybe the Levites didn't volunteer because, back in Jerusalem, they would be responsible for the Temple service, a demanding and disciplined assignment. Since there was no Temple where they were in Persia, they didn't have to work.

Although Ezra didn't ask for military protection for his trip, <u>Nehemiah</u> would many years later as he took a third wave of exiles back to Jerusalem. This difference represents how God often leads different people in different ways. The one thing that never should change is specific Bible doctrine, but styles and methods can change and legitimately should reflect the wonderful diversity of God's people.

Overcoming Struggles

☞ **GO TO:**

Ezra 7:10 (scribe)

Ezra 7:25 (wisdom)

2 Timothy 3:16 (source)

scribe: *a highly trained expert on the Scriptures*

reproof: *encouragement to make a change*

☞ **GO TO:**

Nehemiah 8:9 (teach)

Numbers 1:53 (serve)

Something to Ponder

Remember This . . .

☞ **GO TO:**

Nehemiah 2:9 (Nehemiah)

☞ **GO TO:**

Daniel 2:23 (thank)

Proverbs 21:4 (pride)

Proverbs 22:4 (humility)

Micah 7:18 (mercy)

☞ **GO TO:**

Exodus 34:11–16;
   Deuteronomy 7:1–4
   (against)

What Others are Saying:

impelled: driven

☞ **GO TO:**

Isaiah 53:12 (servant)

Something to Ponder

Ezra gave God the credit for recruiting the Levites. He said he was able to do it *"Because the gracious hand of our God was on us"* (Ezra 8:18). When we see God's hand in our lives, we must be sure to <u>thank</u> God for it. That way, we'll avoid <u>pride</u> and allow God to develop <u>humility</u> in our characters. Ezra also avoided pride when he called a fast so that everyone in the traveling party asked God for protection.

THE BIG PICTURE 🔍

> **Ezra 9** When Ezra arrived in Jerusalem, he discovered that some of the Israelites had married non-Jews. Ezra was so distraught by this that he tore his clothes in grief and prayed to God on their behalf, asking for God's forgiveness and <u>mercy</u>.

A Man Of Passion And Intensity

Intermarriage was specifically <u>against</u> God's law for many reasons. Ezra responded to this news in the customary mode of grief: he tore his garment and robe, and pulled out some of the hair from his head and beard. His righteous response had a profound effect on those around him, and they joined him in his grieving. Ezra kneeled down and stretched out his hands as he prayed. This was a position that showed his dependence on God and his mercy.

Derek Kidner: Something of the devotion and insight of the man praying can be sensed in this confession . . . in the swift transition from "I," in the first sentence, to "our" and "we" for the rest of the prayer. Ezra could have protested his innocence, but like the <u>servant</u> in Isaiah he was **impelled** to reckon himself numbered with the transgressors.[11]

Ezra hadn't sinned himself by marrying outside their religion, yet he came to God with an attitude of repentance as if he had. He sought God's mercy on the people's behalf. That was a very loving thing to do and demonstrated a humble servant's heart. He may have also been motivated by a fear that their actions would again cause God to take them into captivity—since it was that kind of sin that had caused God to discipline them with captivity in the first place.

The sin of intermarrying with those outside the Jewish faith had nothing to do with a racial prejudice, for everyone involved was of the same Semitic race. But God had commanded his chosen people to not marry those who didn't love and follow Jehovah. When someone does, they are more tempted to fall away from worshiping and serving God. That is what happened to King Solomon years earlier and caused the people to turn away from the Lord.

LEADERSHIP PRINCIPLE—A true leader needs to recognize the obstacles and dangers that will destroy the success of his mission. He must use his influence and energies to remain focused and stand against the challenge. Ezra was a man of great influence and action. This influence became magnetic to those he led because he was filled with passion, energy, and intensity. He was fully committed to his God Jehovah, and thus was devastated by the sin that surrounded him. *"O my God, I am too ashamed and disgraced to lift up my face to you, my God, because our sins are higher than our heads and our guilt has reached to the heavens"* (Ezra 9:6).

KEY POINT

Giving God the credit will diminish pride in our lives.

BUILD YOUR SPIRIT: As one man with deep remorse for sin, Ezra knew profound change was needed in these people's hearts. The complacent and easy-going remnant would soon be exposed to a man sold out to heavenly values. We can have that same kind of influence on those around us by taking sin seriously.

THE BIG PICTURE

Ezra 10 When others heard of Ezra's response to their sin, they gathered and wept along with him. Shecaniah confessed the people's sin to Ezra and suggested that the foreign women (and the children of those intermarriages) be put away. To present such a plan to everyone in all of Judah, all Israelites were told to come to Jerusalem. When they arrived, they were encouraged to separate themselves from their foreign wives and children.

Weeping Pays Off

Ezra's heart for God was infectious. His grief pricked the conscience of the people. Everyone was instructed to congregate in Jerusalem in three days to deal with the problem. If anyone refused, he would have to sacrifice everything he owned. At the meeting, leaders of each local area made a list of those who had indeed married foreign women. Only a few men opposed the plan. It took three months to institute it.

Although the plan to divorce their foreign wives and give up their children may seem extreme, some commentators believe it was necessary. Others have wondered, though, whether two wrongs make a right, and suggest that this plan was a wrong.

Regardless, it may be that the careful investigation and listing of those who had wrongly married was because Ezra's leaders needed to find out if any of the foreign women had converted to Judaism. If so, those women were acceptable and in those cases divorce was unnecessary.

Regardless of the depth or degree of sin, God always tells us there is hope. That's why Jesus came to die on the earth. His sacrificial death makes it possible for us to be forgiven and have hope for the future—because every sin was included, no matter how wrong.

LEADERSHIP  PRINCIPLE—One by one others who shared his grief surrounded Ezra. Ezra never told them what to do but set a holy standard that others followed. His subordinates responded with the solution after watching the heart of one man burn for reconciliation with God.

Unfortunately, even after these steps were taken, the Israelites slipped back into their old habits later. Nehemiah will arrive a generation later to find that they had married foreign women again. We also can slip back into our old patterns of sin or spiritual laziness if we don't make a conscious effort to consider ourselves dead to sin and to focus constantly on God. It's a constant battle but God wants us not to grow weary.

Just as the Israelites would suffer the consequences of losing everything they had if they didn't attend the meeting, we should give consequences to our children for their disobedience. That is the only way they will be motivated to change. God gives us that example as he also underlines disciplines his own children. Sometimes, the bad things that happen to us are a result of our sin.

Something to Ponder

Remember This . . .

☞ **GO TO:**

Nehemiah 13:23 (Nehemiah)

Romans 6:11 (dead)

Hebrews 12:2 (focus)

Overcoming Struggles

Galatians 6:9 (weary)

Hebrews 12:6 (disciplines)

Grow Your Family

Nehemiah

. . . Building Walls, Building Bridges

THE BIG PICTURE

Nehemiah 1 Nehemiah was an exiled Jew living in a Persian palace in 445 B.C. He served as the cup bearer to the Persian king. When Nehemiah learned that the walls of Jerusalem had not been rebuilt after the Jews were taken into exile in 586 B.C., he became concerned. Without strong walls, Jerusalem was in danger of being attacked and conquered. He asked God for favor with the king so that he might be allowed to return to Jerusalem.

A Burdened Heart Seeks God

Nehemiah heard the news about Jerusalem's wall being broken down and the gates being destroyed by fire from his brother, Hanani, who had recently returned from a trip to Judah. Nehemiah was so upset that he wept, fasted, and prayed. As he prayed, God created a plan in his mind for seeking permission from the king to leave his duties and go to Jerusalem to rebuild the walls (see illustration, this page).

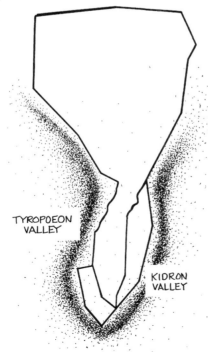

TYROPOEON VALLEY

KIDRON VALLEY

The Walls of Jerusalem

Ancient Jerusalem, situated on Palestine's mountainous ridge, relied on its wall to protect it from attackers approaching from the Tyropean and Kidron valleys.

Max Lucado: We are tempted to wait to pray until we know how to pray. We've heard the prayers of the spiritually mature. We've read of the rigors of the disciplined. And we are convinced we've a long way to transverse.[12]

Something
to Ponder

Nehemiah's prayer contained three elements:

1. Acknowledgment of God's greatness (verse 5)
2. Confession of Israel's sins (verses 6–7)
3. Request for God's help (verses 8–11)

If we pray in this way, we will get God's attention.

Remember
This . . .

A cup bearer had an important position in the king's court. Since he was responsible for tasting the wine and passing it around, he was constantly at the king's disposal. Plus, as the official taster, he would protect the king from any poisoned wine. Being in the royal presence made him privy to confidential information and the king frequently talked things over with him. In the past, a chief cup bearer had been responsible for calling attention to Joseph's ability to interpret dreams.

☞ **GO TO:**

Genesis 41:15 (Joseph)

BUILD YOUR SPIRIT: God loves for us to pray to him like Nehemiah prayed. Although there is not only one way to pray, there are a variety of models given in the Bible. Jesus gave one in Matthew called "The Lord's Prayer." A common formula that people use is:

adoration: praising God

supplication: giving prayer requests

A: **adoration**
C: confession of sin
T: thanksgiving
S: **supplication**

By praying with each of those elements, we know we have covered all the bases. But Nehemiah shows us that we should just pray! Don't worry too much about whether you're doing it correctly. The important thing is to do it!

> **Nehemiah 2–3** For four months, Nehemiah prayed about the situation. He tried to avoid being sad in the king's presence, but his heavy heart showed anyway. When the king noticed and asked about it, Nehemiah told him his concerns. The king asked what he wanted to do. Nehemiah told him he wanted to go to Jerusalem and rebuild the walls and gates. The king approved and sent him with military protection.
>
> Once he arrived in Jerusalem, he secretly inspected the wall at night. The next day, he encouraged the people to rebuild. Although there was some opposition from those who were not Israelites, many people began working on rebuilding the wall.

Nehemiah's Sadness Shows

Nehemiah answered the king's inquiry carefully. However, his prayers had paved the way. The king supported his idea and he was given permission to go to Jerusalem. When he arrived, he reviewed the walls of Jerusalem without telling anyone what he was doing.

This demonstrates what a careful planner Nehemiah was.

Max Lucado: Our prayers may be awkward. Our attempts may be feeble. But since the power of prayer is in the one who hears it and not the one who says it, our prayers do make a difference.[13]

What Others are Saying:

Nehemiah certainly was persistent and <u>patient</u> in prayer. Four months is a long time to be praying about something and seeking God's will without saying anything to anyone else. Yet somehow Nehemiah knew it wasn't the right timing to say anything. When the king inquired, Nehemiah quickly prayed in a method some call an "arrow" prayer—something quickly prayed on the spur of the moment. Previously he'd spent extended time in prayer, but in that moment came the opportunity to pray quickly before saying something to the king. Both kinds of prayer are appropriate and effective.

☞ **GO TO:**

Romans 12:12 (patient)

Something to Ponder

Nehemiah was afraid when the king noticed his sadness. Servants weren't supposed to show negative feelings. It could be interpreted by the king as disapproving of his actions or decisions and he might not like that. The servant's position or even his life could be in danger. No wonder Nehemiah prayed immediately.

Remember This . . .

prudent: cautious

LEADERSHIP PRINCIPLE—Evidently, Nehemiah was a thoughtful and **prudent** leader. Although he took risks, he wasn't spontaneous or thoughtless. He planned his risks! And he made sure he was following God's plan. Leaders today need to do the same thing.

THE BIG PICTURE

> **Nehemiah 4:1–6:14** Nehemiah encountered much opposition in the form of seven different destructive plans hatched by his enemies. In each case, Nehemiah proved himself a godly leader, a wise planner, and a spiritual person.

We All Have Opposition And Competition

Nehemiah's enemies tried everything to stop the rebuilding of the walls. Sanballat, a Horonite, Tobiah the Ammonite, and Geshem the Arab may have had plans to take control of Jerusalem. When Nehemiah arrived to rebuild the walls, he threatened their plans. But as we'll see, sometimes the "enemy" was within Nehemiah's own camp.

This chart recaps the kinds of things that happened and how Nehemiah showed himself to be a man who trusted in God completely.

Something to Ponder

Examples of Times Nehemiah Prevailed over Opposition

4:1–6 .... The opposition publicly mocked the Jews before the wealthy people and said the construction was faulty.

* *Nehemiah prayed that God would not forgive them. Everyone kept building and the wall was reestablished to half its original height.*

4:7–9 .... The opposition threatened to attack the people while they were building.

* *Nehemiah and the Jews prayed and set up a guard day and night.*

4:10–23 .... The opposition used the threat of attack and rumors that the people were growing discouraged to make the people fearful and suspicious.

* *Nehemiah encouraged the people by reminding them that God would fight for them. He also positioned half of the workers with weapons.*

5:1–19 .... The Jews faced a food shortage and many people didn't have enough money to pay their taxes. Therefore they were selling their children into slavery to one another. Also, their Jewish brothers were charging **usury**, which was forbidden by God's laws.

- *Nehemiah was angry at the injustices going on and confronted his fellow Jews. He told them to stop charging interest and to be generous with each other. Since he was appointed governor, he also provided food for many but didn't use the governor's food allowance. He also worked on the wall.*

☞ **GO TO:**

Exodus 22:25 (usury)

usury: high interest fees

6:1–4 .... Five times, the opposition invited Nehemiah to meet with them and find a compromise, which Nehemiah knew was a smokescreen to harm him.

- *Nehemiah refused their requests, saying he had too much good work to do.*

6:5–9 .... Sanballat sent a message for everyone to read that accused Nehemiah of planning a revolt against the rulers with the desire to set himself up as the king.

- *Nehemiah wasn't intimidated and sent a message saying that rumor wasn't true. He also prayed for God to strengthen him.*

6:10–14 .... A Jew, hired by Sanballat, tried to get Nehemiah to enter the Temple to get protection from his enemies.

- *Nehemiah identified this as a **ruse** to make him enter the sanctuary of the Temple, which was against God's rules. Only <u>Levites</u> were allowed to go into the inner Temple. If he had done that, his credibility would have been destroyed. He refused the invitation.*

ruse: trick

☞ **GO TO:**

Numbers 3:10 (Levites)

Examples of Nehemiah's Wise Words and Thoughts

4:14 .... "Don't be afraid of them. Remember the Lord, who is great and awesome, and fight for your brothers, your sons and your daughters, your wives and your homes."

- *He reminded people of how great God is.*

4:19–20 .... "The work is extensive and spread out, and we are widely separated from each other along the wall. Wherever you hear the sound of the trumpet, join us there. Our God will fight for us!"

- *He was great at rallying the people with wisdom and enthusiasm.*

5:6, 9 .... "When I heard their outcry and these charges, I was very angry. 'What you are doing is not right. Shouldn't you walk in the fear of our God to avoid the reproach of our Gentile enemies?'"

- *He wasn't afraid to confront those who were sinning.*

5:16 .... "Instead, I devoted myself to the work on this wall. All my men were assembled there for the work; we did not acquire any land."

- *He was selfless and untiring; even involving his own employees.*

6:3 .... "I am carrying on a great project and cannot go down. Why should the work stop while I leave it and go down to you?"

- *He knew his priorities and kept to them.*

6:12 .... "I realized that God had not sent him, but that he had prophesied against me because Tobiah and Sanballat had hired him."

- *He wisely saw the motives behind the actions of people.*

Nehemiah got angry at the injustices of his fellow Jews, but he didn't sin. The first flash of <u>anger</u> isn't wrong, but what we do with our emotions through actions or attitudes can be. God doesn't want us to harbor anger because then it becomes bitterness and resentment.

 **BUILD YOUR SPIRIT:** Nehemiah gives us a process for dealing with anger. He:

- Recognized he was angry and didn't deny it (5:6)
- "Pondered" over his anger until he found the real cause of it (5:7)
- Confronted those who were sinning (5:7)
- Called a meeting to bring the issue to the attention of everyone involved (5:7)
- Suggested a solution (5:11)

Remember
This . . .

☞ **GO TO:**

Ephesians 4:26 (anger)

Anger is something many of us struggle with. At times, we feel justified in our anger and rationalize that if the person who caused our anger would just act differently, we would too. But the truth is, we are responsible for our own reactions. No one else causes our anger. It is our reaction to the way we perceive the situation.

Overcoming Struggles

Here is what the Bible says about anger:

- Psalm 37:8: Anger creates wrongdoing.
- Proverbs 14:17: Being quick-tempered shows a person is foolish.
- Proverbs 15:1: Speaking gently turns away anger.
- Proverbs 16:32: Being slow to anger shows strength.
- Proverbs 19:3: When we don't take responsibility for our actions, we get angry at God.
- Proverbs 19:11: Being slow to anger shows a person is wise.
- Proverbs 19:19: We should allow angry people to suffer consequences for their choices.
- Proverbs 22:24, 25: Don't associate with angry people or else they will influence you.

Remember This . . .

> **Nehemiah 6:15–16** So the wall was completed on the **twenty-fifth of Elul**, in fifty-two days. When all our enemies heard about this, all the surrounding nations were afraid and lost their self-confidence, because they realized that this work had been done with the help of our God.

twenty-fifth of Elul:
about September 20

The Walls Went Tumbling Up

God did an amazing thing in empowering Nehemiah and his fellow builders to quickly complete the project. They completed it so quickly that even the enemies of Israel attributed the feat to God's enabling. Not only were they impressed, those opposing the project were less motivated to criticize and work against the Israelites.

Charles R. Swindoll: That has to be the most thrilling experience in the world—to watch God come to the rescue when you have been helpless. In the middle of the incessant assault of the enemy, in spite of the endless verbal barrage, the wall was built. While the enemy blasts, God builds.[14]

What Others are Saying:

**Something
to Ponder**

WARNING ➤

☞ **GO TO:**

Galatians 1:3–5 (glory)

Exodus 34:14 (jealous)

2 Corinthians 3:18
(vessels)

Isaiah 25:1 (use)

**Something
to Ponder**

☞ **GO TO:**

John 10:3 (listened)

Hosea 6:3
(acknowledged)

Deuteronomy 5:27
(obey)

Job 33:31 (speak)

God loves to do amazing things so that he can get the <u>glory</u>. But he is a <u>jealous</u> God who wants to make sure *only* he receives the credit—because only he deserves it. He is the source and we are his <u>vessels</u>. He doesn't need us but he chooses to <u>use</u> us as his co-laborer. What a mighty privilege that is.

If you are trying to do good things out of your own power, you won't receive any credit for it in heaven. And quite often, your wrong motives will be revealed and people will notice your pride. *"Pride goes before destruction, a haughty spirit before a fall"* (Proverbs 16:18).

> **Nehemiah 7:5** So my God put it into my heart to assemble the nobles, the officials, and the common people for registration by families. I found the genealogical record of those who had been the first to return.

The Amazing Things God Puts On A Heart

The purpose of the census was to re-populate Jerusalem with people of pure Jewish descent. Few people were residing there at that time because it had been a dangerous place to live. When the walls were crumbling, residents were defenseless. But now that the walls were again strong, Jerusalem would be a safer place to live.

Nehemiah was a godly man who constantly <u>listened</u> to God's voice. He <u>acknowledged</u> God for the ideas he came up with. But even more important, when God led him, he obeyed.

BUILD YOUR SPIRIT: We want to be like Nehemiah, always having our "spiritual antennae" out, aware of how God might be leading or speaking. But if we are not willing to <u>obey</u>, then God may not <u>speak</u>. He knows our heart and responds to those who are eager to do what he says.

> **Nehemiah 8–10** Nehemiah called everyone together at the Water Gate, one of the gates of Jerusalem, and Ezra, the priest, read from the Law. As he read, the people began weeping because they were convicted about their sin and their former negligence in following the Law. But Nehemiah, along with Ezra and the Levites, encouraged them not to grieve but to rejoice. They celebrated for seven days in a <u>festival</u> called the Feast of Tabernacles. Then after one day of rest, they assembled for a time of confession and reviewing God's works from the past. Finally, they renewed their covenant with God.

☞ **GO TO:**

Leviticus 23:42 (festival)

Let's Party!

Commentators estimate that there were thirty to fifty thousand people gathered for the reading of the Law. We don't know how everyone heard Ezra in such a large crowd. It may be that portions were read and then the Levites circulated among smaller groups, giving an explanation and answering questions. But regardless, the people were emotionally and spiritually touched.

Ezra, who wrote the book of Ezra and is also credited by many for writing the book of Nehemiah, was a Jew who lived in the time of Nehemiah. He had returned with a group of exiled Jews to Jerusalem fourteen years before Nehemiah brought his group.

The people responded to the reading of the Law by first standing up in respect and then bowing. Then *"Ezra praised the Lord, the great God; and all the people lifted their hands and responded, 'Amen! Amen!' Then they bowed down and worshiped the Lord with their faces to the ground"* (Nehemiah 8:6). Later they wept and mourned so intensely that Nehemiah had to encourage them to stop grieving and start celebrating.

Something to Ponder

The Law is the collection of rules that God gave Moses back in the days when the Israelites wandered through the wilderness. Israelites constantly went through cycles where they would follow the Law closely, then slide into ignoring it. During Nehemiah's time, he made sure they knew the Law and followed it.

Remember This . . .

BUILD YOUR SPIRIT: Just like the Israelites, we should worship God with our minds and our bodies. Different people worship God in different ways, but every position, whether standing, bowing, raising our hands, shouting, or lying **prostrate** on the ground, is acceptable to God if done with a pure heart of worship.

prostrate: *stretched out face down*

The people took the Law to heart and it changed their behavior. Our "Law" as Christians is the Bible, and it should make a difference in our lives. As we read it, we are <u>in-structed</u> in how God wants us to act and what to believe. Although it doesn't address every issue we might face, it gives principles that can be applied to every situation and challenge. If we <u>hide</u> it in our hearts, we will be able to use it when it is needed, moment by moment.

Overcoming Struggles

☞ **GO TO:**

Romans 10:17 (instructed)

Psalm 119:11 (hide)

> **Nehemiah 13:4–31** Nehemiah served as governor of Judah for twelve years and then returned to serve King Artaxerxes. We don't know for how long but some commentators suggest two years. Then Nehemiah returned to Jerusalem and was shocked at the disappointing changes that had occurred since he had left.

A Shocking Return

When Nehemiah returned to Jerusalem after fulfilling his obligations to King Artaxerxes, he found several disappointing or sinful things occurring. He took measures to prevent them from continuing. Here is a chart of the problems and his response.

Examples of How Nehemiah Responded to Sin

13:4–9 .... Tobiah, a Gentile, was given a room in the Temple. That was wrong because he wasn't a Jew and because he had previously <u>opposed</u> the rebuilding.

- *Threw out Tobiah's things and had the room purified.*

13:10–14 ..... Discovered the Levites hadn't been given their portions of the sacrifices; therefore they had abandoned their positions.

- *Reprimanded the officials and restored the Levites' positions.*

☞ **GO TO:**

Nehemiah 2:19 (opposed)

He reinstituted the tithe and appointed reliable men to distribute the tithe money.

13:15–22 ..... Jews were working on the Sabbath.

- *Rebuked the nobles of Judah and made sure the gates were closed during the Sabbath. The merchants weren't allowed into Jerusalem on the Sabbath.*

13:23–29 ..... Jews had married foreign women and their children weren't able to speak the language of Judah.

- *He forcefully contended with those men and convinced them to not give their daughters to foreign men or let their sons marry foreign women.*

Four different times, Nehemiah prayed something like, *"Remember me for this, O my God, and do not blot out what I have so faithfully done for the house of my God and its services"* (Nehemiah 13:14). Nehemiah wasn't afraid to ask for God's help and his blessings. He knew he was serving God faithfully and he trusted that God would reward him.

Nehemiah didn't merely scold people for their sin or negligence. He always had a solution that included action to correct the problem. He wasn't a man solely of negative words; he was also a man of positive action.

BUILD YOUR SPIRIT: Because God is a <u>just</u> God, he will give <u>unpleasant</u> consequences to those who disobey and <u>reward</u> the right choices of those who obey. We may not see those factors always played out here on earth, but for sure we'll see them in heaven. God is faithful and just. He rewards those who have <u>faith</u> in him and who follow him. Like Nehemiah, we can ask to be remembered and rewarded.

Study Questions

1. What indicated that Samuel was a true prophet of God?
2. How was Solomon's great wisdom demonstrated shortly after he asked for it?
3. Ezra was a scribe. What does that mean?
4. When Nehemiah called the people together to hear the reading of the Law, how did they respond?

KEY POINT

Don't just rebuke. Take positive action.

Something to Ponder

Remember This . . .

☞ **GO TO:**

Revelation 16:7 (just)

2 Thessalonians 1:6 (unpleasant)

Psalm 62:12 (reward)

Hebrews 11:6 (faith)

- Samuel began serving God as a child and faithfully served until he was the last judge of Israel. He obeyed God's voice and anointed the first two kings of Israel, Saul and David. (1 Samuel 1–16)

- Solomon was the third king of Israel and God.gave him incredible wisdom, although he didn't always use it to make wise moral choices. He wrote many proverbs, ruled in grand style, and built God a magnificent Temple. (1 Kings 1–11)

- Ezra led the second group of exiled Jews back to Jerusalem. Because of the high value he placed on God's Scriptures, he reinstated the study and obedience to God's Law. (Ezra 7–10)

- Nehemiah led the third group of exiled Jews back to Jerusalem, where he motivated the Jews to rebuild the walls of Jerusalem despite much opposition. (Nehemiah 1–13)

11 MEN OF COURAGE: LESSONS IN STRENGTH AND BRAVERY

Let's Get Started

In this chapter Caleb, Joshua, Gideon, and Jonathan demonstrate a trait many of us wish we had—courage, even in the face of death.

You and I may not face death, but sometimes it's the more common dangers of life that bother us. Let's see how we can apply what these four men of the Bible teach us.

Caleb

. . . a Man of Courage and Faith

> **Numbers 13:30–33** Then Caleb silenced the people before Moses and said, "We should go up and take possession of the land, for we can certainly do it." But the men who had gone up with him said, "We can't attack those people; they are stronger than we are." And they spread among the Israelites a bad report about the land they had explored. They said, "The land we explored devours those living in it. All the people we saw there are of great size. We saw the <u>Nephilim</u> there. . . . We seemed like grasshoppers in our own eyes, and we looked the same to them."

☞ **GO TO:**

Genesis 6:4 (Nephilim)

We Can Do It!

Moses sent twelve brave and confident spies into the Promised Land. When they returned forty days later, ten of these men told everyone the land was everything they hoped for, except it was filled with giants who would kill them all. Fear swept through the crowd but Caleb jumped up and encouraged everyone to believe God's promises.

W. Phillip Keller: These are the sounds of a spirit attuned to God's Spirit. These are the sure trumpet notes of trust in the Almighty. These are the bugle blasts of the believer who sees with the pure perspective of faith in God and confidence in Christ.[1]

Caleb spoke with confidence because he knew that God had promised victory. But the crowd envisioned only loss and death.

Something to Ponder

Caleb's ability to trust God in the face of obstacles was based on:

- Focusing on God rather than the obstacles
- Finding support in Joshua
- Remembering God's faithfulness in the past

Remember This . . .

BUILD YOUR SPIRIT: God's promises are his fuel for faith. "*He has given us his very great and precious promises, so that through them you may participate in the divine nature and escape the corruption in the world caused by evil desires*" (2 Peter 1:4). Caleb was able to resist the evil desire of fear, even though the giants were in the Promised Land. We can resist distrust in God when we remember that he has promised to provide everything we need to live the way he wants us to.

KEY POINT

Focusing on God's promises empowers us to trust.

Numbers 14:6–10 Joshua, son of Nun, and Caleb, son of Jephunneh, who were among those who had explored the land, tore their clothes, and said to the entire Israelite assembly, "The land we passed through and explored is exceedingly good. If the Lord is pleased with us, he will lead us into that land, a land flowing with milk and honey, and will give it to us. Only do not rebel against the Lord. And do not be afraid of the people of the land, because we will swallow them up. Their protection is gone, but the Lord is with us. Do not be afraid of them." But the whole assembly talked about stoning them. Then the glory of the Lord appeared at the Tent of Meeting to all the Israelites.

Don't Focus On The Giants

Joshua and Caleb tore their clothes to demonstrate their passion and to persuade the others to take the land God had promised. They pointed out the fortresses were no defense against God, who was with them.

As the Israelites marched through the desert they experienced a daily intimate relationship with God. They witnessed miracle after miracle and still they refused to capture the Promised Land.

BUILD YOUR SPIRIT: What about the giants we face in our lives? Is fear keeping us from confronting them? Let Caleb's words of confidence seep into your soul. You don't have a <u>pillar of fire</u> to direct you by night, but the Bible is a source of guidance. Read it!

Something to Ponder

THE BIG PICTURE

> **Numbers 14:22–24, 36–38** Because the Israelites embraced the negative report of the ten spies so readily and utterly disbelieved the two positive spies, God said he would not allow the disbelieving generation into the Promised Land. *"But because my servant Caleb has a different spirit and follows me wholeheartedly, I will bring him into the land he went to, and his descendants will inherit it."* The negative spies were struck down by a plague. Only Joshua and Caleb, the believing scouts, survived.

"Has A Different Spirit"

The Israelites were run over by their fear. Caleb saw the same fortresses, he walked next to the same giants, and he was exposed to the same intimidation. Yet he resisted the majority perception.

Oswald Chambers: The forward look is the look that sees everything in God's perspective. . . . Caleb had the perspective of God; the men who went up with him saw only the inhabitants of the land as giants and themselves as grasshoppers. Learn to take the long view and you will breathe the benediction of God among the squalid things that surround you.[2]

☞ GO TO:

Exodus 13:21 (pillar of fire)

KEY POINT

There could be no more fearful thought than making God your enemy.

What Others are Saying:

Something to Ponder

What kept the fear from overwhelming his senses? Caleb knew his purpose in life. He knew God's direction. They were to obey the Lord and possess the land. A simple message from God had brought them this far and Caleb was confident God would lead them all the way. Caleb's different spirit came from knowing obedience would bring victory.

KEY POINT

Purpose and priorities empower us to have courage.

BUILD YOUR SPIRIT: Knowing your purpose in life and your priorities will help you stay true to God when doubt overwhelms you. If you know God has called you to a certain role or position, then he'll equip you for the task. If you are convinced God loves you, then the rejection of others won't bother you as much. If you know God is in control of your life, then fear won't paralyze you.

> **Numbers 34:18–19; Joshua 14:6–14** Caleb was assigned to help apportion the land of Canaan when the Israelites conquered it [see illustration, page 192]. And when that happened, Caleb was given the land that was later called Hebron. He and Joshua were the only ones from the original group of Israelites who were allowed to go into the Promised Land.

Faithful And Strong To The End

Caleb had a different spirit that was evident to everyone. He believed God's promises and was rewarded for his courage, "*because he followed the Lord, the God of Israel, wholeheartedly*" (Joshua 14:14).

What Others are Saying:

☞ **GO TO:**

Luke 21:19 (persistence)

Overcoming Struggles

Charles R. Swindoll: Remember your old friend Caleb? He was 85 and still growing when he gripped an uncertain future and put the torch to the bridges behind him. At a time when the ease and comfort of retirement seemed predictable, he fearlessly faced the invincible giants of the mountain. There was no dust on that fella. Every new sunrise introduced another reminder that his body and rocking chair weren't made for each other. While his peers were yawning, Caleb was yearning.[3]

> When we are struggling with conquering a sin or resisting temptation, we may fear that God has abandoned us. But just as Caleb stayed true to the end, so can we. <u>Persistence</u> will pay off.

Joshua

. . . Mentored into Leadership

> **Exodus 17:8–10** The Amalekites came and attacked the Israelites at Rephidim. Moses said to Joshua, "Choose some of our men and go out to fight the Amalekites. Tomorrow I will stand on top of the hill with the staff of God in my hands." So Joshua fought the Amalekites as Moses had ordered.

Instant Commander-In-Chief

At a young age, Joshua was chosen by Moses to be commander of the army. He had to have the wisdom to choose men who would be good fighters. This was a big leap: from brick maker to military commander with no training. Moses merely told him to prepare for war. Joshua didn't whine about being untrained. He just went into battle expecting victory.

W. Phillip Keller: Yet the amazing thing was Joshua's prompt response. He did not delay! He did not offer up excuses for not going into action. He did not plead inexperience or lack of military training. Instead he simply set out to do this impossible assignment with **alacrity**.[4]

Joshua became the <u>historian</u> for the Israelites, and so he <u>accompanied</u> Moses to the base of the mountain as Moses met with God. Joshua must have been the first person to see Moses after he came down the mountain. Therefore, he may have gotten more information than anyone else.

Joshua may have been confident to fight because of the staff that Moses had used. Joshua had already seen the victories that had come from it. With it, Moses had divided the Red Sea and then made it close so that the Egyptian army was destroyed. What a history to call upon!

LEADERSHIP PRINCIPLE—Joshua was called Moses' "servant." That's where future leadership starts. By being a servant in the beginning, we never forget what that felt like, and as a result, we motivate men better. Even Jesus said he came to <u>serve</u>.

What Others are Saying:

alacrity: eagerness

Something to Ponder

Remember This . . .

☞ **GO TO:**

Exodus 17:14 (historian)

Exodus 24:13 (accompanied)

Matthew 20:28 (serve)

BUILD YOUR SPIRIT: We build our spiritual strength as we remember what God has done in the past. We may not have a staff to depend upon, but we have other valuable spiritual resources: the Bible, answered prayers, and fellowship with other believers.

> **Numbers 11:26–29** However, two men, whose names were Eldad and Medad, had remained in the camp. They were listed among the elders, but did not go out to the Tent. Yet the Spirit also rested on them, and they prophesied in the camp. A young man ran and told Moses, "Eldad and Medad are prophesying in the camp." Joshua son of Nun, who had been Moses' aide since youth, spoke up and said, "Moses, my lord, stop them!" But Moses replied, "Are you jealous for my sake? I wish that all the Lord's people were prophets and that the Lord would put his Spirit on them!"

A Man Jealous For Righteous Living

Because Moses' burden of leading the Israelites was too much, God shared his spirit with others. Joshua was an aid to Moses and in this passage shows his loyalty to his leader by objecting to two prophets that he felt were not qualified.

Maybe Joshua hadn't been at the meeting to know what was going on, but regardless, he interpreted what had happened as a threat to Moses' leadership. Joshua showed his loyal spirit right from the start.

Something to Ponder

LEADERSHIP PRINCIPLE—God often prepares us for leadership by easing us into our role. He gives us smaller problems at first. If we prove <u>faithful</u> with little, he will give us opportunities to be faithful with much.

☞ **GO TO:**

Matthew 24:45–47
(faithful)

> **Numbers 27:15–23** When Moses inquired of God who would continue to lead the Israelites into the Promised Land after his death, God chose Joshua. Then Moses commissioned him before the priests, and he was given a portion of Moses' spirit.

Forty More Years

Joshua spent an additional forty years in leadership training as the Israelites marched through the wilderness because they had wanted to return to Egypt. During that time, his trust, faith, and patience were strengthened. Joshua's skill as a military man was unquestioned.

Charles R. Swindoll: Along this pilgrimage of faith there will be times of wandering, times of darkness, times of fear, times of uncertainty. In these fearful moments . . . humbly seek Him. You will feel His mighty hand lift you and lead you onward.[5]

What Others are Saying:

THE BIG PICTURE

> **Joshua 1:1–18** After Moses died, God spoke to Joshua and assured him that he would help guide the Israelites successfully into the land that he had promised them. He commanded Joshua to follow his commands and then Joshua would have courage and success. Joshua then began planning a strategy for attacking the people of Canaan (see illustration, page 192).

Obey And There Will Be Success

Joshua had taken Leadership 101 and learned a simple lesson for success. *"Be strong and very courageous. Be careful to obey all the law my servant Moses gave you; do not turn from it to the right or to the left, that you may be successful wherever you go. Do not let this Book of the Law depart from your mouth; meditate on it day and night, so that you may be careful to do everything written in it. Then you will be prosperous and successful. Have I not commanded you? Be strong and courageous. Do not be terrified; do not be discouraged, for the Lord your God will be with you wherever you go"* (Joshua 1:7–9). Joshua knew he would have success if he made decisions courageously, obeyed God's Law, and studied the Book of the Law—God's Word.

Map of Conquest

Canaan was not a united nation when the Israelites invaded. It had been settled by a number of ethnic groups, each of which lived in small fortified city-states. When the Israelites arrived, the kings of these city-states united against them. Joshua's first thrust into Canaan cut the country in two, and the Israelites defeated first the southern and then the northern coalitions. The campaign against the Canaanites is still studied in U.S. and Israeli war colleges.

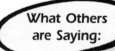

What Others are Saying:

Something to Ponder

☞ **GO TO:**

Joshua 5:14–15 (Captain)

Alan Redpath: It was not a question of what resources or equipment Joshua had, or the numerical strength of his people. The situation was under the control of the <u>Captain</u> of the invisible host, who could defeat any strategy of the enemy.[6]

Over the many years that Joshua led the children of Israel into conquering the Promised Land, he modeled the characteristics and strengths of a courageous leader.

Joshua's Key Leadership Moments

3:1–17 .... Commanded the ark to accompany them; waters of Jordan parted for the crossing.
* *Desired God to be glorified.*

4:1–24 .... Set up twelve stones in middle of Jordan where Israelites crossed; God exalted Joshua and the people revered him like Moses.

- *Set up a memorial for everyone to remember what God had done for them; pointed their attention to God and away from himself.*

5:1–15 .... Practiced rites of circumcision and the Passover; God appeared and Joshua worshiped him.

- *Called himself a "servant."*

6:1–27 .... Marched around Jericho to conquer it.

- *Was willing to follow a bizarre command from the Lord.*

7:1–26 .... Israelites defeated at Ai because there was sin among them.

- *Underestimated the strength of the enemy and didn't initially take care of sin in the camp.*

8:1–35 .... Conquered Ai and completely destroyed it and its people.

- *Didn't let previous defeat prevent him from persevering.*

9:1–27 .... <u>Gibeonites</u> tricked the Israelites into making a treaty with them even though the Gibeonites were a people that Israel wasn't supposed to make peace with.

- *Didn't seek counsel of the Lord and was deceived.*

☞ **GO TO:**

Exodus 23:32
(Gibeonites)

10:1–43 .... Defeated the Amorites in the Promised Land.

- *Joshua fought courageously because God said they would be victorious; Joshua believed him.*

11–17 .... Israelites waged war for at least five years, conquering main sections of the Promised Land.

- *Joshua faithfully persevered in the face of continuing battles.*

18:1–10 .... Seven of the tribes had not taken possession of their land inheritance.

- *Joshua encouraged and motivated them to take the remaining steps necessary to take possession.*

23:1–16 .... Joshua called all the Israelites together to speak to them.

- *Joshua rehearsed God's faithfulness from the past and directed their attention to him. He told them not to worship other gods.*

Joshua was a great military commander, but after his death the importance of his spiritual leadership really became apparent. When he died there was no spiritual giant waiting in the wings. Israel had become dependent upon one leader to keep their spiritual focus. When he was gone, it became apparent they had no individual trust and hope in God. They began to wander spiritually, and Israel began to lose its firm grip on the land.

KEY POINT

Don't become too dependent on men.

🚶 **BUILD YOUR SPIRIT:** Although God wants us to be mentored by others and encouraged through their wise counsel, we shouldn't become too dependent upon one person. Our ultimate counselor is God himself. He doesn't want anyone to become more important than him.

Gideon

. . . a Man Who Grew in Spiritual Strength

> **Judges 6:11–13** The angel of the Lord came and sat down under the oak in Ophrah [see illustration, page 199] that belonged to Joash the Abiezrite, where his son Gideon was threshing wheat in a winepress to keep it from the Midianites. When the angel of the Lord appeared to Gideon, he said, "The Lord is with you, mighty warrior." "But sir," Gideon replied, "if the Lord is with us, why has all this happened to us? Where are all his wonders that our fathers told us about when they said, 'Did not the Lord bring us up out of Egypt?' But now the Lord has abandoned us and put us into the hand of Midian."

Where Has God Been?

It had been two hundred years since the days of Joshua's leadership and God's mighty victories. Now Israel had been invaded numerous times and most recently by a nomadic mob called the Midianites. The Israelites were so oppressed that they hid underground and in caves.

When the angel visited Gideon, he was **threshing** wheat in a winepress, an unusual place to be harvesting. Normally it was done out in the open where the wind could blow away the chaff. Gideon was trying to work and hide at the same time.

Michael Wilcock: It is of the essence of the story that Gideon is not at the beginning a mighty man of valor, as is brought out, I think, by the way his courage grows so gradually; the angel is speaking prophetically about what God intends to make of him.[7]

The nation was defeated and demoralized and Gideon was hiding from the Midianites the day the angel of the Lord approached him and called him a valiant warrior. That must have sounded strange to Gideon. His father had told him stories of God's deliverance but they all seemed empty tales after seven years of Midian terror. He wanted to know why his nation was suffering and why he was hiding in that hole.

BUILD YOUR SPIRIT: Isn't that a typical response? We always want to know the reason for our suffering and pain. His answer to the angel shows just how low Gideon and his countrymen had fallen. When you are that low any opportunity to climb up seems impossible. But God worked with Gideon and he will work with us to give us the courage we need.

> **Judges 6:14–16** The Lord turned to him and said, "Go in the strength you have and save Israel out of Midian's hand. Am I not sending you?" "But Lord," Gideon asked, "how can I save Israel? My clan is the weakest in Manasseh, and I am the least in my family." The Lord answered, "I will be with you, and you will strike down all the Midianites together."

Not Me, I'm The Youngest!

Upon hearing this powerful challenge, Gideon whined some more. He tried to explain that considering his youth and the Midianite domination, he was the wrong guy for the job. The angel promised to see him through to victory. In effect, the angel said, "I see a warrior's heart in you even if you don't. Go and deliver Israel."

☞ **GO TO:**

Ruth 2:3 (threshing)

What Others are Saying:

threshing: separating wheat from chaff

Remember This . . .

KEY POINT

As long as God is with us, we can't fail.

Jamie Buckingham: Gideon was a harassed and discouraged man. He bore the burdens of long defeat. He had not one to stand with him and no traditions to fall back on. He had no concept of the law of Moses and knew virtually nothing of the Bible of the day. . . . He was a very unlikely man to call to lead the nation. Yet God saw something in him that he didn't even see in himself.[8]

Remember
This . . .

Moses tried to use the same excuse to refuse God's anointing of him as deliverer. Moses said he wasn't qualified. God gave him the same reason to obey as God gave Gideon: "I'll be with you."

☞ **GO TO:**

Exodus 3:12 (Moses)

Proverbs 15:23
(encouraging)

LEADERSHIP PRINCIPLE—When we are beaten down or depressed, it is difficult to see the positive qualities in our lives. It often takes an encouraging word to help push away those dark clouds that confuse and slow us down. As leaders when we see others struggling, we must resist the temptation to fix the problem at first. Take the time to give an encouraging word. Recognize one of their strengths and tell them how you admire them for it.

THE BIG PICTURE

> **Judges 6:17–24** Gideon asked for a sign as a confirmation that God wanted to use him to defeat Midian. He brought an offering of a goat and bread and the Angel of God consumed the offering with a spontaneous burst of fire. Gideon then realized it truly was God.

How About A Sign, Lord?

For the first time in his life Gideon realized what was really possible—with God's help. Perhaps, just perhaps, he thought, the angel was correct. Those words, "Deliver Israel, valiant warrior," must have hit a resonant chord in his heart because he asked for some confirmation. Afterwards the frightened farmer stood straighter. He climbed from that winepress a different man and built an altar named "The Lord Is Peace."

Kay Arthur: In the dark hours of Israel's history, God revealed Himself to Gideon as Jehovah-shalom, the Lord is peace.[9]

> **Judges 6:25–32** God directed Gideon to tear down his father's altar of worship to Baal (see illustration, page 133) in their city of Ophrah. Still afraid, he did it at night. When the people of the city found out, they wanted to kill Gideon. His father defended him, saying, *"Are you going to plead Baal's cause? Are you trying to save him? Whoever fights for him shall be put to death by morning! If Baal really is a god, he can defend himself when someone breaks down his altar"* (Judges 6:31). As a result, Gideon got a new name: Jerub-Baal, which means "let Baal contend."

Clean Your Own House First

Before he could deliver Israel, God directed Gideon to take care of business at home. His father had an altar to Baal and an Asherah pole beside it. These were great offenses to God. Gideon gathered some help and did as the Lord instructed—but at night!

The man of valor didn't have the courage to move boldly during the day. But word leaked out about his activities and the next day many came to kill him. His father defended his action with logic, and the crowd accepted the challenge from the old man. Gideon had his first convert.

Bill Hybels: God wants us all to experience a deeper level of security. He wants **emasculated** men to become secure enough to confront timidity and fear, to take risks and make commitments. He wants macho men to become secure enough to crawl out from under the false **pretensions** and quit trying to impress people.[10]

LEADERSHIP 🦅 PRINCIPLE—Leaders should use this same principle for their philosophy. They can't be effective with others until they clean up their own lives. Hypocrisy was something Jesus identified readily in the people who opposed him. To say one thing and do another is a sin worthy of discipline in God's eyes.

> **What Others are Saying:**

emasculated: weakened

pretensions: a phony show of something

☞ **GO TO:**

Luke 18:11 (hypocrisy)

> **Judges 6:33–40** The Midianites and Amalekites attacked the Israelites. Gideon drew together the Israelites with a trumpet blast and sent messengers throughout the tribes. But Gideon still asked for another sign to make sure he was the chosen one to deliver the Israelites, so God showed him two miracles with a wet and dry piece of wool.

Give Me Another Sign, Lord

Courage was contagious. This farmer was now recruiting thousands and was proving to be a skilled and powerful deliverer. The Midianites formed an alliance with another warring tribe, so Israel was threatened again.

What Others are Saying:

diffident: timid

Something to Ponder

fleece: a piece of lamb's woolskin

Overcoming Struggles

Michael Wilcock: We ought not to blame Gideon for putting out his famous fleece. Here the Lord is coaxing along a reluctant leader who really is "**diffident**, modest, and shy," and who needs to have his confidence built up step by step by a patient, loving, but determined God.[11]

Gideon wanted assurance God was with him so he asked God for a demonstration to prove he was in God's will. If a **fleece** was wet and the ground dry when he woke up, he would know God's hand was on him.

🚶 **BUILD YOUR SPIRIT:** God's most powerful guidance tool is his Word, the Bible. It provides every promise and every life-changing assurance we need. Read it because God said, *"Meditate on it day and night, so that you may be careful to do everything written in it. Then you will be prosperous and successful"* (Joshua 1:8).

Demanding extra signs is an indication of unbelief. Fear often makes us wait for more confirmation when we should be taking action. Visible signs are unnecessary if they only confirm what we already know to be true.

Judges 7:1–8 When Gideon gathered everyone together, there were thirty-two thousand men in the army. But God didn't want to use that many. So he instructed Gideon in two different encounters to decrease the number. Only three hundred end up fighting for Israel.

Some Tactics!

From thirty-two thousand men to three hundred? That was an amazing step of faith for Gideon and for everyone else. But Gideon obeyed. First he allowed those who were afraid to leave. Twenty-two thousand left. Then God told Gideon that any man who knelt down to drink from the river was to be dismissed. But a man who lapped the water from his hands was retained. Only three hundred men lapped and God said he would defeat their enemies with those.

Jamie Buckingham: Gideon was a person just like us . . . when he obeyed God, miracles happened. . . . God can achieve great things with a few dedicated people who will give Him the Glory. God, who looks on the heart, is able to take a person who seems to be a coward and turn him or her into a hero—as long as that person is willing to do things God's way.[12]

God wanted to ensure this new leader and his loyal troops would know who gave them the victory. If there had been a lot of men fighting, then everyone could say that the victory came from their sheer numbers. But God wanted to bring glory to himself.

Letting the men go who were fearful is based on Deuteronomy 20:8. *"Then the officers shall add, 'Is any man afraid or fainthearted? Let him go home so that his brothers will not become disheartened too.'"* We need to surround ourselves with those who are not fainthearted. That way we'll be strengthened and not brought down spiritually and emotionally.

LEADERSHIP 🦅 PRINCIPLE—Do you want to receive the <u>glory</u> for what you do for the Lord? Whether you're in the ministry or in the secular world, God wants to make sure he receives the glory and believe it or not, sometimes our failures actually work toward that. When we admit failure or ask forgiveness, we show our humility and <u>dependence</u> upon God. Sometimes that's more glorifying to him than when our plans go perfectly.

What Others are Saying:

Something to Ponder

◄ **WARNING**

☞ **GO TO:**

John 8:50 (glory)

2 Corinthians 4:17 (dependence)

Gideon's trust gave him courage to lead his small army against their enemies. Against all odds Gideon's army defeated their rivals. The map shows the route Gideon traveled to gather his army and to pursue and defeat the enemy.

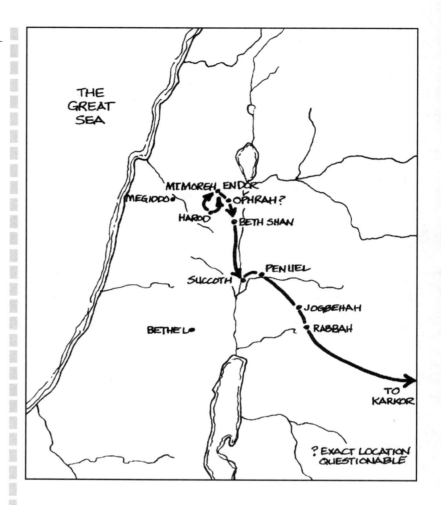

THE GREAT SEA

MEGIDDO
MT. MOREH ENDOR
HAROD
OPHRAH?
BETH SHAN
PENUEL
SUCCOTH
JOGBEHAH
BETHEL
RABBAH
TO KARKOR

? EXACT LOCATION QUESTIONABLE

THE BIG PICTURE

Judges 7:9–25 God provided a further assurance by telling Gideon to listen to the Midianites as they encamped nearby. When he did, he heard two men say they knew Gideon would defeat them. Bolstered, Gideon called the Israelites to attack and defeated the enemy in an unusual way (see illustration, this page).

Smash Those Pitchers

Shortly after 10:00 P.M. a new watch of guards in the Midian camp were shocked by the sound of smashing jars and hundreds of horns blaring. Gideon had instructed his people to make those noises so that they would sound like a much greater army than they were.

This collection of desert tribesmen never trusted each other and in the dark and confusion, they started fighting each other. The death and disarray caused the enemy to flee. It was a rout for Gideon's army and a victory for God.

Because of the recent change of guards, many more men were milling around than normal, which made the **melee** even more confusing. Gideon used the enemy's fear and confusion to make them kill each other while Gideon and his men watched from the sidelines.

Remember This . . .

melee: confused struggle

LEADERSHIP PRINCIPLE—Before the battle Gideon had sneaked into the enemy camp and overheard a soldier say the battle belonged to Gideon. Since God told him this would happen, he quickly returned. *"Watch me,"* he told them. *"Follow my lead. When I get to the edge of the camp, do exactly as I do"* (Judges 7:17). Gideon told them, "Don't do as I say, do as I do." There is no better way to demonstrate our resolve during threatening times than putting ourselves into the tough jobs.

BUILD YOUR SPIRIT: Symbolically, we could listen in on Satan's conversations with his demons and hear the same kind of comments that the Midianites said. Satan knows he is a <u>defeated</u> foe, but he keeps hoping he'll win. God has already written the script. He will be <u>victorious</u> and his children will reign with him in glory.

☞ **GO TO:**

Romans 16:20 (defeated)

Revelation 15:2 (victorious)

THE BIG PICTURE

> **Judges 8:1–21** The men of the tribe of Ephraim complained that they hadn't been called to the battle. Gideon dealt with them by complimenting them. Then he and his men asked for help from the men of Succoth, but they refused. God gave Gideon the victory and he took revenge on the men of Succoth.

Warrior Turned Diplomat

The rout of the Midianites roared through the nation like a lightning bolt. Men from every tribe began chasing the invaders out of the land. The tribe of Ephraim joined the battle and helped capture two enemy generals. However, they complained they were

☞ **GO TO:**

Proverbs 15:1 (soothed)

Something to Ponder

not included in the initial battle plans. Gideon told them their brilliant move in capturing the generals outshined the early work of his army. This diplomatic answer <u>soothed</u> the hurt egos.

This was a masterful stroke. Gideon was on top of his world. He led a broken and defeated nation of twelve different tribes into a great victory. The tribe of Ephraim was known for their troublesome, arrogant attitude. Gideon could have brushed aside their complaints and inflamed tribal rivalries. After all, he was used by God to bring a mighty victory. Instead, in humbleness and wisdom, he paid tribute to their contribution.

LEADERSHIP PRINCIPLE—As leaders we need to remember those we lead respond best to sincere compliments. They need to know their contribution was meaningful and appreciated. If we don't credit what they do, even if it's incomplete, they won't be encouraged to try the next time.

THE BIG PICTURE

> **Judges 8:22–32** Although the Israelites wanted Gideon to rule over them, he told them God should. But he did ask for the gold earrings the people had gotten from the defeated Midianites. He took that gold and made an **ephod**, which turned into a kind of god for the people and they worshiped it. Israel had forty years of peace under his leadership.

☞ **GO TO:**

Exodus 25:7 (ephod)

ephod: *garment of a priest*

Gold Keeps Turning Into Gods

In just a few days Israel had gone from bondage to freedom. Drunk on that freedom, they focused their attention on the man who made it happen, not God. Gideon could have been the first monarch. The nation wanted him to rule, but wisely Gideon pointed them back to God.

What Others are Saying:

W. Phillip Keller: In spite of the distraction caused by Gideon's golden ephod, he himself remained a remarkable force in Israel for the next forty years. It is indeed a measure of the man that without either pretense or ostentation his strong quiet presence among his people provided a base for peace. He had no need to take power into his hands nor assume undue authority over his contemporaries. Just being there was a guarantee of his great and godly influence in Israel.[13]

This farmer, whom God had used in a special way, did have a weak spot—gold. Gideon asked for an earring from each soldier's plunder. The gold from the rings alone weighed nearly forty-three pounds. With a portion of this gold he made a special tunic called an ephod. His intentions were probably to create a remembrance commemorating the victory, but the people began to worship the ephod as an idol.

Something to Ponder

LEADERSHIP PRINCIPLE—As leaders we usually measure our behavior by our best intentions while others react to our actions alone. We need to think things through before acting. Good intentions will not help the consequences of a bad decision.

Jonathan
. . . a Faithful Friend

> **1 Samuel 13:2–4** Saul chose three thousand men from Israel; two thousand were with him at Micmash and in the hill country of Bethel, and a thousand were with Jonathan at Gibeah in Benjamin. The rest of the men he sent back to their homes. Jonathan attacked the Philistine outpost at Geba, and the Philistines heard about it. Then Saul had the trumpet blown throughout the land and said, "Let the Hebrews hear!" So all Israel heard the news: "Saul has attacked the Philistine outpost, and now Israel has become a stench to the Philistines." And the people were summoned to join Saul at Gilgal.

No Credit For A Courageous Fighter

Jonathan was the eldest son of Saul, the King of Israel. His name meant, "Yahweh has given." Jonathan proved himself over and over as a gift from God. In this instance, he was a man of courage as he fought for the glory of Israel, leading his father's army. Jonathan attacked a Philistine outpost and obtained a great victory. He was building a solid reputation as a military leader.

☞ **GO TO:**

1 Samuel 14:49 (eldest)

☞ GO TO:

1 Samuel 13:19–20
(blacksmiths)

Bruce H. Wilkinson and Larry Libby: Saul's valiant son Jonathan had come to the firm opinion that it would be disastrous to allow the Philistine army to establish itself in the southern hill country of Judah. Not one to waste time on formalities, Jonathan leaped into action by leading a surprise attack on a Philistine garrison at Geba.[14]

LEADERSHIP PRINCIPLE—Although it was common for a king to take credit for a military victory he had no part in, it was still wrong. It is still wrong today to take credit for a great accomplishment that belongs to a subordinate. It is just like stealing, and it will destroy your credibility.

THE BIG PICTURE

> **1 Samuel 14:1–23** Saul, Jonathan, and the army of Israel were being attacked by the Philistines. They were at a great disadvantage because the Philistines had removed all the <u>blacksmiths</u>. Therefore no one in the army had swords or spears except Saul and Jonathan. Jonathan secretly went behind the enemy lines to see what God would do for them. As a result, he killed many of the Philistines, and it caused the whole Philistine camp to become fearful. Then Israel had victory against them.

Going Out On A Limb Of Faith

Jonathan said to his young armor bearer, *"Come, let's go over to the outpost of those uncircumcised fellows. Perhaps the Lord will act in our behalf"* (1 Samuel 14:6). What a statement! Faith and courage controlled Jonathan's life. Unknown to his father, he mounted an assault with two warriors—his armor-bearer and himself.

Jonathan used the word "perhaps." He wasn't presumptuous by dictating to God what God should do. Instead, he felt a nudge to do something and was curious to find out how God would use it. It demonstrated his willingness to risk all for God.

John Hercus: The Philistines are one of the great world powers. They were the iron makers of the world; they were fighters to a man. You should talk about Philistines in the way you talk about the Egyptians, the Greeks, the Romans, the British. And Jonathan, the daring young spark, had been reckless enough to clean up one of their outpost garrisons. It is almost as though a band of American Indians had blown up West Point.[15]

Jonathan had previously proven himself in battle but now he would prove his faith in God as the foundation for his warrior's spirit. Jonathan wasn't empowered by his own power or ability, but by God, whom he trusted.

THE BIG PICTURE 🔍

> **1 Samuel 14:24–46** Saul foolishly forbade the men of his army to eat until he had complete victory over the Philistines. Jonathan hadn't heard about it and ate some honey. When Saul couldn't get God to give him direction for the battle, he knew something was wrong and vowed that whoever was the source of the problem would be killed. That person turned out to be Jonathan. Saul would have killed him if the Israelites hadn't intervened.

Wrongfully Accused

In great haste Saul had pronounced a death sentence for something ridiculous. Jonathan's actions were innocent, and thus he could not be charged with disobedience. However, his father backed it with a curse upon himself if he did not see the sentence executed. Faced with certain death, Jonathan told Saul, "*I merely tasted a little honey with the end of my staff. And now must I die?*" (1 Samuel 14:43).

KEY POINT

Everyone needs a close friend—even men.

Luis Palau: God chose Saul to reign. Saul chose to reign without God. In Saul's hand, the authority of the king became hard, brittle, arbitrary, and cruel. Saul held the scepter but the scepter held him. He issued commands simply to command.[16]

What Others are Saying:

Something to Ponder

Talk about a man filled with peace. Jonathan didn't offer any excuses or make a passionate plea for mercy. He just stated the facts. The king's men recognized the injustice of it and saved Jonathan from this outrage.

Jonathan was the son of a mentally unstable father. It's amazing that Jonathan was such a stable individual himself with that kind of influence around him.

> **1 Samuel 18:1–4** After David had finished talking with Saul, Jonathan became one in spirit with David, and he loved him as himself. From that day Saul kept David with him and did not let him return to his father's house. And Jonathan made a covenant with David because he loved him as himself. Jonathan took off the robe he was wearing and gave it to David, along with his tunic, and even his sword, his bow, and his belt.

Souls Knit Together In Friendship

Jonathan recognized David had the same faith and courage that was in his heart when he had attacked the Philistine army. That brought them together as friends and their hearts were *"one in spirit"* (1 Samuel 18:1) or "knit together in love."

What Others are Saying:

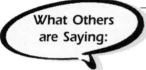

Something to Ponder

Gene A. Getz: The word knit literally means "chained"; that is, the soul of Jonathan was chained to the soul of David. They were bound to each other in an inseparable relationship and union. They were in a true sense "soul brothers."[17]

So strong were Jonathan and David's mutual feelings that they made a covenant with each other. Although Jonathan was heir to the throne, he would willingly lose the kingdom rather than his friendship with David.

> **1 Samuel 20:1–42** David returned from hiding and contacted Jonathan, who couldn't believe his father really intended to kill David. So they set up a test to see how Saul would react when David wasn't at his usual seat for dinner. When David was repeatedly gone from meals, Saul got angry and accused Jonathan of defending David. Saul even tried to kill Jonathan with a spear. This caused Jonathan to be depressed and he communicated with David through their pre-determined signal that David should flee the area completely.

Choices: Father Or Friend

Jonathan was such a loyal person that he couldn't believe his father harbored evil thoughts toward David, even though he'd seen evidence of it in the past. Although he loved David as a best friend, he was also loyal to his father. He wanted to think the best about his own father and king.

Jonathan's loyalty was certainly praiseworthy but his naiveté almost got him killed. While it is good to be loyal and to think the best about people, we should also be discerning so that we don't walk into trouble.

BUILD YOUR SPIRIT: God especially wants us to be discerning about false <u>doctrine</u>. There are many false teachers that could call themselves Christians. We must be careful to analyze whether they are truly teaching principles from the Bible. Otherwise, we'll be feeding our souls false information.

> **1 Samuel 23:15–18** While David was at Horesh in the Desert of Ziph, he learned that Saul had come out to take his life. And Saul's son Jonathan went to David at Horesh and helped him find strength in God. "Don't be afraid," he said. "My father Saul will not lay a hand on you. You will be king over Israel, and I will be second to you. Even my father Saul knows this." The two of them made a covenant before the Lord. Then Jonathan went home, but David remained at Horesh.

Jonathan's Encouraging Heart

Even though Jonathan could rightfully claim the throne, he was convinced that God had <u>called</u> David to be king. Jonathan proved his friendship when he encouraged David even though Jonathan's own father was hunting him.

Alan Redpath: It is apparent that Jonathan showed greater faith in the promises of God than did David at this point. Jonathan asked him if he would remember him and his family, and show kindness to his house when the Lord had long since taken him to be with Himself.[18]

Jonathan laid aside his own potential to be king and believed that God knew best in choosing David as the next king. He had a loyal heart to David and to God. His faith was strong enough to **subjugate** his own desire for exaltation as king.

Jesus had the same loyal and subservient heart to his father, being willing to sacrifice his claim as God in heavenly glory to arrive on earth as a baby to fulfill his father's gracious plan.

Something to Ponder

☞ **GO TO:**

1 Timothy 4:16 (doctrine)

☞ **GO TO:**

1 Samuel 16:13 (call)

What Others are Saying:

Remember This . . .

subjugate: *put under; deny*

GO TO:

Philippians 2:9 (glorify)

LEADERSHIP PRINCIPLE—God did glorify Jesus—not because Jesus asked for it, but because he wanted his son to be given the glory he deserved. If we can trust that God will provide everything we need—even praise—then we will be at peace.

THE BIG PICTURE

> **1 Samuel 31:1–13** Jonathan, Saul, and the Israelite army were fighting the Philistines when Jonathan was killed in battle, along with Saul and his two other sons. The Philistines found their bodies and mounted them on their temple wall. Some brave men of Jabesh-gilead rescued the bodies and burned them for burial.

Loyal To The End

All loyalty entails sacrifice. Jonathan's loyalty put him in harm's way and he was killed. His faith and courage provided the fertile ground from which his loyalty selflessly grew. When loyalty conflicts occurred between his father, David, and God, he let truth and love guide his decisions.

Something to Ponder

Love is not just a feeling or an emotion. The best definition for love is making a choice for the highest good of the person loved. Jonathan made that choice often.

Remember This . . .

David was also loyal as a friend. Later, as the new king, David would honor his friendship with Jonathan by singing about his bravery and by providing for the needs of his crippled son, Mephibosheth.

GO TO:

1 Samuel 1:17 (singing)

2 Samuel 9:7 (Mephibosheth)

LEADERSHIP PRINCIPLE—As leaders, the loyalty conflicts that occur will drive us to examine the core values that direct our lives. The easy choice is quite often the wrong one. Integrity, honesty, and a desire for justice are inner motivations we get from God. They must be used as a plumb line to measure choices that seem right but aren't.

Study Questions

1. When the Israelites were afraid of the giants in the Promised Land, what did Caleb say to them?

2. What requirements did God give Joshua in order for him to have courage?

3. How did Gideon respond when God told him he would be Israel's deliverer?

4. How did Jonathan find out that the Philistines were afraid of the Israelite army?

5. How did Jonathan show his committed friendship with David?

6. How did Jonathan encourage David?

CHAPTER WRAP-UP

- Caleb was one of the spies sent into the Promised Land when the Israelites first arrived. Although others were afraid, he believed they could go in and take the land. Of the original group that left Egypt to go into the Promised Land, only Caleb and Joshua made it. (Numbers 13:30–33; Joshua 14:6–14)

- Joshua was Moses' assistant and after Moses died, he took over the leadership of the Israelites, leading them into the Promised Land in great dependence upon God. (Exodus 17:8–10; Joshua 23:1–16)

- Gideon started out being fearful but God developed his courage and used him to defeat the Midianites. Gideon's diplomacy held the nation in unity and strength for forty years. (Judges 6:8)

- Jonathan was a mighty warrior, risking his life to go to the Philistine camp and test whether God wanted to give them victory. He also became best friends with David, and they made a covenant with each other to protect each other and one another's families. (1 Samuel 14:8–52; 18:1–4)

- Even though Jonathan's father was seeking to kill his friend, Jonathan affirmed that David would become king. (1 Samuel 23:15–18)

12 THE PROPHETS: LESSONS IN SPEAKING THE WORDS OF GOD

Let's Get Started

Have you ever been afraid to speak about your faith? How would you like to share Christ for twenty or forty years and have hardly anyone turn to him for salvation? A pretty discouraging thought, huh?

Well, that's exactly what the prophets of God encountered in the Old Testament times. Many of them saw very little results from their ministries. Most of the time they were laughed at and mocked. Yet, they faithfully believed the message they'd been given from God and proclaimed it anyway. That's consistency! Let's see what they did and how they can inspire us.

Isaiah

. . . a Willing Servant

THE BIG PICTURE

Isaiah 6:1–13 Isaiah had a vision of God seated on his throne in great holiness and majesty, and the prophet recognized his unworthiness to stand before Jehovah. He thought he would die. But a **seraph** touched a burning coal to his mouth and said he was forgiven. When he heard God's voice wondering whom they—the Trinity—would send to speak on their behalf, he volunteered. Isaiah then got his marching orders to speak to the people of Judah, even though very few would respond.

seraph: angel

A Job We Don't Usually Volunteer For

Isaiah most likely started out as a scribe in the palace in Jerusalem but was called by God to be his prophet through a direct vision. He was called to give the Israelites both judgment and comfort. He was married to a prophetess and they had at least two <u>sons</u>. Also, he:

☞ **GO TO:**

Isaiah 7:3; 8:3 (sons)

- Prophesied throughout the reigns of four kings (Uzziah, Jotham, Ahaz, and Hezekiah)
- Ministered for over forty years
- Gave a lot of prophecies about the coming Messiah
- Encountered little success in the response of the people
- Had a way with words and wrote the book of Isaiah
- Died by being sawed in two during the reign of Manasseh (Hezekiah's successor)
- Is quoted over 50 times in the New Testament

His name means "salvation is of the Lord"—the theme of his prophetic ministry.

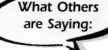

What Others are Saying:

Barry G. Webb: Chapter 6 [of Isaiah] towers like a majestic peak over the surrounding terrain and is clearly of central importance for the message of the book. It was in this encounter with the Lord that Isaiah's understanding of both God and his own mission was crystallized.[1]

Something to Ponder

Isaiah knew right from the beginning that the people he was a prophet to would not respond to him. God told him, "*Make the heart of this people callused; make their ears dull and close their eyes. Otherwise they might see with their eyes, hear with their ears, understand with their hearts, and turn and be healed*" (Isaiah 6:10). God wasn't actually telling Isaiah that he should try to turn the people away, but that God knew they wouldn't respond well because God knew everything. But he still wanted Isaiah to tell of the Lord's love and judgment because a few would respond.

It's amazing to think that any of us would sign up for a job that we knew wasn't going to be successful. Isaiah had a deep faith and trust in God and that gave him the power to persevere in the face of deep rejection.

Isaiah's Prophecies Of A Coming Savior

Isaiah gave some of the most specific prophecies about the Messiah. Here are just a few.

Verse in Isaiah	The Prophecy	Where Fulfilled
7:14	Born of a virgin A descendant of Jesse and King David	Matthew 1:22, 23; 11:1, 10 Luke 3:23
50:6	Voluntarily suffer	Matthew 26:67
53:4	Take the sins of the world upon himself	Romans 5:6
53:9	Be buried in a rich man's grave	Matthew 27:57–60

The chances for even a few of the three hundred Old Testament prophecies about Christ to be fulfilled are astronomical. Isaiah contributed the most to that incredible collection of true prophecies.

Isaiah didn't volunteer for his position flippantly. He asked the Lord how long he would preach with no one responding. We shouldn't make ourselves available to God unless we're really willing to stay <u>faithful</u>, regardless of the response we get.

BUILD YOUR SPIRIT: When Isaiah appeared before God's throne, he knew he was sinful. God provided his forgiveness. None of us are worthy to stand before God or to be used by him, but he provided for our sins to be forgiven through Jesus' death on the cross.

Jeremiah
. . . Weeping Prophet

> **Jeremiah 9:1–2** Oh, that my head were a spring of water and my eyes a fountain of tears! I would weep day and night for the slain of my people. Oh, that I had in the desert a lodging place for travelers, so that I might leave my people and go away from them; for they are all adulterers, a crowd of unfaithful people.

Something to Ponder

WARNING

☞ **GO TO:**

Revelation 14:12 (faithful)

KEY POINT

Whether or not we experience success in God's role for us, we can be faithful.

Cistern

Cisterns were bottle-shaped hollows in the ground where rainwater was collected. They served both individual households and entire communities, depending on their size. The Bible records that Jeremiah and Jacob's son Joseph were both held captive in cisterns.

☞ **GO TO:**

Jeremiah 1:6–7 (adequate)

Jeremiah 38:9 (cistern)

cistern: reservoir

☞ **GO TO:**

Jeremiah 13:17 (wept)

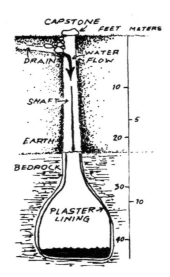

Hope From A Broken Heart

Jeremiah was called to be a prophet at a young age and didn't feel <u>adequate</u> for the job. But he was willing to obey God and ended up preaching for forty years to the rebellious people of Judah.

Jeremiah:

- Was hated and treated harshly by the people, even dropped into an empty **cistern** (see illustration, this page) and left to die
- Was not allowed to marry, as a visual aid of the coming judgment when many people would be without their spouses because of death
- Was persecuted by a false prophet named Hananiah, but predicted his death
- Was alive at the time when the prophets Zephaniah, Habakkuk, Daniel, and Ezekiel prophesied
- Wrote the Biblical book of Lamentations after Jerusalem's destruction at the beginning of the exile
- Frequently <u>wept</u> because of his deep grief over the sins of the people (that's how he has the nickname "the Weeping Prophet")

His message to the Israelites of Judah was that if they would not repent, calamity would come. But he spoke without anger. He covered his prophecies with tears of compassion. Because the people did not repent, they were taken into captivity into Babylon.

Irving L. Jensen: Jeremiah was the gentle and compassionate type. . . . He knew that within a short time the proud, beautiful city of Jerusalem with its magnificent temple would be in ruins, and that his beloved people would be in captivity. . . . No wonder Jeremiah wept.[2]

What Others are Saying:

As an intensely emotional person, Jeremiah wrote about his feelings a lot. He honestly expressed deep sadness over his people's rebellion against God. He even wrote of the <u>horrible</u> ways he was treated and his <u>desire</u> at times to quit. In his lifetime, Jeremiah endured being publicly humiliated, threatened, put in stocks, dropped in a cistern, running for his life, and being carried away from his home land against his will.

Something to Ponder

Commentators believe that Jeremiah's book is a collection of his sayings but they are not put in any particular order. Therefore, prophecies appear together that occurred years apart.

Remember This . . .

LEADERSHIP PRINCIPLE—Like so many of the Israelite prophets, Jeremiah's job was to try to turn the people's hearts back toward God even though God knew it wouldn't happen. Yet Jeremiah persevered. If you are in a ministry or job where you feel like your actions aren't bearing much fruit, hang in there like Jeremiah. Your responsibility is not to make results happen, but to be faithful and obedient to God.

☞ **GO TO:**

Jeremiah 20:7 (horrible)

Jeremiah 20:9 (desire)

Ezekiel

. . . the Watchman

> **Ezekiel 24:16–18; 33:7** "Son of man, with one blow I am about to take away from you the delight of your eyes. Yet do not lament or weep or shed any tears. Groan quietly; do not mourn for the dead. Keep your turban fastened and your sandals on your feet; do not cover the lower part of your face or eat the customary food [of mourners]." So I spoke to the people in the morning, and in the evening my wife died. The next morning I did as I had been commanded" . . . "Son of man, I have made you a watchman for the house of Israel; so hear the word I speak and give them warning from me."

Total Commitment

Ezekiel was chosen by God to be a prophet when he was thirty. Five years earlier, he had been among the Judeans who were exiled from Jerusalem by the Babylonians. He was married and had two children. His wife was the delight of his eyes and a prophetess in his ministry. But God told him she would die. When Jerusalem fell once more, Ezekiel used his wife's death to drive home a message to the surviving exiles in Babylon.

Ezekiel's ministry overlapped the ministries of Jeremiah and Daniel, coming at the end of Jeremiah's and at the beginning of Daniel's. Ezekiel:

- Was a priest before he was a prophet.
- Showed a concern for the priesthood, sacrifices, and the **Shekinah.**
- Saw God in a <u>vision</u> several times.
- Was instructed by God to use many different kinds of visual aids like a <u>linen</u> garment, two <u>eagles</u>, and a <u>withered vine</u>.
- Was likely killed by fellow exiles because he stood against their idolatry.

☞ **GO TO:**

Ezekiel 3:23 (Shekinah)

Ezekiel 8:2 (vision)

Ezekiel 16:10 (linen)

Ezekiel 17:3 (eagles)

Ezekiel 19:10 (withered vine)

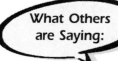

What Others are Saying:

Something to Ponder

Shekinah: glory of God in the Temple

KEY POINT

Like Ezekiel, we are watchmen looking for opportunities to tell others about Jesus.

H. A. Ironside: When his neighbors questioned Ezekiel as to his strange behavior he explained that his loss was but a small one compared with the sorrows and bereavements that were to come to the inhabitants of Jerusalem and all the people of Israel.[3]

Ezekiel did many unusual things. They were supposed to be signs to the people that God loved them and wanted them to draw closer to him. Ezekiel:

Shut himself up inside his house .... Ezekiel 3:24–27
Drew the city of Jerusalem on a
    clay tablet .... Ezekiel 4:1
Lay on his left side for 390 days .... Ezekiel 4:4, 5
Lay on his right side for 40 days .... Ezekiel 4:6
Baked bread over cow manure
    (see GWHN, pages 35–48) .... Ezekiel 4:12–15
Shaved his head and beard .... Ezekiel 5:1–4
Left home to represent exile .... Ezekiel 12:3–7
Sang a song of mourning about
    the leaders .... Ezekiel 19:1

God called Ezekiel a watchman on a watchtower. Such a job in those days was dangerous for the watchman and the city. If the watchman wasn't careful, the city could be overrun and destroyed. God was telling Ezekiel that he had a very important job to do—one which affected a lot of people. He faithfully preached to the people as a result.

As Christians, we are responsible to tell others about God's wonderful gift of grace through his Son, Jesus. Like a watchman, we are supposed to be faithful in looking for opportunities to speak of him.

LEADERSHIP PRINCIPLE—Loneliness, isolation, and troubles frequently touch the life of a leader. Attacks come toward all who stand for something. When your feet are firmly planted in principle and pressure mounts to compromise, steel yourself with courage. God will fill your life with boldness when standing for him. When bold conflicts approach, it takes bold leaders to say no. As Ezekiel stood against his own people, God told him, *"But I will make you as unyielding and hardened as they are. I will make your forehead like the hardest stone, harder than flint. Do not be afraid of them or terrified by them, though they are a rebellious house"* (Ezekiel 3:8–9). Be encouraged, God will help you. Deep, resounding confidence comes from an intimate relationship with him. The prophet Isaiah said, *"Because the Sovereign Lord helps me, I will not be disgraced. Therefore have I set my face like flint, and I know I will not be put to shame"* (Isaiah 50:7). The Lord can help us.

BUILD YOUR SPIRIT: God considers us so important that he calls us his <u>ambassadors</u>. The responsibility of an ambassador is to represent his native country and to look out for its interests in a foreign land. As Christians, we are <u>aliens</u> on this earth, watching for Jesus' return and representing him to the inhabitants of the earth. We are looking out for the best interests of our future country, heaven.

☞ **GO TO:**

2 Corinthians 5:20 (ambassadors)

Ephesians 2:19 (aliens)

Daniel
... Man of Integrity and Insight

> **Daniel 1:8–9, 17** But Daniel resolved not to defile himself with the royal food and wine, and he asked the chief official for permission not to defile himself in this way. Now God had caused the official to show favor and sympathy to Daniel ... And Daniel could understand visions and dreams of all kinds.

Destined For The Lion's Den

Judah was raided by King Nebuchadnezzar, and Daniel was taken to Babylon. There Daniel studied the Babylonian culture and language in preparation for serving his captors (see GWDN, pages 21–26).

While being schooled and trained in Babylon, Daniel refused to eat anything from the king's table because he wanted to keep true to his Jewish laws for eating. Therefore, he lived on a vegetarian diet (see GWHN, pages 49–63). He risked death by not eating from the king's offerings, yet God made sure his "strange" opinions and practices didn't offend the king—at this point. In fact, Daniel became a high official.

When Daniel was serving under his third king in Babylon, Darius, his power and influence had grown so that he was one of the highest ranking officials in the empire. The king liked Daniel so much that he intended to place him above his Babylonian peers. They were jealous and hunted for something to accuse Daniel of (see GWDN, pages 151–160). Daniel always prayed three times a day. He would kneel in his home, open a window facing Jerusalem, and talk to God. Knowing this, his enemies talked the king into issuing a decree that prevented anyone from praying for thirty days. If Daniel prayed once more it would cost him his life. The choice was: conform or perish.

He chose to continue his daily prayers. As a result, the king was forced to give the predetermined consequence: the offender had to be thrown into the den of hungry lions (see illustration, page 219). God miraculously intervened and closed the lions' mouths. Then the king caused Daniel's accusers to be thrown in, and they were promptly eaten. The king issued a decree which honored Daniel's God. Throughout his interaction in a foreign land, Daniel kept his integrity and prophesied many events that were to come true later (see GWDN, pages 222–223). Some won't be fulfilled until the **End Times.**

End Times: when Jesus returns

Lion's Den

Daniel trusted God for deliverance and the lions did not harm him.

Steve Farrar: Prayer is to the soul what exercise is to the body. A spiritual self-starter is a man who is in good spiritual shape. That means he does two things: (1) He consistently eats the nutritious diet of the Scripture; and (2) he consistently spends time in aerobic kneeling. Prayer is the exercise of the man who is a spiritual self-starter.[4]

What Others are Saying:

When Nebuchadnezzar plundered Israel, he had the most talented and skillful young people brought back to Babylon. Daniel was <u>described</u> as good-looking, intelligent, and knowledgeable. Daniel could have gone home each day, closed the windows to his house, and prayed in secret. But everyone knew his commitment to pray. Therefore it would be dishonest. His choices were to either stand fast or compromise.

Something to Ponder

☞ **GO TO:**

Daniel 1:4 (described)

The Four Kings Daniel Served

Name	Empire	Chapter	Events
Nebuchadnezzar	Babylonia	1–4	Daniel was rescued from a death sentence by interpreting a dream. Three faithful Jewish friends, thrown into the fiery furnace, were unharmed.
Belshazzar	Babylonia	5, 7, 8	Daniel read the writing on the wall, which signaled the end of the Babylonian empire. He turned down any reward for this feat.
Darius	Medo-Persia	6	Daniel was thrown into a lion's den and emerged unharmed.
Cyrus	Medo-Persia	10–12	The exiles returned to their homeland in Judah but Daniel stayed to serve the King.

☞ **GO TO:**

1 Corinthians 1:8
(blame)

Romans 12:2 (conform)

KEY POINT

If we compromise, we
can lose our ability to
speak honestly about
Jesus.

When the world pressures you to conform, will you
choose to compromise, or will you choose to stand firm
in your faith? Daniel was able to stand on his integrity
and faith. There are three things you need to know
before stepping into your own lion's den:

1. Daniel knew his heart was right with God. You need
   to know you are forgiven and all known sin is out of
   your life. Having no <u>blame</u> comes only from a right
   relationship with Jesus. *"My God . . . shut the mouths
   of the lions . . . because I was found innocent in his
   sight"* (Daniel 6:22).

2. Daniel knew his heart was right with others. Duty and
   honor to others were more than words to Daniel. He
   treated everyone with respect, fairness, and an honest
   day's work. *"Nor have I ever done any wrong before
   you, O king"* (Daniel 6:22).

3. Daniel trusted God for every part of his life. *". . . no
   wound was found on him, because he had trusted in
   his God"* (Daniel 6:23).

BUILD YOUR SPIRIT: The world seeks to <u>conform</u> us. Our
Christianity is fine with them if we keep it private. Daniel
served four kings for over sixty-five years. The story of the
lion's den is a classic story of one man's integrity and God's
intervention. But when he first arrived he had three choices.
One, give in to the culture and compromise his faith. Two,
live like a hermit and isolate himself from all the sinners around
him. Three, influence those he touched with his faith in God.
You and I have the same choices. What will you choose?

Jonah

. . . You Can Run, but You Can't Hide

> **Jonah 1:1–3** The word of the Lord came to Jonah son
> of Amittai: "Go to the great city of Nineveh and preach
> against it, because its wickedness has come up before
> me." But Jonah ran away from the Lord and headed for
> Tarshish. He went down to Joppa, where he found a
> ship bound for that port [see illustration, page 221].
> After paying the fare, he went aboard and sailed for
> Tarshish to flee from the Lord.

Jonah Runs But God Is Faster!

2 Kings 14:25 mentions Jonah as a prophet who lived during the reign of Jeroboam II in the Northern Kingdom of Israel. Jonah predicted that a portion of the Syrian territory would be recaptured and returned to Jewish control. However, six hundred miles northeast of Israel was the Assyrian city of Nineveh. One hundred twenty thousand people filled its streets, and they were feared and hated by the Israelites. They presented a grave military threat to Israel.

God told Jonah to go there to give them a prophetic word. Instead of going to Nineveh, Jonah rebelled and ran. He booked passage on a ship headed for Tarshish, a city in Spain, about as far in the opposite direction as one could sail in those days. After boarding, he went down into the hold and fell asleep.

But God turned the sea stormy and got Jonah's attention by having a huge fish swallow him (the Bible never actually calls it a "whale"). As a result, Jonah repented, and stopped running from God. After he preached at Ninevah, the entire city repented. But Jonah was mad. Jonah's hatred for the Ninevites was so great, he resented God's merciful choices. He basically told God, "I just knew you would do this but it's wrong to love and redeem my enemies."

God allowed a shade plant to grow and shade Jonah. Then it withered, exposing Jonah to fierce heat. Sullen and hot, Jonah asked to die. He wanted that silly plant to live but not the masses in Nineveh. God asked Jonah that if the prophet could care so deeply about a mere plant, why couldn't he believe the Creator would care for the people of Nineveh?

Charles R. Swindoll: Take Jonah. (No one else wanted to.) He was prejudiced, bigoted, stubborn, openly rebellious, and spiritually insensitive. Other prophets ran to the Lord. He ran from him. Others declared the promises of God with fervent zeal. Not Jonah. He was about as motivated as a six-hundred-pound grizzly in mid-January.[5]

D. Stuart Briscoe: As we look into the portrayal of God in this story, it is obvious to me that the aspect of God's character the writer is most concerned to project is his kindness.[6]

*Something
to Ponder*

☞ **GO TO:**

2 Corinthians 5:21
(paid)

If you are running from God, you might know the darkness Jonah experienced. Condemnation and guilt bring powerful anxiety. Sleep brings the only relief. But when you wake up, the emotional struggle resumes, only more intense.

If this describes you, you can be sure God is designing a storm to get your attention. He loves you and the blood of Christ <u>paid</u> for your sins. If you have booked passage on the same trip the backslider Jonah took, think twice. He cares for you too much to leave you alone. You may be tossed about while God battles for your heart. He tells us, *"But like a woman unfaithful to her husband, so you have been unfaithful to me, O house of Israel, declares the Lord. A cry is heard on the barren heights, the weeping and pleading of the people of Israel, because they have perverted their ways and have forgotten the Lord their God. Return faithless people; I will cure you of back-sliding"* (Jeremiah 3:20–22).

*Remember
This . . .*

KEY POINT

Love your enemies
because God does.

The sailors were awake and calling on their gods, but Jonah, a prophet of God, was asleep. Not for long, though. The captain of the ship came down to chasten him and ask why he wasn't praying. It wasn't until the ship's crew cast lots and the lot fell on Jonah that he finally admitted he was running from the God of Heaven. At his insistence, the crew threw him into the ocean, where a great fish swallowed him. He expected to die, and he finally realized the miraculous fish was for his benefit. As a result, he prayed a thankful song to God.

Jesus taught, *"Love your enemies and pray for those who persecute you"* (Matthew 5:44). How much of Jonah's bias is echoed in your heart? Do you find it difficult to pray for your enemies? Jesus' command is difficult, but it cannot be ignored.

If we don't choose to love our enemies, we'll be filled with bitterness. Bitterness is like a poison inside us. We may think our anger hurts others, but it's really only hurting us. The solution is to forgive and give up thinking we must make people pay for hurting or disappointing us. If we remember how much we've been <u>forgiven</u> by God, we may find it easier to forgive others.

 Overcoming Struggles

☞ **GO TO:**

Ephesians 4:32
(forgiven)

Study Questions

1. How did Isaiah become cleansed so that he wouldn't die in God's presence?
2. What caused Jeremiah to be known as "the weeping prophet"?
3. What was the most difficult situation Ezekiel experienced as a prophet?
4. Why did Daniel not want to eat the royal food and wine?
5. Who did God want Jonah to preach to?

CHAPTER WRAP-UP

- Isaiah began his ministry by seeing a vision of God's throne and volunteering to become a prophet. He served for forty years, yet had little success in making the people change. Regardless, he served faithfully. (Isaiah 6:1–13)

- Jeremiah was a prophet who saw his nation's unwillingness to repent and felt very sad about it. As a result, he cried often and was known as the weeping prophet. (Jeremiah 9:1–2)

- Ezekiel was known as God's watchman because he was assigned by God to watch the sins of Judah and warn them to change. (Ezekiel 33:7)

- Daniel set a strong example through his obedience to proper dietetic laws and by his great discernment. God prevented hungry lions from eating him when he was thrown into the lion's den. (Daniel 1:8–9:17)

- Jonah didn't want to preach to the people of Ninevah because he knew God would withhold judgment upon Israel's enemies if they repented. They did, and Jonah was angry. But God taught Jonah about grace and compassion. (Jonah 1:1–3)

Part Two

MEN OF THE
NEW TESTAMENT

REVEREND FUN

"I'm actually Second Peter. This is First Peter to my right and Third Peter is on First Peter's right . . . You'll have to forgive us as we are out of order again."

13 PAUL: PASSIONATE WRITER FOR GOD

Let's Get Started

The work of Paul was a huge contribution to the cause of Christ in the first century. Paul started out as a Jewish Pharisee who hated those "new believers" of Jesus Christ. But God grabbed his heart in a unique fashion and turned it into a heart of love for himself and followers of Jesus.

Paul has had a powerful influence in the lives of Christians throughout the centuries. His story is told in the book of Acts and his heart is shown in his letters to groups of Christians, which we now use as books of the New Testament.

From his strong example of faithful living in spite of the most horrible conditions, you and I will learn to love and value God more. We'll also be inspired to regard our lives as only important for the wonderful task of representing Jesus to others. That was Paul's mission statement.

> **Acts 8:3** But Saul began to destroy the church. Going from house to house, he dragged off men and women and put them in prison.

I'm Gonna Get Those Christians!

Saul hated Christians. He hunted them without mercy. He wasn't some hired thug; he was a highly trained Pharisee, a religious man, and he intended, with every ounce of his being, to rid his world of this heretical group of Christians. He saw them as a threat to the Jewish Law. He was single-minded in his hunt. He took care of people's coats who were <u>stoning</u> a young Christian preacher named Stephen. It was a bloody sight, yet Saul watched and later said he was <u>pleased</u> about it. Later, Saul would be called Paul. Saul is his Jewish name and Paul is his Roman name.

What Others are Saying:

Remember This . . .

☞ **GO TO:**

Acts 7:54–60 (stoning)

Acts 8:1 (pleased)

Acts 7:60 (blame)

Charles R. Swindoll: He was a zealot who despised the very name of Jesus of Nazareth. . . . He was mean. He was merciless. He burst into people's houses, dragging off both men and women and throwing them into prison. He hated Christians![1]

As Stephen faced death, he graciously asked the Lord not to <u>blame</u> the murderers. Stephen went into the Lord's presence in front of Paul. Even in his bloody thirst, Paul had to wonder about the light and life in Stephen's heart, and may have compared it with the darkness and death that filled his own.

> **Acts 9:1–8** Meanwhile, Saul was still breathing out murderous threats against the Lord's disciples. He went to the high priest and asked him for letters to the synagogues in Damascus, so that if he found any there who belonged to the Way, whether men or women, he might take them as prisoners to Jerusalem. As he neared Damascus on his journey, suddenly a light from heaven flashed around him. He fell to the ground and heard a voice say to him, "Saul, Saul, why do you persecute me?" "Who are you, Lord?" Saul asked. "I am Jesus, whom you are persecuting," he replied. "Now get up and go into the city, and you will be told what you must do." The men traveling with Saul stood there speechless; they heard the sound but did not see anyone. Saul got up from the ground, but when he opened his eyes he could see nothing. So they led him by the hand into Damascus.

Light Brings A Changed Heart

Stephen's death caused the Christians to flee in all directions. Saul knew Damascus would be one spot to find those refugees. Little did he know who was chasing whom. On the way there, Saul met Jesus on that dusty road. After encountering Jesus and being struck blind, Paul was led to a believer in Damascus. There he was filled with the Holy Spirit and baptized. His vision returned.

Oswald Chambers: But the humility Paul manifests was produced in him by the remembrance that Jesus, whom he had scorned and despised, whose followers he had persecuted, whose Church he had harried, not only had forgiven him, but made him His chief apostle.[2]

Paul later referred to his conversion experience by writing, *"but I press on to take hold of that for which Christ Jesus took hold of me"* (Philippians 3:12). Paul was saying that Jesus apprehended him. The one man who made a living apprehending those who loved Jesus was now apprehended by Jesus' love.

Something to Ponder

Paul immediately began telling about Jesus and his own conversion experience in the synagogue. Obviously he was a man who had been drastically changed. Just as he had thrown himself totally into wanting to kill Christians, now he was totally involved in speaking of his new Savior. With Paul, it was all or nothing.

Remember This . . .

> **Acts 13:1–3** In the church at Antioch there were prophets and teachers: Barnabas, Simeon called Niger, Lucius of Cyrene, Manaen (who had been brought up with Herod the tetrarch), and Saul. While they were worshiping the Lord and fasting, the Holy Spirit said, "Set apart for me Barnabas and Saul for the work to which I have called them." So after they had fasted and prayed, they placed their hands on them and sent them off.

I'll Send You Letters While I'm Away

Some personality traits don't change. Saul, whose name was changed to Paul, shifted his power and energy from pursuing Christians to spreading Christianity. He and Barnabas became the first Christian missionaries (see Appendix B—Paul's Missionary Journeys).

Warren W. Wiersbe: Until now, Jerusalem had been the center of ministry, and Peter had been the key apostle. But from this point on, Antioch in Syria would become the new center and Paul the new leader. The Gospel was on the move![3]

What Others are Saying:

Significant Events on Paul's Journeys

Trip	Significant Event
FIRST (A.D. 46–48)	The people of Lycia wanted to make Paul and Barnabas gods. Of course, the missionaries refused (Acts 14:11–18).
SECOND (A.D. 49–52)	A Philippian jailer was converted after a big earthquake caused the chains of Paul, Silas, and the other prisoners to unfasten (Acts 16:25–34).
THIRD (A.D. 53–57)	God performed many miracles through Paul. Even handkerchiefs and aprons he had touched were powerful enough to heal and cast out evil spirits (Acts 19:11–12).
FOURTH (A.D. 59–60)	On the way to Rome where he would be imprisoned and tried in court, Paul was shipwrecked, but many were brought to salvation in Jesus. Some commentators do not actually call this a missionary journey; others do.

Something to Ponder

☞ **GO TO:**

Galatians 1:17 (Arabia)

Galatians 2:1 (fourteen)

Paul didn't immediately become a missionary after his conversion. Commentators believe he spent some years in Tarsus (<u>Arabia</u>) before returning to become more involved with the early church fathers. At one point, he spent <u>fourteen</u> years learning more about what he should believe.

> **2 Corinthians 11:24–28** Five times I received from the Jews the forty lashes minus one. Three times I was beaten with rods, once I was stoned, three times I was shipwrecked, I spent a night and a day in the open sea, I have been constantly on the move. I have been in danger from rivers, in danger from bandits, in danger from my own countrymen, in danger from Gentiles; in danger in the city, in danger in the country, in danger at sea; and in danger from false brothers. I have labored and toiled and have often gone without sleep; I have known hunger and thirst and have often gone without food; I have been cold and naked. Besides everything else, I face daily the pressure of my concern for all the churches.

Winner Of The Unpopularity Contest

vilified: hated

Talk about a changed man. Paul traded all the privileges of his birth and position for the Gospel. That choice got him whipped, beaten, stoned, plotted against, and **vilified**. This man was truly transformed by his relationship with Christ.

Patrick M. Morley: To the same degree Paul persecuted the Christians, he was persecuted in return. It was not an easy-street life. For Paul, following Christ and God's purpose for his life was not an option, not a cushy desk job, but a mandate to exist and function in the way God directed, whatever the cost.[4]

Wherever Paul went, trouble was soon to follow. *"For when we came into Macedonia, this body of ours had no rest, but we were harassed at every turn—conflicts on the outside, fears within"* (2 Corinthians 7:5). Paul was no different than anyone else. He not only dealt with fear, he admits he had many fears! But his life was marked by victory over those fears.

Something to Ponder

Life always offers difficulties, even if a person isn't a Christian. But if you are a Christian, at least you have a purpose in hardship. And you have a great God who wants to help you. Jesus said we would have tribulation, Peter asked why we would be surprised at our tribulations, and Paul said that no one is exempt from suffering for the Lord. You're not alone. God wants you to be strengthened through it all.

Overcoming Struggles

> **Acts 15:12** The whole assembly became silent as they listened to Barnabas and Paul telling about the miraculous signs and wonders God had done among the Gentiles through them.

Gentiles Need Jesus Too

After Paul and Barnabas returned from their first missionary journey, a controversy began within the new Christian church about whether the Gospel should be preached to those who weren't Jews. The Apostle Peter had brought it up after God, in a **vision,** told him to preach to the Gentiles. Some said that the Gentiles had to be circumcised in order to qualify Christianity. A great discussion began among the leaders. Paul and Barnabas told them of how God had used them among the Gentiles. As a result, the leadership group <u>decided</u> to allow Gentiles to hear about Jesus, without being circumcised.

☞ **GO TO:**

Hebrews 2:18 (help)

John 16:33 (Jesus)

1 Peter 4:12 (Peter)

KEY POINT

Difficulties transform us into the <u>image</u> of Christ.

☞ **GO TO:**

Acts 10:9–16 (vision)

Acts 15:28–30 (decided)

vision: *something seen supernaturally*

Warren W. Wiersbe: Their emphasis was on the miracles that God had enabled them to perform among the Gentiles. These miracles were proof that God was working with them and that they were God's chosen messengers.[5]

> **Acts 15:36–41** Some time later Paul said to Barnabas, "Let us go back and visit the brothers in all the towns where we preached the word of the Lord and see how they are doing." Barnabas wanted to take John, also called Mark, with them, but Paul did not think it wise to take him, because he had deserted them in Pamphylia and had not continued with them in the work. They had such a sharp disagreement that they parted company. Barnabas took Mark and sailed for Cyprus, but Paul chose Silas and left, commended by the brothers to the grace of the Lord. He went through Syria and Cilicia, strengthening the churches.

KEY POINT

Everyone needs Jesus.

I Won't Let Him Flake Out On Us Again!

There is a common saying in management circles: "You only can expect what you inspect." Paul was concerned for the growth of the new churches and wanted to revisit them. Barnabas, the encourager, wanted to give John Mark another chance. Paul flatly refused to take him. He probably believed the mission would be compromised. At this point, Paul may not have thought John Mark was trying hard enough, but later he would have more grace toward him.

What Others are Saying:

John Pollock: Paul saw it as rank desertion. Mark's excuse has been variously guessed. Some think Paul had fallen ill of malaria, and made for the mountains to seek cooler air rather than from deliberate intent, and Mark was frightened. Whatever the cause, Mark's withdrawal left a wound in Paul which took years to heal.[6]

Remember This . . .

Paul focused exclusively on the task, while Barnabas saw only the man. Barnabas took John Mark on his own trip. Later in life Paul's thinking about John Mark turned around, because Paul asked for his help. *"Only Luke is with me. Get Mark and bring him with you, because he is helpful to me in my ministry"* (2 Timothy 4:11). (John Mark later became known as Mark.) The hurt feelings were healed. Obviously, Paul learned a valuable lesson.

LEADERSHIP PRINCIPLE—For many leaders it is so easy to focus on the task. Results count and the job needs to be done. That is a short-term view and never addresses our responsibility to develop those we are leading. Paul, in his perfectionism, didn't want to risk the success of "the mission" with a weak team member. Barnabas was able to see that developing "the man" would make "the mission" even stronger. Barnabas was right, the job got done, and the man was restored. When we allow a long-term viewpoint to influence our leadership skills we will become better leaders.

Other Attitudes Paul Expressed

Paul grew from a hateful, revenge-seeking Pharisee intent on fulfilling the Law, to a Christian who lived out the very fruit of the Spirit he wrote about to the Galatians. *"But the fruit of the Spirit is love, joy, peace, patience, kindness, goodness, faithfulness, gentleness and self-control. Against such things there is no law"* (Galatians 5:22–23). Here are some of the qualities he revealed:

- Humility (Acts 20:19, 24)
- Selflessness (Philippians 2:3–5)
- Joy regardless of circumstances (2 Corinthians 7:4)
- Deep love and concern for other believers (2 Timothy 1:4)
- Willingness to sacrifice himself for the cause of Christ (Philippians 1:19–21)

Paul gained those qualities the same way the rest of us do: he had problems that forced him to trust in Christ continually.

Books Paul Wrote

Paul was the most prolific writer of letters to the Christian churches. He cared about them so much that he wanted to keep in touch with them and instruct them in continued growth. Here are the letters he wrote and the main premise of each one. Most often, his message is one of stressing God's salvation through grace, and eliminating his readers' desires to be **legalistic** about faith.

Max Lucado: All the world religions can be placed in one of two camps: legalism or grace. Humankind does it or God does it. Salvation as a wage based on deeds done—or salvation as a gift based on Christ's death.[7]

☞ **GO TO:**

Ephesians 2:8, 9
(legalistic)

What Others are Saying:

legalistic: having to do it by the rule book

Books Paul Wrote

Biblical Book	Main Premise
Romans	Paul presented God's gift of salvation through Jesus Christ, rather than through good works.
1 & 2 Corinthians	Paul addressed problems going on within the church in Corinth.
Galatians	Paul encouraged Galatian believers not to go back into thinking their salvation was based on doing good things.
Ephesians	Paul inspired the Christians at the Ephesian church to know the power they have to live as Christians.
Philippians	Paul **exhorted** the Christians at Philippi to know how they can have unity and joy.
Colossians	Paul instructed the Colossian church to have the right priorities of putting Christ first in their lives.
1 Thessalonians	Paul directed the believers at Thessalonica to grow in their new faith in Christ.
2 Thessalonians	Paul encouraged the believers in Thessalonica to remove the false teaching that some teachers had been putting in their minds.
1 & 2 Timothy	Paul wrote to the young pastor, Timothy, to encourage and instruct him in responsibilities at the Ephesian church.
Titus	Paul stressed to Titus, a young pastor on the island of Crete, how to run his church both administratively and as a counselor to spiritual problems.
Philemon	Paul subtly asked Philemon to accept back as a brother in Christ a runaway slave named Onesimus.

exhorted: *encouraged urgently*

> **Acts 28:30–31** For two whole years Paul stayed there in his own rented house and welcomed all who came to see him. Boldly and without hindrance he preached the kingdom of God and taught about the Lord Jesus Christ.

Paul's Death

Although the end of Paul's life was not chronicled in Scripture, **tradition** says that he was released after no charges were brought against him in Rome at his trial. After his release, he supposedly made another trip to the provinces of Macedonia, Achaia, Asia, and finally Spain. Tradition also alleges he was eventually beheaded by the Roman government.

tradition: *what people have said through the years*

What Others are Saying:

John Pollock: Of Paul's final trial nothing is known beyond the tradition that he was condemned by resolution of the Senate on the charge of treason against the divine Emperor. How long Simon Peter and Paul were in prison together before being executed the same day, as an early and strong belief asserts, cannot be fixed: possibly as much as nine months.[8]

Paul was taken to Rome in order to be tried for treason against the Roman state because the Roman state said Caesar was god. The Jews who wanted to get rid of Paul claimed he was preaching against Rome's authority in Jerusalem and hoped the Roman officials would kill him for it. But they couldn't supply any specific evidence and no one who was accusing him showed up at his first Roman trial. Later at another Roman trial he was found guilty and executed.

Remember This . . .

Study Questions

1. What brought about Paul's change of heart concerning Jesus and Christians?
2. How did the Christians know what God wanted Paul and Barnabas to do?
3. What are some of the things that happened to Paul while he was on his missionary journeys?
4. How did Paul participate in the controversy about whether Christians should preach to Gentiles?
5. What did Paul and Barnabas disagree about?

CHAPTER WRAP-UP

- Paul had been trying to kill or stop Christians from preaching Jesus as the Messiah but when Jesus appeared to him in a bright light, Paul was converted and became a Christian himself. (Acts 9:18)

- After God's directions became known, the Christian leaders sent off Paul and Barnabas on their first missionary journey. They ended up making three more trips. (Acts 13:1–3)

- While Paul was on his missionary journeys, he had a lot of horrible things happen to him, including being beaten, stoned, shipwrecked, attacked, and falsely accused. He went without sleep, food, and drink. But he stayed faithful to God throughout everything. (2 Corinthians 11:24–28)

- When a controversy arose about whether Gentiles could also become Christians, Paul and Barnabas explained how much the Gentiles were responding to their preaching. As a result, the early Christian leaders saw the need to preach to Gentiles too without requiring them to become circumcised. (Acts 15:12)

- Paul and Barnabas had a big disagreement about whether John Mark should go on their next missionary journey, since he had left them prematurely on their previous trip. Paul and Barnabas went in separate directions as a result, but God used it to impact even more people. (Acts 15:36–41)

14 PETER: GROWING IN FAITH

CHAPTER HIGHLIGHTS

- Walking on Water
- Peter Has All the Answers
- The Painful Denial
- An Opportunity to Repent
- The Church Has Begun

Let's Get Started

Peter was the impulsive and expressive disciple of Jesus who said some silly things and did some impetuous stuff, but proved himself a faithful follower in the end. He is an example to many of us who are impulsive. Jesus saw Peter's potential and gave him a new name representing his future position in the church. We'll be focusing on only a few of the many verses that refer to Peter, but even those few will show us what kind of person he was and how he changed.

> **Matthew 4:18–20** As Jesus was walking beside the Sea of Galilee [see illustration, page 239], he saw two brothers, Simon called Peter and his brother Andrew. They were casting a net into the lake, for they were fishermen. "Come, follow me," Jesus said, "and I will make you fishers of men." At once they left their nets and followed him.

Ready, Fire, Aim!

Peter immediately left his nets to follow Jesus. He was just that type of man. He was the first one in line, the first to raise his hand, and the first to move. Decisions came quickly to him. Inaction was intolerable and he avoided it at all costs.

KEY POINT

Peter was a natural go-getter.

Herschel H. Hobbs: No man should ever limit God by his own power or understanding. When faith is tested to the utmost, we should rest in God and leave the unknown to him. It is better to walk with God in the dark than to walk alone in the light. In his own time God will make all things plain.[1]

Something to Ponder

Peter was independent and confident and our society admires and rewards men like him. He was a self-made man who got things done. Of course, he could come across a little pushy now and then, but you couldn't help admiring a self-starter like Peter.

☞ **GO TO:**

Proverbs 3:5–6 (understanding)

LEADERSHIP PRINCIPLE—You may have many wonderful qualities, but are they controlled by the Holy Spirit or are you operating in your own power? God wants us to depend upon him, not our own <u>understanding.</u>

> **Matthew 14:22–32** Immediately Jesus made the disciples get into the boat and go on ahead of him to the other side, while he dismissed the crowd. After he had dismissed them, he went up on a mountainside by himself to pray. When evening came, he was there alone, but the boat was already a considerable distance from land, buffeted by the waves because the wind was against it. During the fourth watch of the night Jesus went out to them, walking on the lake. When the disciples saw him walking on the lake, they were terrified. "It's a ghost," they said, and cried out in fear. But Jesus immediately said to them: "Take courage! It is I. Don't be afraid." "Lord, if it's you," Peter replied, "tell me to come to you on the water." "Come," he said. Then Peter got down out of the boat, walked on the water and came toward Jesus. But when he saw the wind, he was afraid and, beginning to sink, cried out, "Lord, save me!" Immediately Jesus reached out his hand and caught him. "You of little faith," he said, "why did you doubt?" And when they climbed into the boat, the wind died down.

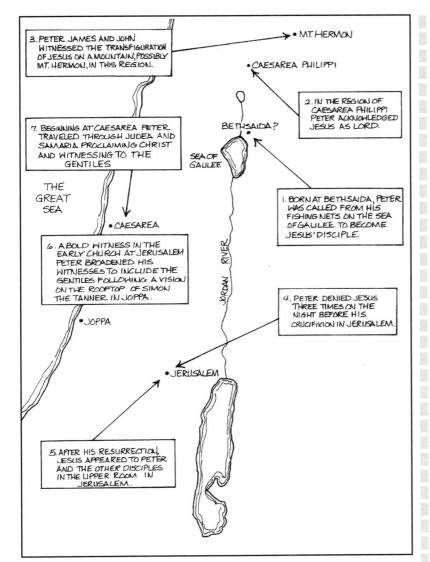

This map shows where major events occurred in Peter's life. The events are numbered chronologically.

3. PETER, JAMES AND JOHN WITNESSED THE TRANSFIGURATION OF JESUS ON A MOUNTAIN, POSSIBLY MT. HERMON, IN THIS REGION.

• MT. HERMON

• CAESAREA PHILIPPI

2. IN THE REGION OF CAESAREA PHILIPPI PETER ACKNOWLEDGED JESUS AS LORD.

BETHSAIDA?

SEA OF GALILEE

7. BEGINNING AT CAESAREA PETER TRAVELED THROUGH JUDEA AND SAMARIA PROCLAIMING CHRIST AND WITNESSING TO THE GENTILES

THE GREAT SEA

• CAESAREA

1. BORN AT BETHSAIDA, PETER WAS CALLED FROM HIS FISHING NETS ON THE SEA OF GALILEE TO BECOME JESUS' DISCIPLE.

6. A BOLD WITNESS IN THE EARLY CHURCH AT JERUSALEM PETER BROADENED HIS WITNESSES TO INCLUDE THE GENTILES FOLLOWING A VISION ON THE ROOFTOP OF SIMON THE TANNER IN JOPPA.

JORDAN RIVER

4. PETER DENIED JESUS THREE TIMES ON THE NIGHT BEFORE HIS CRUCIFIXION IN JERUSALEM.

• JOPPA

• JERUSALEM

5. AFTER HIS RESURRECTION, JESUS APPEARED TO PETER AND THE OTHER DISCIPLES IN THE UPPER ROOM IN JERUSALEM.

Jump Now, Float Later

Look up the word "zest" in the dictionary and you might see Peter's likeness. Peter loved Christ with his whole heart and it showed. He would be the first one jumping out of a boat to meet Jesus on the shore. It comes as little surprise he would ask to meet Jesus on the water!

It also comes as no surprise to see Peter sink beneath the waves when he took his eyes off Jesus. He was quick to jump in, but lacked the staying power to follow through. You and I also sink into our difficult circumstances when we take our eyes off Jesus. *"Let us fix our eyes on Jesus, the author and perfecter of our faith, who for the joy set before him endured the cross, scorning its shame, and sat down at the right hand of the throne of God"* (Hebrews 12:2).

LEADERSHIP PRINCIPLE—All of us have seen leaders like Peter jump quickly into situations without counting the cost. They try relying on their own skill to push through stormy times. Their resolve is strong, their courage is unquestioned, and they want to make a difference. Intentions are good, but the outcomes can be erratic. We need to remember that we should move fast with decisions that can be reversed, and slower with irreversible ones.

BUILD YOUR SPIRIT: Peter was quick to sign up but often faltered in continuing strong. We should also be careful about staying faithful and not growing <u>weary</u>. The Christian life isn't a sprint, it's a marathon.

☞ **GO TO:**

Galatians 6:9 (weary)

> **Matthew 16:13–20** When Jesus came to the region of Caesarea Philippi, he asked his disciples, "Who do people say the Son of Man is?" They replied, "Some say John the Baptist; others say Elijah; and still others, Jeremiah or one of the prophets." "But what about you?" he asked. "Who do you say I am?" Simon Peter answered, "You are the Christ, the Son of the living God." Jesus replied, "Blessed are you, Simon son of Jonah, for this was not revealed to you by man, but by my Father in heaven. And I tell you that you are Peter, and on this rock I will build my church, and the gates of Hades will not overcome it. I will give you the keys of the kingdom of heaven; whatever you bind on earth will be bound in heaven, and whatever you loose on earth will be loosed in heaven." Then he warned his disciples not to tell anyone that he was the Christ.

I Know Who You Are!

How come no one was surprised Peter answered the big question for everyone else? Peter knew where Jesus was leading the discussion. Like a bubble ready to burst, Peter was ready to jump when Jesus asked, "Who do you say I am?" Peter was ready and answered on behalf of everyone, "You are the Christ, the Son of the living God" (verse 16). His answer shot from his lips because it was the honest confession of his heart.

Philip Yancey: According to Jesus, what I think about him and how I respond will determine my destiny for all eternity.[2]

Every person in the world will some day <u>answer</u> that question and it will determine whether they are allowed into heaven or sent to eternity without God's presence. If we say Jesus is the Christ, we are acknowledging our need of a Savior and that he is actually God.

When Jesus said "I AM" he was calling himself God for that's how God referred to himself in the Old Testament. That is why the religious leaders wanted to <u>stone</u> him.

> **Matthew 16:21–23** From that time on Jesus began to explain to his disciples that he must go to Jerusalem and suffer many things at the hands of the elders, chief priests and teachers of the law, and that he must be killed and on the third day be raised to life. Peter took him aside and began to rebuke him. "Never, Lord!" he said. "This shall never happen to you!" Jesus turned and said to Peter, "Get behind me, Satan! You are a stumbling block to me; you do not have in mind the things of God, but the things of men."

Open Mouth, Insert Foot

Peter had it all figured out. Jesus was the Messiah, the Son of God. This returning king would deliver the Jews from their persecutors.

Philip Yancey: Jesus' most devoted followers usually come off as scratching their heads in wonderment—Who is this guy?—more baffled than conspiratorial.[3]

What Others are Saying:

Something to Ponder

Remember This . . .

☞ **GO TO:**

Matthew 10:32 (answer)

John 8:59 (stone)

What Others are Saying:

Peter loved Christ, but he wasn't ready to hear anything contrary to his own plans. He had it all worked out in his mind. No one was going to tell him anything different. Not even Jesus.

> **Matthew 17:1–8** After six days Jesus took with him Peter, James and John the brother of James, and led them up a high mountain by themselves. There he was transfigured before them. His face shone like the sun, and his clothes became as white as the light. Just then there appeared before them Moses and Elijah, talking with Jesus. Peter said to Jesus, "Lord, it is good for us to be here. If you wish, I will put up three shelters—one for you, one for Moses and one for Elijah." While he was still speaking, a bright cloud enveloped them, and a voice from the cloud said, "This is my Son, whom I love; with him I am well pleased. Listen to him!" When the disciples heard this, they fell face down to the ground, terrified. But Jesus came and touched them. "Get up," he said. "Don't be afraid." When they looked up, they saw no one except Jesus.

Open Mouth, Insert Foot II

Shooting from the hip, Peter blurted out that they should build a memorial. How fitting that God interrupted the zealous Peter. In mid-sentence Peter got the message. His only response was to fall face down to the ground before Jesus Christ and the presence of God.

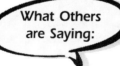

**What Others
are Saying:**

Max Lucado: Stand in God's presence. Stand in his sight. Stand still and wait. Sometimes that's all a soul can do.[4]

**Something
to Ponder**

What an appropriate response for Peter: to fall face down in worship before God's presence. Instead of trying to make plans and do things, we should humble ourselves by being quiet. When we see Jesus in heaven, we're not going to talk; we'll bow.

Peter continued to reveal his impetuousness many times. When Jesus wanted to wash Peter's feet, he protested. *"You shall never wash my feet."* Only when Jesus answered, *"Unless I wash you, you have no part with me,"* did Peter agree and say, *"not just my feet but my hands and my head as well!"* (John 13:6–8).

When Jesus was arrested in the garden, Peter impulsively cut off the <u>ear</u> of the servant of the high priest. Peter was trying to make things turn out the way he wanted. To Peter's credit, whenever the truth was revealed, he quickly changed his thinking.

Remember This . . .

☞ **GO TO:**

John 18:7–11 (ear)

BUILD YOUR SPIRIT: There is so much of Peter in all of us. We busy ourselves with activities that seemingly honor the Lord, when we need to take time to worship him. We worship when we focus on his graciousness, mercy, love, faithfulness, kindness, and goodness.

> **Matthew 26:31–35** Then Jesus told them, "This very night you will all fall away on account of me, for it is written: "'I will strike the shepherd, and the sheep of the flock will be scattered.' But after I have risen, I will go ahead of you into Galilee." Peter replied, "Even if all fall away on account of you, I never will." "I tell you the truth," Jesus answered, "this very night, before the rooster crows, you will disown me three times." But Peter declared, "Even if I have to die with you, I will never disown you." And all the other disciples said the same.

Pride Before The Downfall

Peter was telling the Lord, "You have trained me. I love you. I am a changed man. I will never leave you." But Peter was unprepared for total commitment because too much of Peter stood in the way.

John MacArthur, Jr.: Peter was a man of action—impulsive and eager. I call him the Apostle with the foot-shaped mouth because he was always sticking his foot in it. He was always blurting out, charging ahead in a mad hurry.[5]

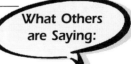

What Others are Saying:

KEY POINT

Don't let self-confidence ruin your God-confidence.

Peter's great confidence was his greatest weakness. Peter loved the Lord, was forgiven, and desired to serve him forever. However, Peter was just hours away from catastrophic failure, even as he boasted his fidelity to the Lord.

It will take Peter's broken heart to allow that last drop of his pride to spill out. Then Peter will be ready to die for Christ. Pride always stands in the way of being able to see God's purposes and of knowing how to respond the way he wants us to.

Someone has said, "He who is disappointed in himself is he who first trusted in himself." We will avoid that kind of disappointment if we recognize that we can only do anything good through the Holy Spirit's power in our lives.

> **Matthew 26:69–75** Now Peter was sitting out in the courtyard, and a servant girl came to him. "You also were with Jesus of Galilee," she said. But he denied it before them all. "I don't know what you're talking about," he said. Then he went out to the gateway, where another girl saw him and said to the people there, "This fellow was with Jesus of Nazareth." He denied it again, with an oath: "I don't know the man!" After a little while, those standing there went up to Peter and said, "Surely you are one of them, for your accent gives you away." Then he began to call down curses on himself and he swore to them, "I don't know the man!" Immediately a rooster crowed. Then Peter remembered the word Jesus had spoken: "Before the rooster crows, you will disown me three times." And he went outside and wept bitterly.

Peter And The Wail

Peter wrapped his whole life around Jesus. His confidence seemed to be an asset. But his confidence failed, and when he denied Christ, his world fell apart. "Wept bitterly" in Greek actually means "a piercing, violent cry." For the next three days after Jesus hung on the cross and died, Peter lived in agony. He most likely repeatedly rehearsed his denial. He may have asked himself a thousand times, "Why did I respond like that, I love Jesus!" But he had no peace.

F. B. Meyer: Then, forgetting his own grief, he turned and looked at Peter, not with anger or reproach, but remembering and reminding. Many waters cannot drown his love! We too may fail him, deny, and crucify him afresh. But when our heart turns back in an agony of grief and remorse, he will renew us again unto repentance.[6]

Such a grievous failure would have driven most men into depression. Some men might have even committed <u>suicide</u> like Judas Iscariot did after he betrayed Jesus. But Peter somehow had the courage to persevere. He was even meeting with the disciples, which was a wise thing to do.

Remember This . . .

BUILD YOUR SPIRIT: When we are feeling discouraged or depressed because we have failed, the best thing we can do is meet with other Christians. Most of the time, that's the thing we least want to do, but to let us know there is hope we need the <u>support</u> of others who have also failed.

☞ **GO TO:**

Matthew 27:5 (suicide)

1 Thessalonians 2:11, 12 (support)

> **John 21:3–7** "I'm going out to fish," Simon Peter told them, and they said, "We'll go with you." So they went out and got into the boat, but that night they caught nothing. Early in the morning, Jesus stood on the shore, but the disciples did not realize that it was Jesus. He called out to them, "Friends, haven't you any fish?" "No," they answered. He said, "Throw your net on the right side of the boat and you will find some." When they did, they were unable to haul the net in because of the large number of fish. Then the disciple whom Jesus loved said to Peter, "It is the Lord!" As soon as Simon Peter heard him say, "It is the Lord," he wrapped his outer garment around him (for he had taken it off) and jumped into the water.

I'll Pick Jesus Over A Huge Catch

As a fisherman, this was Peter's big score. He had struck it rich. However, when he learned that Jesus was on the shore, he compared the wealth in his net to the relationship he had with Jesus. No more denials, no more water walking attempts, and no more fish! Peter threw himself into the water and swam to Jesus.

Warren W. Wiersbe: It was time for Jesus to take over the situation, just as he did when he called Peter into discipleship. He told them where to cast the net; they obeyed, and they caught 153 fish! We are never far from success when we permit Jesus to give the orders, and we are usually closer to success than we realize.[7]

Something to Ponder

The word "friends" in Greek is literally "little children" or perhaps "lads." Even though the disciples had given up on their former discipleship life, Jesus' compassionate calling to them shows his understanding and desire to woo them back to the mission he started to train them for.

LEADERSHIP PRINCIPLE—At times we may become discouraged and leave the calling or mission God has given us. But if we'll hear him call us "friends" and "lads" in a compassionate voice, we may be inspired again to serve him in the way he wants us to.

> **John 21:15–19** When they had finished eating, Jesus said to Simon Peter, "Simon son of John, do you truly love me more than these?" "Yes, Lord," he said, "you know that I love you." Jesus said, "Feed my lambs." Again Jesus said, "Simon son of John, do you truly love me?" He answered, "Yes, Lord, you know that I love you." Jesus said, "Take care of my sheep." The third time he said to him, "Simon son of John, do you love me?" Peter was hurt because Jesus asked him the third time, "Do you love me?" He said, "Lord, you know all things; you know that I love you." Jesus said, "Feed my sheep. I tell you the truth, when you were younger you dressed yourself and went where you wanted; but when you are old you will stretch out your hands, and someone else will dress you and lead you where you do not want to go." Jesus said this to indicate the kind of death by which Peter would glorify God. Then he said to him, "Follow me!"

Career Move: From Fisherman to Shepherd

Jesus had a meal of fish all ready to be eaten when Peter and the disciples arrived from their huge catch. After eating, Jesus concentrated on Peter and gave him a chance to redeem himself. Jesus asked Peter if he loved his Savior more than the disciples sitting there. Peter was able to put aside his great guilt and tell Jesus that he did indeed love him. How healing that must have been to be able to express it to Jesus' face after denying him.

Jesus was giving Peter his marching orders for the future, indicating he would be the shepherd of the flock of new Christians. He was also predicting that Peter would die in a stretched out position—which is exactly what happened—through crucifixion. Peter may not have been able to comprehend Jesus' meaning at that time.

What Others are Saying:

Max Lucado: What did he do? He met them at their point of pain. Though death has been destroyed and sin **annulled**, he has not retired. The resurrected Lord has once again wrapped himself in flesh, put on human clothes, and searched out hurting hearts.[8]

annulled: *repealed*

Something to Ponder

What must the disciples have said to Jesus as he sat beside them in his resurrected body? Did they want to know what the future held for them? Did they believe he would now be around forever in his new body? Did Peter feel the most uncomfortable? Did Peter want to say something about the denial but couldn't? Or maybe he did say something and that's why Jesus started to give him new hope.

> **Acts 2:14** Then Peter stood up with the Eleven, raised his voice and addressed the crowd: "Fellow Jews and all of you who live in Jerusalem, let me explain this to you; listen carefully to what I say.

The Church Has Begun

After Jesus <u>rose</u> into heaven, the disciples waited to be filled with the Holy Spirit as Jesus had <u>instructed</u> them. After they were filled with the Spirit, Peter truly became a new person filled with more of God's power and less of himself.

☞ **GO TO:**

Acts 1:9 (rose)

Acts 1:8 (instructed)

What Others are Saying:

Lloyd John Ogilvie: There is no need I have ever heard articulated by individuals or the Church that could not be met by the Holy Spirit. Our need for wisdom, knowledge, faith, healing, discernment, and freedom are his gifts.[9]

Peter's Leadership Activities

Peter revealed his changed nature in the following ways.

☞ **GO TO:**

Leviticus 23:16
(Pentecost)

Pentecost: Jewish Feast
of Weeks

2:14–36 .... Peter was the first one to give a sermon and explained **Pentecost**.
- *He was quickly established as a primary leader of the new church.*

3:1–26 .... Peter healed a lame man at the temple gates and then gave a sermon to those watching. He also healed Aeneas (9:32–35) and Dorcas (9:36–43).
- *He had great power and looked for every opportunity to share.*

4:1–31 .... Peter and others were imprisoned for preaching but refused to stop.
- *He was more interested in pleasing God than man.*

5:1–11 .... Peter confronted Ananias and Sapphira about their lie.
- *He was able to confront with love and strength.*

12:3–19 .... Peter was asleep in prison and an angel miraculously set him free. Peter didn't worry much.
- *He could sleep in prison when his life was in danger.*

1 Peter .... Peter wrote this letter to Christians in Asia Minor encouraging them to see their sufferings as opportunities to represent Jesus.
- *He himself suffered persecution and persevered.*

2 Peter .... Peter wrote this letter to the same Christians, most likely just before his death as a martyr. He addressed the problems of false doctrine and teachers.
- *He was concerned about the condition of the church and made every effort to help other Christians.*

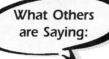

What Others are Saying:

F. B. Meyer: It seemed as though a very special illumination had been given him by the Holy Spirit of Inspiration, that he might understand the Scriptures and perceive the relevance to Jesus of all things written in the Law of Moses, the Prophets, and the Psalms.[10]

Peter's Death

Peter died most likely between 64 and 66 A.D. He died as a martyr through crucifixion. Some commentators believe, based on some first century writers, that he was forced to watch the crucifixion of his wife before his death. He then requested he be put on the cross upside down because he felt he wasn't worthy of dying the same way Jesus did.

Jesus told Peter he would die for his faith. That makes some of the last words he ever wrote even more significant. He was a bold man who came full circle from mountaintop to deepest valley, yet finished his life strong and dedicated to the Lord. We can learn from his words and live with real purpose in our lives.

Something to Ponder

Study Questions

1. When Peter was walking on the water toward Jesus, what distracted him and caused him to sink?
2. Who did Jesus say had inspired Peter's answer as he identified Jesus as the Messiah?
3. What did Peter do when he realized he had denied Jesus?
4. After Peter denied knowing Jesus, how did Jesus make Peter feel better and know he was forgiven?
5. Who was the first person to give a sermon after the disciples experienced the infilling of the Holy Spirit?

CHAPTER WRAP-UP

- Peter was one of the first disciples of Jesus and impulsively offered to walk on the water toward Jesus. When he grew fearful, he began to sink. He called to Jesus and Jesus rescued him. This incident serves as a picture of how we can overcome life's storms if we stay focused on Jesus. (Matthew 14:22–32)

- When Jesus asked the disciples who they thought he was, Peter quickly answered for them saying Jesus was the Christ, the Son of God. (Matthew 16:13–20)

- Peter was accused of being with Jesus while Jesus was being tried as a traitor. Peter denied ever knowing him. When he realized he had fulfilled Jesus' prediction of his denials, he wailed with grief. (Matthew 26:69–75)

- After Jesus was resurrected and appeared to many, he had a meal with Peter and the disciples. Jesus asked Peter three times whether he loved him. Peter said he did and Jesus gave him the mission of shepherding his followers. (John 21:15–19)

- After the Holy Spirit was given to the disciples on Pentecost, Peter established himself as a primary leader by giving the first sermon, and with powerful results. (Acts 2:14)

15 MEN IN MINISTRY: LESSONS IN FOLLOWING CHRIST

Let's Get Started

Whether during Jesus' walk here on earth or after, powerful men spread the news that Jesus offered God's unconditional love. John the Baptist was his forerunner and prepared the way. Then others wrote about him, like Luke, Mark, Matthew, John, and James. Others, such as Philip and Andrew, were part of Jesus' hearty band of disciples. And then there were the ones in the early church, like Stephen. We'll have a better chance of succeeding by understanding those who did a good job before us.

John the Baptist

. . . Not to Name-drop or Anything, but the Messiah's My Cousin

Matthew 3:13–17 Then Jesus came from Galilee to the Jordan to be baptized by John. But John tried to deter him, saying, "I need to be baptized by you, and do you come to me?" Jesus replied, "Let it be so now; it is proper for us to do this to fulfill all righteousness." Then John consented. As soon as Jesus was baptized, he went up out of the water. At that moment heaven was opened, and he saw the Spirit of God descending like a dove and lighting on him. And a voice from heaven said, "This is my Son, whom I love; with him I am well pleased."

"Bulldozer" Baptist Levels The Ground For The Messiah

☞ **GO TO:**

Luke 1:36 (cousins)

Luke 1:80 (wilderness)

Matthew 14:10 (beheaded)

John the Baptist and Jesus were <u>cousins</u> born six months apart. They may not have had much contact because they lived far from each other and John began living in the <u>wilderness</u> as a young man.

In a prophetic utterance his father foretold John's ministry when he was born. He predicted, *"And you, my child, will be called a prophet of the Most High; for you will go on before the Lord to prepare the way for him, to give his people the knowledge of salvation through the forgiveness of their sins, because of the tender mercy of our God, by which the rising sun will come to us from heaven to shine on those living in darkness and in the shadow of death, to guide our feet into the path of peace"* (Luke 1:76–79).

John the Baptist was <u>beheaded</u> because of his strong witness to the evil King Herod's court.

What Others are Saying:

John A. Martin: When a king traveled the desert, workmen preceded him to clear debris and smooth out the roads to make his trip easier. In Luke the leveling of the land was a figurative expression denoting that the way of the Messiah would be made smooth because through John a large number of people were ready to receive Jesus' message.[1]

Something to Ponder

Isaiah had prophesied about John the Baptist's ministry many years previously when he wrote, *"A voice of one calling: 'In the desert prepare the way for the Lord; make straight in the wilderness a highway for our God. Every valley shall be raised up, every mountain and hill made low; the rough ground shall become level, the rugged places a plain. And the glory of the Lord will be revealed, and all mankind together will see it. For the mouth of the Lord has spoken'"* (Isaiah 40:3–5). Yet, even after John the Baptist baptized Jesus and heard of his continuing ministry, John had <u>doubts</u> about Jesus' authority. He sent a message from prison and asked Jesus if he was indeed the one who was predicted to come. Jesus sent a message back saying that his works proved he was the Messiah.

☞ **GO TO:**

Matthew 11:1–6 (doubts)

1 Peter 3:21 (baptism)

Remember This . . .

John the Baptist was named that because his ministry was to call people to repentance and then baptize them. The <u>baptism</u> itself did not save them from their sins, but their repentance did.

BUILD YOUR SPIRIT: Baptism is a formal and public declaration of the cleansing work that God does in your heart when you ask Jesus to come into your life and forgive you. Baptism represents a burial into water that symbolizes your death to sin. And just as you rise up out of the water, some day, you will be resurrected from the grave to reside in heaven.

Luke

. . . Chronicler of Jesus and the Early Church

> **Luke 1:1–4** Many have undertaken to draw up an account of the things that have been fulfilled among us, just as they were handed down to us by those who from the first were eyewitnesses and servants of the word. Therefore, since I myself have carefully investigated everything from the beginning, it seemed good also to me to write an orderly account for you, most excellent Theophilus, so that you may know the certainty of the things you have been taught.

Apparently Not All Doctors Have Horrible Writing

If your doctor told you he'd written a book, would you imagine that it would be detailed and specific? Most of us imagine a doctor as one who is interested in details and is careful in evaluations. Luke must have been that kind of doctor. He was very meticulous as he interviewed people and researched the material for his two-volume book.

There's a good possibility that Luke interviewed Mary, the mother of Jesus, in order to gain the information that only he included in his book. Plus, Luke's goal in writing his gospel account was to present Jesus as the Son of Man. He showed Jesus' human side through the details of his birth and youth. Luke is the only Gospel writer who mentioned any part of Jesus' growing up years.

Luke wanted to communicate in both volumes of his book (Vol. 1: Luke; Vol. 2: Acts) that Jesus wanted both Jews and Gentiles to know of his salvation. Thus, Acts also chronicles the decision of the early church fathers to support giving Jesus' message to the Gentiles.

☞ **GO TO:**

Colossians 4:14 (doctor)

Luke 1:26–2:20 (birth)

Luke 2:41–52 (youth)

Acts 15:7 (Gentiles)

Robert H. Schuller: Acts presents the origin of our faith with extreme accuracy. Archaeologists confirm that Luke was among the most reliable historians of antiquity. A master of the Greek language, Luke gives the most detailed account of the early church of all the Gospels and Epistles.[2]

Something to Ponder

We can tell when Luke joined Paul's traveling missionary group in the book of Acts. It was while Paul was in Troas. Luke didn't name himself but he wrote, *"After Paul had seen the vision, we got ready at once to leave for Macedonia, concluding that God had called us to preach the gospel to them"* (Acts 16:10). Previously in the account, there was no mention of "us" or "we." It was "he" or "they." Luke must have written the first part of the book based on his interviews of others. Then he included his own first-hand account of Paul's missionary activities and did so throughout the end of the book.

Remember This . . .

The writings of Luke make up a little over a fourth of the Greek <u>New Testament</u>. Although he's not mentioned specifically as the author of Luke and Acts, he is mentioned in other parts of the New Testament.

☞ **GO TO:**

Colossians 4:14;
  2 Timothy 4:11;
  Philemon 24
  (New Testament)

🥾 **BUILD YOUR SPIRIT:** Humility is a worthy goal that Luke seemed to have made a part of his life. He doesn't try to take credit for what he did. He was content to give the great news about Jesus' gift of salvation. If we can have the same perspective, we'll be able to respond with more humility in our actions and thinking.

Mark

. . . the Original Comeback Kid

KEY POINT

God wants us to be unconcerned with who gets credit for his work within us.

Acts 15:37–41 Barnabas wanted to take John, also called Mark, with them, but Paul did not think it wise to take him, because he had deserted them in Pamphylia and had not continued with them in the work. They had such a sharp disagreement that they parted company. Barnabas took Mark and sailed for Cyprus, but Paul chose Silas and left, commended by the brothers to the grace of the Lord. He went through Syria and Cilicia, strengthening the churches.

I Can Succeed . . . Mark My Words

Mark and his mother used their home as a meeting place for the Christians. He was exposed to Christ's claim on his life and was a believer. He later wrote the book of Mark and many scholars believe Mark was writing about himself when he mentioned a young man who fled during Jesus' arrest.

☞ **GO TO:**

Mark 14:51–52 (fled)

Warren W. Wiersbe: Here were two dedicated men who had just helped bring unity to the church, and yet they could not settle their own disagreements! Disturbing and painful as these conflicts are, they are often found in church history; and yet God is able to overrule them and accomplish his purposes.[3]

What Others are Saying:

Mark's weakness of leaving when the going got tough would pop up again when he left Paul and Barnabas on their first missionary journey. Paul rejected any suggestion that Mark would accompany him on the next trip. As a result, Barnabas took Mark under his wing and went to Cyprus. Barnabas made an investment in Mark that paid off in dividends. Mark later became the author of one of the gospels of the Bible.

Something to Ponder

Later, Paul became a close friend of the young disciple when Mark redeemed himself through faithful service. Mark also became a missionary partner of Paul, Peter, and Barnabas. Paul changed his mind about Mark and in the end considered him an important asset. He wrote, *"Only Luke is with me. Get Mark and bring him with you, because he is helpful to me in my ministry"* (2 Timothy 4:11).

Remember This . . .

We don't know why Mark left, but missionaries had it really hard in those days. We need to consider when we sign up for something in the Lord's work whether we will carry through to the end no matter what.

WARNING

BUILD YOUR SPIRIT: If you have gotten off on the wrong foot with your manager at work, or a leader at church, or a co-worker, you can trust God to change their mind about you if you will serve faithfully and cheerfully over the long haul. If God can change the strong-willed Paul's mind about Mark, then he can change anyone's mind.

KEY POINT

Count the cost before agreeing to serve the Lord so that you'll persist until the end.

Barnabas

. . . More Encouraging Than a Purple Dinosaur

> **Acts 4:36, 37; 9:26, 27** Joseph, a Levite from Cyprus, whom the apostles called Barnabas (which means Son of Encouragement), sold a field he owned and brought the money and put it at the apostles' feet. . . . When [Paul] came to Jerusalem, he tried to join the disciples, but they were all afraid of him, not believing that he really was a disciple. But Barnabas took him and brought him to the apostles. He told them how Saul on his journey had seen the Lord and that the Lord had spoken to him, and how in Damascus he had preached fearlessly in the name of Jesus.

Mensch: Jewish word for genuinely helpful person

Trouble-Shooting Mensch

Barnabas was born a Levite. He was a generous and wealthy man who sold land and gave the proceeds to the disciples to be shared with others. Barney's commitment to Christ was apparent, for he sacrificed a comfortable life to walk the countryside for Jesus.

News of this reached the ears of the church at Jerusalem, and they sent Barnabas to Antioch. *"When [Barnabas] arrived and saw the evidence of the grace of God, he was glad and encouraged them all to remain true to the Lord with all their hearts. He was a good man, full of the Holy Spirit and faith, and a great number of people were brought to the Lord"* (Acts 11:23–24).

What Others are Saying:

Lloyd John Ogilvie: While the church in Jerusalem resisted, Barnabas was a reconciler. His response to Jesus always spelled responsibility for someone who was misunderstood or resisted. Barnabas threw opinion and caution aside and interceded for Paul with the Jerusalem church. The Greek actually implies that he took him by the hand and led him in among the Apostles to assert his belief in the authenticity of Paul's conversion, convictions, and new character.[4]

Something to Ponder

Will Rogers once said he never met a man he didn't like. Good ol' Barney was a lot like that because he could see the potential in others. He never let a tough exterior persona or a shy, insecure personality keep him at arm's length. He knew each person's worth and invested his time and energy in their lives. That's how Barnabas saw Saul, even before he was known as Paul. *"Then Barnabas went to Tarsus to look for Saul, and when he found him, he brought him to Antioch"* (Acts 11:25–26). Saul was feared and a **pariah** in the Christian community. It was Barnabas who came <u>alongside</u> and eased him into Christian history.

Barnabas possessed exceptional people skills. It was no surprise he was sent to provide leadership for the new church in Antioch. It was also no surprise he picked up Paul along the way. Barnabas was content to support others with his inspiring influence. He would never shy away from the spotlight, but his real skill was putting others on stage.

LEADERSHIP PRINCIPLE—The responsibility to develop those we lead lands nears the top of every priority list. However, it is one of the most neglected leadership skills. It takes work. The excuses are endless: it takes too much time to delegate, I'll do it myself, I can do it better. . . . Each may be true but those who look to our leadership should expect us to support them and provide opportunities for growth. Not all of us can be an inspirational Barnabas, but if we commit in our heart to care for those we lead, we will find the energy and time to develop others.

pariah: *a person rejected by others, an outcast*

☞ **GO TO:**

Acts 11:24–26 (alongside)

Remember This . . .

Matthew
. . . a Despised Tax Collector Turned Disciple

> **Matthew 9:9, 10** As Jesus went on from there, he saw a man named Matthew sitting at the tax collector's booth. "Follow me," he told him, and Matthew got up and followed him. While Jesus was having dinner at Matthew's house, many tax collectors and "sinners" came and ate with him and his disciples.

Show Me The Mon—Nah, Forget It

Since tax collectors normally skimmed money from the collections they made, they were despised throughout the land. Jesus challenged Matthew to leave behind a cushy job, high pay, and special benefits. If anyone had to really count the cost, it was

itinerant: nomadic

Matthew. Yet, he left it all to live an **itinerant** disciple's life following Jesus around.

Matthew, also called Levi, brought two things into his service as an apostle. First, his immediate and active faith. He abandoned wealth for a relationship with Jesus. He felt so strongly about Jesus that he invited his fellow tax collectors and other sinners to a dinner date with Jesus. Second, his pen and keen sense for collecting information. Matthew was probably the type of guy who had a bunch of pens filling a pocket protector on his shirt. No detail was too small to escape his notice when he wrote the first book of the New Testament, carefully linking the Old Testament prophecies to Jesus' fulfillment of them.

What Others are Saying:

R. C. Sproul: Jesus, as was the case with other rabbis in the ancient world, was what we call a peripatetic teacher. That is a fancy way of saying he was a teacher who walked around as he taught. As Jesus walked around the land of Palestine his disciples would literally walk behind him, committing to memory the words he would utter to them on their travels.[5]

Something to Ponder

Matthew referred to himself as "Matthew the tax collector." This referred to his former distasteful—in fact, hated—occupation and his humility about being chosen as a disciple of Jesus. Another aspect of his low-key persona was revealed when he referred to the dinner he hosted for Jesus. In his own account, he called it a "dinner." But in Luke's account, Luke referred to it as a "great <u>banquet</u>." Apparently, Matthew didn't want to brag about the big shindig he had put on for Jesus.

Matthew's gospel account has more references to coins than anywhere else in the other three gospels. It even included three different terms for coins: the <u>two-drachma</u>, the <u>four-drachma</u>, and <u>talents</u>. Of course, this goes along with his former occupation as a tax collector. He had been very interested in money!

☞ GO TO:

Luke 5:29 (banquet)

Matthew 17:24 (two-drachma)

Matthew 17:27 (four-drachma)

Matthew 18:24 (talents)

Overcoming Struggles

Finances can be a source of great strain in a Christian's life. Although Jesus doesn't call everyone to sacrifice everything, like he did Matthew, he does want us to have the correct perspective about any money that we do have. "*Command those who are rich in this present world not to be arrogant nor to put their hope in wealth, which is so uncertain, but to put their hope in God, who richly provides us with everything for our enjoyment*" (1 Timothy 6:17).

Andrew

. . . He Passed along the Good News

> **John 1:40–42** Andrew, Simon Peter's brother, was one of the two who heard what John had said and who had followed Jesus. The first thing Andrew did was to find his brother Simon and tell him, "We have found the Messiah" (that is, the Christ). And he brought him to Jesus. Jesus looked at him and said, "You are Simon son of John. You will be called Cephas" (which, when translated, is Peter).

Sibling Revelry, Or, Wow Bro, I Found the Messiah!

Only the book of John gives us three brief glimpses of Andrew. Each time he was found bringing others to Jesus. First, he brought his brother, Peter. That was like bringing Mark McGwire to play baseball in your friends' sandlot game. Within seconds the star of the game changed and all the attention focused away from Andrew. But Andrew didn't care. He loved his brother and he loved Jesus. Next, Andrew knew Jesus needed to feed a large crowd, so he found a small <u>boy</u> with some fishes and bread. He saw a need and his faith was acted upon by Jesus. Finally, some men wanted to <u>see</u> Jesus, and he took them to Jesus.

John MacArthur, Jr.: Andrew is the picture of all those who labor quietly in humble places; not with eye service as men pleasers, but as servants of Christ doing the will of God from the heart. Andrew is not a pillar like Peter, James, and John—he is a humbler stone.[6]

His brother, Peter, was filled with a passion that spilled onto everyone. Andrew was filled with a passion that seeped into other's hearts. His passion for Christ and others was never played with power but with grace and gentleness.

KEY POINT

How willing are you to surrender control of your money to God? That serves as an indicator of your commitment to Christ.

☞ **GO TO:**

John 6:8, 9 (boy)

John 12:20–22 (see)

What Others are Saying:

Something to Ponder

LEADERSHIP 🦅 **PRINCIPLE**—Every leader worth his salt will include a man like Andrew on his team; a salt of the earth guy that just gets the job done with dignity and class. Fanfare doesn't motivate him, appreciation does. Ambition is not his power source, commitment is. When you find men like this, hire them. If you hire them, keep them.

Thomas

. . . Doubter but No Coward

> **John 11:16; 20:24–29** Then Thomas (called Didymus) said to the rest of the disciples, "Let us also go, that we may die with him." . . . Now Thomas (called Didymus), one of the Twelve, was not with the disciples when Jesus came. So the other disciples told him, "We have seen the Lord!" But he said to them, "Unless I see the nail marks in his hands and put my finger where the nails were, and put my hand into his side, I will not believe it." A week later his disciples were in the house again, and Thomas was with them. Though the doors were locked, Jesus came and stood among them and said, "Peace be with you!" Then he said to Thomas, "Put your finger here; see my hands. Reach out your hand and put it into my side. Stop doubting and believe." Thomas said to him, "My Lord and my God!" Then Jesus told him, "Because you have seen me, you have believed; blessed are those who have not seen and yet have believed."

A Half-Empty Glass Beats No Glass At All

Jesus had just announced he was going back to Bethany, which is only two miles west of Jerusalem. All the disciples tried to talk him out of the trip because they believed he—and they—would be killed. It was Thomas who first affirmed his love and commitment for Christ when he in essence said, "If we go with him, we'll die, but let's go anyway." So, when Jesus insisted on leaving, Thomas tried to rally his peers, in his own pessimistic way. It took courage and initiative to make that statement. Thomas may have been a doubter, but he was no coward.

Like the other disciples, Thomas fled after Jesus was arrested. He was depressed and confused. This confusion was rooted in his pessimism. Earlier, Jesus told the disciples he would leave and prepare a place for them. Thomas had asked, *"Lord, we don't know where you are going, so how can we know the way?"* (John 14:5). His mind was spinning with confusion. He had found the Messiah and now he discovered Jesus would leave them behind.

What Others are Saying:

Warren W. Wiersbe: We call him "Doubting Thomas," but Jesus didn't rebuke him for unbelief: "Be not faithless, but believing." Doubt is often an intellectual problem: we want to believe, but the faith is overwhelmed by problems and questions. Unbelief is a moral problem; we simply will not believe.[7]

Thomas appears to be a pessimist. His glass was always half-empty. Faced with Jesus' death, the glass was no longer half-empty, but shattered on the ground. Ten men told Thomas that Jesus was alive. But Thomas would not listen to unsubstantiated claims, even from trustworthy men. He had to see for himself. The good news is that he got the proof he sought, but Jesus proclaimed a special blessing to those who believe more readily than Thomas.

Something to Ponder

Although depression can have physical causes, it is often the result of pessimistic thinking about life. Believing that God hasn't <u>abandoned</u> you can help to restore confidence in God, life, and yourself. Even though he may seem far away, he's always there.

Overcoming Struggles

☞ **GO TO:**

Hebrews 13:5
(abandoned)

John
. . . the One Jesus Loved

> **John 13:21–23** After he had said this, Jesus was troubled in spirit and testified, "I tell you the truth, one of you is going to betray me." His disciples stared at one another, at a loss to know which of them he meant. One of them, the disciple whom Jesus loved, was reclining next to him.

He Came A Long Way, Baby!

Originally, John (see illustration, page 262) wanted to call down fire from heaven upon some Samaritan villagers who didn't welcome Jesus. After that incident, Jesus named John and his brother, James, the "sons of thunder." But after a long walk with Jesus,

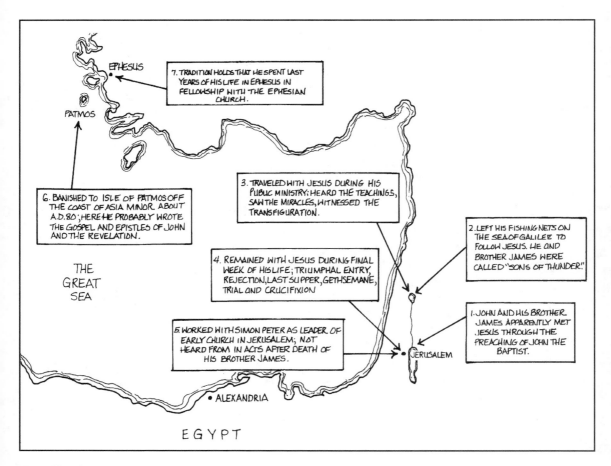

The Life of John

This map shows where major events occurred in John's life. The events are numbered chronologically.

The map contains the following labels:

EPHESUS

7. TRADITION HOLDS THAT HE SPENT LAST YEARS OF HIS LIFE IN EPHESUS IN FELLOWSHIP WITH THE EPHESIAN CHURCH.

PATMOS

6. BANISHED TO ISLE OF PATMOS OFF THE COAST OF ASIA MINOR ABOUT A.D. 80; HERE HE PROBABLY WROTE THE GOSPEL AND EPISTLES OF JOHN AND THE REVELATION.

3. TRAVELED WITH JESUS DURING HIS PUBLIC MINISTRY; HEARD THE TEACHINGS, SAW THE MIRACLES, WITNESSED THE TRANSFIGURATION.

2. LEFT HIS FISHING NETS ON THE SEA OF GALILEE TO FOLLOW JESUS. HE AND BROTHER JAMES WERE CALLED "SONS OF THUNDER."

THE GREAT SEA

4. REMAINED WITH JESUS DURING FINAL WEEK OF HIS LIFE; TRIUMPHAL ENTRY, REJECTION, LAST SUPPER, GETHSEMANE, TRIAL AND CRUCIFIXION

1. JOHN AND HIS BROTHER JAMES APPARENTLY MET JESUS THROUGH THE PREACHING OF JOHN THE BAPTIST.

5. WORKED WITH SIMON PETER AS LEADER OF EARLY CHURCH IN JERUSALEM; NOT HEARD FROM IN ACTS AFTER DEATH OF HIS BROTHER JAMES.

JERUSALEM

• ALEXANDRIA

EGYPT

The Books of the Bible Written by John

Books John Wrote	Purpose
Gospel of John	Represent Christ's deity so that others will believe.
1 John	Encourage believers to enjoy fellowship with God because of his great love for them.
2 John	Love others with discernment.
3 John	Letter to <u>Gaius</u> encouraging faithful service and generosity.
Revelation	A recounting of the revelatory messages John received from the resurrected Christ about the end of the world.

John changed, and he became known as the author of love. The theme of 1 John, which he penned, is love.

John had been transformed. The jealous, fiery follower of Christ wrote the gospel of John and never used his own name. The fact that Jesus could love a man who had wanted to kill the Samaritans and had connived for a place of honor in heaven filled John's heart with gratitude. Referring to himself as "the disciple whom Jesus loved" was recognition of his sinful past and God's forgiveness (see GWRV, pages 13–14).

John ended his days in exile on the island of Patmos. While there, he received the revelation of the last days of the world.

John, and his brother James, of course, had assertively asked Jesus for the privilege of sitting at Jesus' right hand in heaven. They prefaced it this way: *"Teacher,"* they said, *"we want you to do for us whatever we ask"* (Mark 10:35). Better add presumption and pride to John's resume. His desire to be closer to Jesus demonstrated some spiritual growth, but can you imagine the audacity of making a request like this behind the backs of the other disciples? This was an important moment for John. Jesus replied, *"Whoever wants to become great among you must be your servant, and whoever wants to be first must be slave of all. For even the Son of Man did not come to be served, but to serve, and to give his life as a ransom for many"* (Mark 10:43–45). John seemed to gain control of his zeal and strong convictions as he put Jesus' words into action. Love and service turned his heart around.

John had some issues of anger and narrowmindedness to deal with before he matured. Look how he responded when he found other believers raining on his parade. *"Teacher,"* said John, *"we saw a man driving out demons in your name and we told him to stop, because he was not one of us"* (Mark 9:38). He was very assertive and rigid in his thinking. But God changed even that.

BUILD YOUR SPIRIT: Anyone can change. John changed from a man of anger to a man of love. You can too. No matter what people say about you. No matter what your reputation is. No matter how your childhood has affected you. God can do an inside transformation of you. It may take time but he has the power and desire to do it. All you have to do is obey.

☞ **GO TO:**

Acts 19:29 (Gaius)

Mark 10:35–40 (place of honor)

Revelation 1:9 (Patmos)

Something to Ponder

Remember This . . .

☞ **GO TO:**

Romans 12:2 (transformation)

James

... Not to Name-drop or Anything, but the Messiah's My Brother

THE BIG PICTURE 🔍

> **Acts 15:13–21** In the early church family, a disagreement arose among the leadership about whether the good news about Jesus should be presented to Gentiles and if so, whether they should be circumcised. Several people shared their opinions and experiences and then James, the brother of Jesus, spoke up and offered a solution. The Gentiles should be welcomed into the church. They didn't need to become circumcised, but they should abstain from food polluted by idols, from sexual immorality, from the meat of strangled animals and from blood. Everyone agreed.

... I Just Wish I'd Believed Him When He Was Here

James was just like every other new believer, except that he had a distinction: he was the <u>brother</u> of Jesus. He grew up in the same home and was raised by the same parents. James is actually Jesus' half brother because they had the same mother but not the same father. Joseph was the father of James but Mary was a virgin when she conceived Jesus by the Holy Spirit. Even though James saw Jesus' selfless life, he didn't <u>believe</u> at first. He believed only after Jesus' death and resurrection.

In the early church, James was president of the first council. He was martyred by being thrown off the pinnacle of the Temple. When that didn't kill him, he was stoned to death.

☞ **GO TO:**

Matthew 13:55 (brother)

John 7:5 (believe)

What Others are Saying:

Max Lucado: It may surprise you to know that Jesus had a difficult family. It may surprise you to know that Jesus had a family at all! And it may surprise you to know that his family was less than perfect. They were. If your family doesn't appreciate you, take heart, neither did Jesus'.[8]

Something to Ponder

James' name was often listed first when church leaders were named. The Apostle Paul wrote, *"James, Peter, and John, those reputed to be pillars, gave me and Barnabas the right hand of fellowship when they recognized the grace given to me. They agreed that we should go to the Gentiles, and they to the Jews"*

(Galatians 2:9). In the writings of the Bible, the most prominent person was often listed first. It showed respect for his position.

James wrote the letter to Christians that became the book of James. James wanted his readers to focus on staying joyful in the midst of great difficulties or persecution. He also stressed the definition of real faith versus faith based on works. Since he was known as "The Man with Camel's Knees" because of the extensive time he spent on his knees praying, we aren't surprised that his letter also emphasizes prayer.

BUILD YOUR SPIRIT: Prayer is one of the main ways to build our spiritual life. In fact, without prayer it is impossible to grow as a Christian. James wrote, "*Therefore confess your sins to each other and pray for each other so that you may be healed. The prayer of a righteous man is powerful and effective*" (James 5:16). We can pray for others, confess our own sins in prayer, refuse to worry through prayer, and ask for God's direction in prayer.

Remember This . . .

KEY POINT

Prayer makes the Christian grow.

Study Questions

1. Why didn't John the Baptist want to baptize Jesus?
2. Why did Luke feel qualified to write a history of Jesus' life on earth?
3. Why didn't Paul want to take John Mark with him and Barnabas on their next missionary trip?
4. How did Barnabas first establish himself as an encouraging kind of person in the early church?
5. What kind of life did Matthew leave in order to become a disciple of Jesus?
6. How did Andrew share his faith with others?
7. Why didn't Thomas believe that Jesus had risen from the dead?
8. What special quality was John known for and why?
9. Who was a brother of Jesus who didn't believe in him at first but then became a leader of the Christian church?

CHAPTER WRAP-UP

- John the Baptist was Jesus' cousin and prepared the hearts of men to receive the teaching of Jesus. (Matthew 3:13–17)

- Luke was a physician who was a part of Paul's missionary journeys. He investigated Jesus' life and the early Christian church and wrote about them. (Luke 1:1–4)

- John Mark (later called Mark) grew stronger after Barnabas believed in him and took him on their own missionary trip. (Acts 15:37–41)

- Barnabas was quickly established in the early church as an encouraging kind of person who saw the best in everyone. (Acts 4:36, 37; 9:26–27)

- Matthew, the tax collector, left behind his dishonest work in order to become a full-time follower of Jesus. He also ended up writing the gospel account named for him. (Matthew 9:9–10)

- Andrew, one of the original disciples, quietly and subtly influenced people to believe in Jesus. (John 1:40–42)

- Thomas was a whole-hearted follower of Jesus, even willing to die with him. But when he'd been told Jesus had risen from the dead, he didn't believe it until he saw Jesus personally. (John 11:16; 20:24–29)

- John was changed from an angry man to one whom Jesus loved. He was later given the privilege of writing the last book of the Bible: Revelation. (John 13:21–23)

- James was Jesus' half-brother who, after believing Jesus' death and resurrection, became an early church father. (Acts 15:13–21)

APPENDIX A — TIME LINE

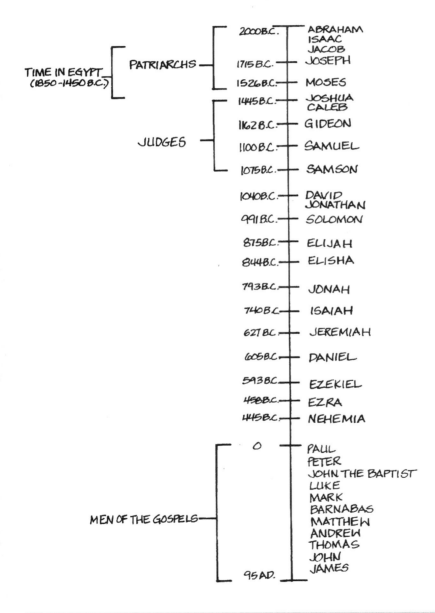

TIME IN EGYPT
(1850-1450 B.C.)

PATRIARCHS

- 2000 B.C. — ABRAHAM
  ISAAC
  JACOB
- 1715 B.C. — JOSEPH
- 1526 B.C. — MOSES

JUDGES

- 1445 B.C. — JOSHUA
  CALEB
- 1162 B.C. — GIDEON
- 1100 B.C. — SAMUEL
- 1075 B.C. — SAMSON

- 1040 B.C. — DAVID
  JONATHAN
- 991 B.C. — SOLOMON

- 875 B.C. — ELIJAH
- 844 B.C. — ELISHA

- 793 B.C. — JONAH

- 740 B.C. — ISAIAH

- 627 B.C. — JEREMIAH

- 605 B.C. — DANIEL

- 593 B.C. — EZEKIEL
- 458 B.C. — EZRA
- 445 B.C. — NEHEMIA

MEN OF THE GOSPELS

- 0 — PAUL
  PETER
  JOHN THE BAPTIST
  LUKE
  MARK
  BARNABAS
  MATTHEW
  ANDREW
  THOMAS
  JOHN
- 95 A.D. — JAMES

APPENDIX B

KEY:

→ FIRST

- - -→ SECOND

****→ THIRD

•••••→ TO ROME

Paul's Missionary Journeys

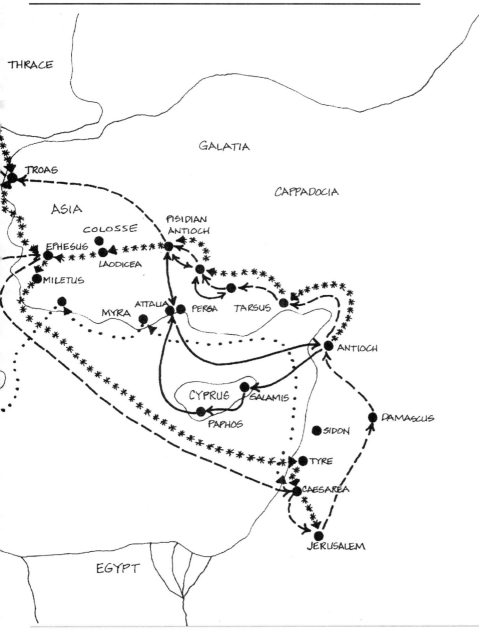

THRACE

GALATIA

CAPPADOCIA

TROAS

ASIA

PISIDIAN
ANTIOCH

COLOSSE

EPHESUS

LAODICEA

MILETUS

MYRA ATTALIA

PERGA

TARSUS

ANTIOCH

CYPRUS SALAMIS

PAPHOS

DAMASCUS

SIDON

TYRE

CAESAREA

JERUSALEM

EGYPT

APPENDIX C — THE BIBLE, SECTION BY SECTION

Bible (66 books)

Old Testament (39 books)

Law	*5 books*	Genesis, Exodus, Leviticus, Numbers, Deuteronomy
History	*12 books*	Joshua, Judges, Ruth, 1 & 2 Samuel, 1 & 2 Kings, 1 & 2 Chronicles, Ezra, Nehemiah, Esther
Wisdom	*5 books*	Job, Psalms, Proverbs, Ecclesiastes, Song of Songs
Prophecy	*17 books*	Isaiah, Jeremiah, Lamentations, Ezekiel, Daniel, Hosea, Joel, Amos, Obadiah, Jonah, Micah, Nahum, Habakkuk, Zephaniah, Haggai, Zechariah, Malachi

New Testament (27 books)

Gospels/Acts	*5 books*	Matthew, Mark, Luke, John, Acts
Letters	*21 books*	Romans, 1 & 2 Corinthians, Galatians, Philippians, Ephesians, Colossians, 1 & 2 Thessalonians, 1 & 2 Timothy, Titus, Philemon, Hebrews, James, 1 & 2 Peter, 1 & 2 & 3 John, Jude
Revelation	*1 book*	

APPENDIX D — THE ANSWERS

CHAPTER 1

1. God told Adam he could eat from any tree in the garden except from the Tree of the Knowledge of Good and Evil. If he did eat from the forbidden tree, he would die (Genesis 2:16–17).
2. God called all of creation "very good" except the fact that Adam was alone (Genesis 2:18).
3. None of the animals was sufficient as Adam's "helper" (Genesis 2:19–20).
4. Adam's job of taking care of the earth began to be painful toil and he would have to work hard. Eve's pain in childbearing was greatly increased, and her husband would rule over her. The serpent would crawl on his belly from then forward, and the woman's offspring was destined to "crush the head" of the serpent (Genesis 3:17–19).
5. Adam named Eve. Eve means "living" because Adam was recognizing her ability to create a new life (Genesis 20).

CHAPTER 2

1. God promised to make Abram a great nation, receive blessings, have a great name, be a blessing to others, and cause those who cursed him to be cursed themselves (Genesis 12:2–3).
2. Abram initially thought his heir would be his servant, Eliezer (Genesis 15:2).
3. Sarai offered her maid, Hagar, to be a substitute wife. Abraham's son, Ishmael, was born from this union (Genesis 16:1–16).
4. God changed Abram's and Sarai's names to Abraham and Sarah (Genesis 17:5, 15).
5. Abimelech saw the miracle of Isaac's birth and the great blessings God gave Abraham (Genesis 21:22).
6. God told Abram to sacrifice Isaac on an altar on Mt. Moriah (Genesis 22:2).

CHAPTER 3

1. "Isaac" means "laughter," so named because of the improbability of a woman birthing a son at age ninety and because of the joy his birth brought (Genesis 17:19).
2. Isaac was praying and meditating when Rebekah arrived (Genesis 24:63).
3. Isaac favored Esau because Esau was a skillful hunter and man of the field (Genesis 25:27).
4. Isaac lied because Rebekah was very beautiful and he thought the king would want to kill him in order to take her as his wife (Genesis 26:9).
5. Isaac was easily deceived because he was blind and was spiritually blinded by his appetites (Genesis 27:1, 9).

CHAPTER 4

1. Rebekah favored Jacob because he was peaceful and a man of the tents. Isaac favored Esau because he hunted game and Isaac loved meat (Genesis 25:27–28).
2. By putting Esau's clothing and an animal's skin on Jacob to simulate Esau's smell and hairy arms, Rebekah and Esau fooled Isaac. Rebekah also cooked a goat into tasting like venison (Genesis 27:14–23).
3. Laban justified marrying the "wrong" daughter to Jacob because customarily the younger sister could not be married before the older one (Genesis 29:26).
4. Israel means "he who strives with God" (Genesis 32:28).
5. Jacob thought Joseph had died because his sons produced Joseph's coat with blood on it, and allowed Jacob to conclude wild animals had killed his son (Genesis 37:33).

CHAPTER 5

1. Jacob preferred Joseph over his other sons because Joseph was born to him in his old age (Genesis 37:3).
2. When the other brothers wanted to kill Joseph, Reuben suggested they put him into a pit. He planned to rescue Joseph later (Genesis 37:22).
3. God first provided the dreams of the cup bearer and baker for Joseph to interpret correctly and then the cup bearer told Pharaoh about Joseph when Pharaoh had a dream that no one could interpret (Genesis 40–41).
4. Joseph caused his brothers' grain money to be replaced in their sacks when they returned to their homeland on the first trip and he put one of his silver cups in Benjamin's bag on their second trip (Genesis 42:25; 44:12).
5. Joseph's brothers were afraid that he would punish them for the cruel ways they had treated him thirteen years before (Genesis 50:18).

CHAPTER 6

1. Moses fled his princely existence when people found out that he had killed an Egyptian and Pharaoh wanted to kill him (Exodus 2:15).
2. Moses said he would not be able to deliver Israel because he didn't think he was anyone special (Exodus 3:11), the Israelites wouldn't believe him (Exodus 4:1), and he couldn't speak well (Exodus 4:10).
3. Miracles leading up to Israel's release from Egypt included: the Nile River turned to blood, frogs, gnats, flies, animal diseases, boils, hail, locusts, darkness, and death of first born (Exodus 7–11).
4. Moses didn't feel as weary once he delegated his work and God provided meat for the people to eat (Numbers 11:16–23).
5. Moses prayed for Miriam's healing and didn't hold a grudge (Numbers 12:1–13).

CHAPTER 7

1. Saul ridiculed David's offer to battle Goliath by saying David was an inexperienced youth while Goliath was a seasoned warrior (1 Samuel 17:33).
2. Saul's son, Jonathan, became David's best friend (1 Samuel 18:1).
3. David took care of Jonathan's son, Mephibosheth (2 Samuel 9:1–13).
4. David should have been fighting with his men on the battlefield (2 Samuel 11:1).
5. Though David fled the kingdom, he had one advantage because his adviser, Hushai, became an adviser to Absalom and gave him wrong advice (2 Samuel 17:7–14).

CHAPTER 8

1. The Ark was 450 feet long, 75 feet wide, and 45 feet high (Genesis 6:15).
2. The rainbow was a sign of God's promise to never destroy everything on the earth through a flood again (Genesis 9:15).
3. God permitted Satan to hurt Job only with God's limitations (Job 1:12; 2:6).
4. Job reasoned that if he accepted good from God, he should accept adversity too (Job 2:10).

CHAPTER 9

1. Samson nagged his parents into getting him a wife from the Philistines (Judges 14:1–4).
2. Delilah nagged Samson until he was sick of resisting her (Judges 16:1–22).

3. Elijah called down fire from heaven to burn up a sacrifice that was covered with water, while the prophets of Baal could not (1 Kings 18:1–39).
4. God provided physical nourishment, a time for Elijah to vent his feelings, and a new purpose in life (1 Kings 19:9–21).
5. Elisha asked Elijah for a double portion of God's power (2 Kings 2:7–10).
6. Elisha showed his "double portion" by doing many more miracles for God than Elijah did (2 Kings 2:19–22; 4–6; 13).

CHAPTER 10

1. Samuel was a true prophet of God because everything he predicted came true (1 Samuel 3:19).
2. Solomon showed wisdom by his unique solution to the problem of two women claiming the same baby (1 Kings 3:27).
3. Scribes were highly trained men who were well educated in the Scriptures (Ezra 7:10).
4. The people praised God, lifted their hands in praise, bowed down and worshiped God with their faces to the ground (Nehemiah 8:6).

CHAPTER 11

1. Caleb tried to overcome the Israelites' fear by insisting the land was good and that God would give it to them because God was with them (Numbers 14:7–9).
2. Joshua was commanded to obey the Law and meditate on it day and night (Joshua 1:7–9).
3. Gideon said he was too young and from a weak family (Judges 6:14–16).
4. Jonathan snuck into the Philistine camp and told his armor bearer that if the Philistines invited them to come ahead, that meant the Israelites would have victory. The Philistines did call to Jonathan, and Jonathan and his armor bearer started a victory right then (1 Samuel 14:10–15).
5. Jonathan made a covenant with David and put his robe and armor on David so that he would be protected (1 Samuel 18:1–4).
6. Jonathan encouraged David by affirming that David would indeed live to become king (1 Samuel 23:15–18).

CHAPTER 12

1. An angel touched a burning coal to Isaiah's lips and pronounced him clean (Isaiah 6:6–7).
2. Jeremiah expressed grief and sadness over his nation's sins by crying all the time (Jeremiah 9:1–2).
3. One of Ezekiel's toughest challenges was the death of his wife (Ezekiel 24:16–18).
4. Daniel did not want to eat unclean food (food not prepared God's way) (Daniel 1:8–9, 17b).
5. Jonah was called to preach to the people in Ninevah (Jonah 1:1–3).

CHAPTER 13

1. Jesus appeared to Paul in a bright light, spoke to Paul, and blinded him. This Damascus road encounter convinced Paul that Jesus was the Messiah (Acts 9:1–8).
2. The Christians in Antioch heard the Holy Spirit's direction through prayer and fasting (Acts 13:1–3).
3. Paul was beaten, stoned, shipwrecked, attacked, falsely accused, and went without sleep, food, and drink (2 Corinthians 11:24–28).
4. Paul and Barnabas shared with the early church leaders their exciting results from preaching to the Gentiles (Acts 15:12).
5. Paul did not want John Mark to join their missionary trip since Mark had left prematurely on the previous trip (Acts 15:36–41).

CHAPTER 14

1. Peter could no longer walk on water when he focused on the wind and grew afraid (Matthew 14:22–32).
2. Jesus said God had revealed to Peter that Jesus was the Christ (Matthew 16:13–20).
3. Peter left and wept bitterly, even wailed, upon realizing he had denied Jesus (Matthew 26:75).
4. Jesus showed his forgiveness to Peter by giving Peter three opportunities to express his love for Jesus, and by asking Peter, *"feed my sheep"* (John 21:15–19).
5. Peter gave the world's first Holy Ghost–filled Christian sermon (Acts 2:14).

CHAPTER 15

1. John the Baptist believed he wasn't worthy to baptize the Son of God (Matthew 3:13–17).
2. Luke made a careful investigation into Jesus' life and death (Luke 1:1–4).
3. Paul did not trust John Mark because John Mark had left them while they were in Pamphylia before their work was done (Acts 15:37–41).
4. Barnabas took Saul (later called Paul) and introduced him around to the early Church fathers when other believers feared Saul (Acts 4:36–37; 9:26–27).
5. Matthew was formerly a tax collector (Matthew 9:9–10).
6. Andrew took his brother, Peter, to go see Jesus, telling him Jesus was the Messiah (John 1:40–42).
7. Thomas doubted because he wasn't there when Jesus first appeared in physical form to the other disciples (John 20:24–29).
8. John was called the one whom Jesus loved (John 13:21–23).
9. James was Jesus' half-brother (Acts 15:13–21).

APPENDIX E — THE EXPERTS

Kay Arthur—Author of many books and well-known speaker.

J. Sidlow Baxter—Preacher and author, born in Australia and grew up in England.

D. Stuart Briscoe—Pastor of Elmbrook Church in Waukesha, Wisconsin. Speaker and author of many books including *Tough Truths For Today's Living*.

Jamie Buckingham—Ordained minister who wrote more than forty books. Former spiritual overseer of the Tabernacle Church in Melbourne, Florida.

Oswald Chambers—Itinerant evangelist and Bible college teacher. Most of his works were compiled posthumously by his wife in 1917.

Edwin Louis Cole—Founder and president of Christian Men's Network. Speaks to men across the world.

Charles Colson—Former presidential advisor who went to prison during the Watergate era. While in prison Colson came to Christ and is the founder of Prison Fellowship, a worldwide ministry.

Thomas L. Constable—Director of D. Min. Studies and Associate Professor of Bible Exposition at Dallas Theological Seminary.

Dr. Tony Evans—Senior pastor of Oak Cliff Bible Fellowship in Dallas and author of many books.

Steve Farrar—President of Point Man Leadership Ministries in Dallas, Texas. He is an active speaker today and has authored a number of books.

F. Charles Fensham—Professor of Semitic Languages at University of Stellenbosch in South Africa.

Leslie Flynn—Former pastor of Grace Conservative Baptist Church in Nanuet, New York. Author of several books including *Me Be Like Jesus?*

Gene A. Getz—Pastor of Fellowship Bible Church of Dallas, Texas. Associate Professor of Practical Theology at Dallas Theological Seminary.

Billy Graham—Widely known around the world as an evangelist and author.

Howard Hendricks—Professor at Dallas Theological Seminary. Author and speaker at Promise Keepers events.

Matthew Henry—Pastor and biblical expositor who wrote a seven-volume *Commentary on the Bible* for which he is still remembered 250 years later.

John Hercus—Writer and Australian eye-specialist.

Herschel H. Hobbs—Well-known pastor of the international "Baptist Hour" broadcast. Former president of the Southern Baptist Convention.

Bill Hybels—Senior pastor of Willow Creek Community Church and the author of many books including *Honest to God*.

H. A. Ironside—Internationally known Bible teacher and preacher with more than sixty volumes of writings.

Irving L. Jensen—Author, professor, and chairman of the department of Bible at Bryan College.

John Jewell—Bishop of Salisbury and exiled by Queen Mary. He was active in the British Reformation movement.

W. Phillip Keller—Writer known for insightful devotional commentaries.

Derek Kidner—Author of several biblical works and former Warden of Tyndale House, Cambridge, U.K.

Larry Libby—Editor at Multnomah Press, Portland, Oregon. Co-authored a book with Bruce Wilkinson.

Max Lucado—Pastor, writer, and speaker. He is the voice of "UpWords," a daily fifteen-minute radio program.

John MacArthur, Jr.—Senior Pastor of Grace Community Church in Southern California and author of many books.

John A. Martin—Assistant Professor of Bible Exposition and Assistant Academic Dean and Director of summer school of Dallas Theological Seminary, Dallas, Texas.

J. Vernon McGee—Well-known radio preacher who created a five-year Bible study program, *Through the Bible*. This program is still widely popular today.

F. B. Meyer—Pastor, speaker, supporter of missions, and prolific writer.

Patrick M. Morley—Founder and chairman of Morley Properties. Also writes and speaks to men and women across the country.

Harold Ockenga—Religious leader and educator, co-founder of Fuller Theological Seminary, Pasadena, California. First president and one of the founders of the National Association of Evangelicals.

Lloyd John Ogilvie—Chaplain to the United States Senate. Frequent speaker on radio and television. Author of many books.

Raymond C. Ortlund, Jr.—Assistant Professor of Old Testament at Trinity Evangelical Divinity School and ordained minister.

James I. Packer—Teaches systematic and historical theology at Regent College in Vancouver, British Columbia. Author of numerous books.

Luis Palau—International evangelist who was born in Argentina. His daily radio programs in Latin America and Spain reach millions of people. Author of many books.

Jessie Penn-Lewis—Christian author during the late 1800's.

John Pollock—Ordained Anglican priest who has authored several books on history and biography, including an authorized biography of Billy Graham.

Alan Redpath—Pastor of Charlotte Chapel in Edinburgh, Scotland, Scotland's largest Baptist congregation. Writer and speaker.

Larry Richards—Award-winning editor of several study Bibles and the author of over one hundred books that cover subjects such as theological and biblical studies, church leadership, and devotional writings.

Larry (a.k.a. Lawrence O.) Richards is general editor of the *God's Word for the Biblically-Inept* and *What's in the Bible for . . .* series (Starburst Publishers).

Allen P. Ross—Chairman and Professor of Semitics and Old Testament Studies, Dallas Theological Seminary.

Robert H. Schuller—Pastor of the Crystal Cathedral in Southern California. Author of numerous books, Schuller is well known for his weekly television broadcast, *Hour of Power*.

R. C. Sproul—Theologian, minister, teacher, and chairman of the board for Ligonier Ministries. Author of many books.

Ray Stedman—Pastor and author of many books.

Charles R. Swindoll—President of Dallas Theological Seminary. Author and pastor in the Dallas, Texas, area.

Merrill F. Unger—Former pastor and professor of Old Testament studies at Dallas Theological Seminary. Author of many books and reference works.

Barry G. Webb—Head of the Old Testament department at Moore Theological College in Sydney, Australia.

Warren W. Wiersbe—Author of more than eighty books. Speaker, writer, and radio minister.

Smith Wigglesworth—English preacher and author of a number of books.

Michael Wilcock—Vicar of St. Nicholas' Church, Durham, England, and former director of pastoral studies at Trinity College, Bristol. Author of *The Message of Chronicles* and other books.

Bruce H. Wilkinson—Founder and president of "Walk Thru the Bible Ministries" in Atlanta, Georgia.

Philip Yancey—Editor-at-large for *Christianity Today*. Author of six Gold Medallion Award-winning books, including *Where Is God When It Hurts?*

NOTE: To the best of our knowledge, all of the above information is accurate and up to date. In some cases we were unable to obtain biographical information.
—THE STARBURST EDITORS

ENDNOTES

Chapter 1

1. Allen P. Ross, *The Bible Knowledge Commentary,* editors John F. Walvoord and Roy B. Zuck (Victor Books, 1985), 30.
2. Charles R. Swindoll, *Laugh Again* (Dallas, TX: Word Publishing, 1991), 193–194.
3. Raymond C. Ortlund, Jr., *Recovering Biblical Manhood and Womanhood* (Wheaton, IL: Crossway Books, 1991), 100.
4. Ibid., 101.
5. Herschel H. Hobbs, The *Origin of All Things* (Waco, TX: Word, 1975), 48.
6. Alan Redpath, *The Making of a Man of God* (Old Tappan, NJ: Revell, 1979), 67.
7. Hobbs, *The Origin of All Things,* 52.

Chapter 2

1. Charles R. Swindoll, *The Living Insights Study Bible* (Grand Rapids, MI: Zondervan Publishing House, 1996), 21.
2. Harold Ockenga, *Women Who Made Bible History* (Grand Rapids, MI: Zondervan Publishing House, 1979), 22.
3. Gene A. Getz, *Abraham: Trials & Triumphs* (Glendale, CA: Gospel Light Publications, 1976), 30.
4. Jamie Buckingham, *The Promise of Power* compiled by Judith Couchman (Ann Arbor, MI: Servant Publications, 1998), 62.
5. Charles R. Swindoll, *The Living Insights Study Bible,* 24.
6. Smith Wigglesworth, *Dare to Believe,* compiled by Judith Couchman (Ann Arbor MI: Servant Publications, 1997), 40.
7. Gene A. Getz, *Abraham: Trials & Triumphs,* 81.
8. *Life Application Bible Notes* (Wheaton, IL: Tyndale House Publishers, and Grand Rapids, MI: Zondervan Publishing House, 1991) 34.
9. Herschel H. Hobbs, *The Origin of All Things,* 108.
10. Oswald Chambers, *My Utmost for His Highest* (Barbour and Company, 1963), 79.
11. Charles R. Swindoll, *The Living Insights Study Bible,* 29.

Chapter 3

1. Charles R. Swindoll, *The Living Insights Study Bible,* 26.
2. Herschel H. Hobbs, *The Origin of All Things,* 118.
3. J. Vernon Magee, *Genesis: Volume II* (Pasadena, CA: Thru the Bible Books, 1975), 281.
4. William Hendriksen, *New Testament Commentary: Ephesians* (Grand Rapids, MI: Baker, 1967), 261.
5. Charles R. Swindoll, *The Living Insights Study Bible,* 34.

Chapter 4

1. Herschel H. Hobbs, *The Origin of All Things,* 126.
2. Bruce H. Wilkinson and Larry Libby, *Talk Through Bible Personalities* (Atlanta, GA: Walk Thru The Bible Ministries, Inc., 1983), 12–13.
3. Herschel H. Hobbs, *The Origin of All Things,* 131.

4. Smith Wigglesworth, *Dare to Believe,* compiled by Judith Couchman, 127–128.
5. Bruce H. Wilkinson and Larry Libby, *Talk Through Bible Personalities,* 16–17.
6. Gene A. Getz, *Joseph: from Prison to Palace* (Ventura, CA: Regal Books, 1983), 33–34.
7. Charles R. Swindoll, *Living Insights Study Bible,* 43.
8. Gene A. Getz, *Joseph: from Prison to Palace,* 35.
9. Kay Arthur, *Lord I Want to Know You* (Sisters, OR: Multnomah Press, 1992), 64.

Chapter 5

1. Leslie Flynn, *Joseph: God's Man in Egypt* (Victor Books, 1979), 25.
2. Allen P. Ross, *The Bible Knowledge Commentary,* 87.
3. Billy Graham, *Freedom from the Seven Deadly Sins* (Grand Rapids, MI: Zondervan Publishing House, 1955), 41.
4. Gene A. Getz, *Joseph: from Prison to Palace,* 49.
5. Charles R. Swindoll, *Living Insights Study Bible,* 48.
6. Patrick M. Morley, *The Man in the Mirror* (Woglemuth & Hyatt, 1989), 47.
7. Matthew Henry, *Unabridged Commentary Matthew Henry's Commentary on the Whole Bible: New Modern Edition Database* (Hendrickson Publishers, Inc., 1991, 1994, Electronic markup copyright 1995 by Epiphany Software), Genesis 41:14.
8. Merrill F. Unger, *Unger's Bible Dictionary* (Moody Press, 1985), 989.
9. Leslie Flynn, *Joseph: God's Man in Egypt,* 117.
10. Patrick M. Morley, *The Man in the Mirror,* 237.
11. Gene A. Getz, *Joseph: from Prison to Palace,* 136.
12. Max Lucado, *He Still Moves Stones* (Dallas, TX: Word Publishing, 1993), 110.
13. Philip Yancey, quoted in *Men's Devotional Bible* (Zondervan Publishing House, 1993), 42.
14. Edwin Louis Cole, *Manhood 101* (Tulsa, OK: Honor Books, no date given), 9.

Chapter 6

1. Bruce H. Wilkinson and Larry Libby, *Talk Through Bible Personalities,* 29–30.
2. Jamie Buckingham, *The Promise of Power,* compiled by Judith Couchman (Ann Arbor: MI, Servant Publications, 1998), 98.
3. Bruce H. Wilkinson and Larry Libby, *Talk Through Bible Personalities,* 32.
4. Jamie Buckingham, *The Promise of Power,* 99.
5. Max Lucado, *He Still Moves Stones,* 69.
6. John Hercus, *Pages from God's Case-book* (Downers Grove, IL: InterVarsity Press, 1962), 30.

7. Oswald Chambers, *Growing Deeper With God,* compiled by Judith Couchman (Ann Arbor, MI: Servant Publications, 1997), 17.

8. Charles R. Swindoll, *Moses: A Man of Selfless Dedication* (Anaheim, CA: Insight for Living, no date given), 81.

9. Max Lucado, *He Still Moves Stones,* 60–61.

10. Oswald Chambers, *Growing Deeper With God,* 16.

11. Gene A. Getz, *Moses: Moments of Glory, Feet of Clay* (Ventura, CA: Gospel Light, 1976), 138.

12. Ibid., 156.

Chapter 7

1. F. B. Meyer, *Samuel the Prophet* (Fort Washington, PA: Christian Literature Crusade, 1978), 200.

2. Charles R. Swindoll, *David: A Man of Passion & Destiny* (Nashville, TN: Word Publishing, 1997), 75.

3. Alan Redpath, *The Making of a Man of God* (Old Tappan, NJ: Revell, 1962), 107.

4. Oswald Chambers, *Growing Deeper,* 184–185.

5. Thomas Carlyle, *John Bartlett's Familiar Quotations* (Little, Brown and Company, 1980), 474.

6. Max Lucado, *He Still Moves Stones,* 75.

7. John W. Lawrence, *Life's Choices* (Portland, OR: Multnomah Press, 1975), 39.

8. Greg Laurie, *The Great Compromise* (Dallas, TX: Word Publishing, 1994), 120–124.

9. Charles R. Swindoll, *David: A Man of Passion & Destiny,* 248.

10. Steve Farrar, *Point Man* (Sisters, OR: Multnomah Press, 1990), 75.

11. Ibid., 76–77.

Chapter 8

1. Max Lucado, *He Still Moves Stones,* 69.

2. Herschel H. Hobbs, *The Origin of All Things,* 74.

3. Ibid., 67.

4. Robert H. Schuller, *Tough Times Never Last, but Tough People Do!* (Nashville, TN: Thomas Nelson Publisher, 1983), 158.

5. Oswald Chambers, *Growing Deeper,* 34.

6. Charles Colson, as quoted in *Men's Devotional Bible* (Grand Rapids, MI: Zondervan Publishing House, 1993), 517.

7. Jessie Penn-Lewis, *The Story of Job* (The Overcomer Literature Trust, 1902), 99.

8. Max Lucado, *He Still Moves Stones,* 44.

9. Larry Richards, *The Bible: God's Word for the Bibically-Inept* (Lancaster, PA: Starburst Publishers, 1998), 73.

Chapter 9

1. Michael Wilcock, *The Message of Judges* (Downers Grove, IL: InterVarsity Press, 1992), 130.

2. Dr. Tony Evans, *Returning to Your First Love* (Chicago, IL: Moody Press, 1995), 198.

3. Charles R. Swindoll, *Living Insights Study Bible,* 252.

4. Michael Wilcock, *The Message of Judges,* 143.

5. John Jewell, *Near to the Heart of God,* compiled by Bernard Bangley (Wheaton, IL: Harold Shaw, 1998), taken from *Of the Holy Scriptures,* April 8.

6. Oswald Chambers, *Growing Deeper,* 47–48.

7. J. Sidlow Baxter, *Mark These Men* (Grand Rapids, MI: Zondervan Publishing House, 1960), 12.

8. Howard Hendricks, *Standing Together* (Gresham, OR: Vision House, 1995), 26.

9. W. Phillip Keller, *Elijah: Prophet of Power* (Waco, TX: Word Books, 1980), 89.

10. Oswald Chambers, *My Utmost for His Highest,* 215.

11. Howard Hendricks, *Standing Together,* 105.

12. Bruce H. Wilkinson and Larry Libby, *Talk Through Bible Personalities,* 117.

13. Steve Farrar, as quoted in *Men's Devotional Bible,* 360

14. Bruce H. Wilkinson and Larry Libby, *Talk Through Bible Personalities,* 122

15. Dr. Tony Evans, *Returning to Your First Love,* 183.

Chapter 10

1. Bruce H. Wilkinson and Larry Libby, *Talk Through Bible Personalities,* 50.

2. F. B. Meyer, *Samuel the Prophet* (Fort Washington, PA: Christian Literature Crusade), 72.

3. Steve Farrar, *Point Man,* 218.

4. F. B. Meyer, *Samuel the Prophet,* 135.

5. Thomas L. Constable, *The Bible Knowledge Commentary* (Victor Books, 1983), 494.

6. James I. Packer, *Knowing God* (Downers Grove, IL: InterVarsity Press, 1981), 30.

7. Bruce H. Wilkinson and Larry Libby, *Talk Through Bible Personalities,* 104.

8. Ray Stedman, *Is This All There Is To Life?* (Sisters, OR: Multnomah Press, 1985), 35.

9. Patrick M. Morley, *The Man in the Mirror,* 85.

10. F. Charles Fensham, *The Books of Ezra and Nehemiah* (William B. Eerdmans, 1982), 105.

11. Derek Kidner, *Ezra & Nehemiah* (Downers Grove, IL: InterVarsity Press, 1979), 68–69.

12. Max Lucado, *He Still Moves Stones,* 99.

13. Ibid., 102.

14. Charles R. Swindoll, *Hand Me Another Brick* (Nashville, TN: Thomas Nelson, 1978), 137.

Chapter 11

1. W. Phillip Keller, *Joshua: Man of Fearless Faith* (Dallas, TX: Word Books, 1983), 36.

2. Oswald Chambers, *Growing Deeper,* 67.

3. Charles R. Swindoll, *Second Wind: A Fresh Run at Life* (Sisters, OR: Multnomah Press, 1977), 67.

4. W. Phillip Keller, *Joshua: Man of Fearless Faith,* 18.

5. Charles R. Swindoll, *The Living Insights Study Bible,* 135.

6. Alan Redpath, *The Making of a Man of God,* 238.

7. Michael Wilcock, *The Message of Judges,* 79.

8. Jamie Buckingham, *The Promise of Power,* 76.

9. Kay Arthur, *Lord, I Want to Know You,* 129.

10. Bill Hybels, *Men's Devotional Bible,* 243.

11. Michael Wilcock, *The Message of Judges,* 82.

12. Jamie Buckingham, *The Promise of Power,* 77.

13. W. Phillip Keller, *Mighty Man of Valor* (Old Tappan, NJ: Revell, 1979), 115.

14. Bruce H. Wilkinson and Larry Libby, *Talk Through Bible Personalities,* 61.

15. John Hercus, *Pages from God's Case-book,* 91.

16. Luis Palau, *Heart after God* (Sisters, OR: Multnomah Press, 1978), 40.

17. Gene A. Getz, *David: God's Man in Faith and Failure* (Ventura, CA: Gospel Light, 1978), 63–64.

18. Alan Redpath, *The Making of a Man of God,* 61.

Chapter 12

1. Barry G. Webb, *The Message of Isaiah* (Downers Grove, IL: InterVarsity Press, 1996), 58.

2. Irving L. Jensen, *Isaiah Jeremiah: A Self Study Guide* (Chicago, IL: Moody Bible Institute, 1968), 66.

3. H. A. Ironside, *Ezekiel* (New York, NY: Loizeaux Brothers, 1949), 164.
4. Steve Farrar, *Point Man*, 137.
5. Charles R. Swindoll, *Second Wind: A Fresh Run at Life*, 8.
6. D. Stuart Briscoe, *Taking God Seriously* (Dallas, TX: Word Press, 1986), 73.

Chapter 13
1. Charles R. Swindoll, *Living Insights Study Bible,* 1193.
2. Oswald Chambers, *Growing Deeper,* 71.
3. Warren W. Wiersbe, *The Bible Exposition Commentary* (Victor Books, 1983), 456.
4. Patrick M. Morley, *The Man in the Mirror*, 67.
5. Warren W. Wiersbe,, *The Bible Exposition Commentary*, 462.
6. John Pollock, *The Apostle, a Life of Paul,* 54–55.
7. Max Lucado, *He Still Moves Stones*, 128.
8. John Pollock, *The Apostle, a Life of Paul,* 237.

Chapter 14
1. Herschel H. Hobbs, *The Origin of All Things*, 109.
2. Philip Yancey, *The Jesus I Thought I Knew* (Grand Rapids, MI: Zondervan Publishing House, 1995), 17.
3. Ibid., 21.
4. Max Lucado, *He Still Moves Stones*, 140.
5. John MacArthur, Jr., *The Master's Men* (Van Nuys, CA: Word of Grace Communications, 1982), 15.

6. F. B. Meyer, *Peter the Man* (Wheaton, IL: Good News Publishers, 1959), 43.
7. Warren W. Wiersbe, *The Bible Exposition Commentary*, 397.
8. Max Lucado, *He Still Moves Stones*, 88.
9. Lloyd John Ogilvie, *Drumbeat of Love* (Waco, TX: Word Press, 1976), 34.
10. F. B. Meyer, *Peter the Man*, 56

Chapter 15
1. John A. Martin, *The Bible Knowledge Commentary New Testament,* 211
2. Robert H. Schuller, *The New Possibility Thinkers Bible* (Nashville, TN: Thomas Nelson, 1996), 1281.
3. Warren W. Wiersbe, *The Bible Exposition Commentary*, 465–466.
4. Lloyd John Ogilvie, *Drumbeat of Love,* 135.
5. R. C. Sproul, *Before the Face of God* (Grand Rapids, MI: Baker, 1993), 134–135.
6. John MacArthur, Jr., *The Master's Men* (Van Nuys, CA: Word of Grace Communications, 1982), 29.
7. Warren W. Wiersbe, *The Bible Exposition Commentary*, 393.
8. Max Lucado, *He Still Moves Stones*, 41.

INDEX

Boldface numbers refer to defined (What?) terms in the sidebar.

Egypt, rescue of Israelites from, 74, 89
Egypt, return to, 76
Egyptian, killing of, 73, 89
and father-in-law, 73, 76
faith of, 80
faithfulness of, 71, 83–84
as fearful, 10
forty years in wilderness, 73
God's appearance to, 74, 89
God, argument with 75–76, 89
God's plan for, 80
and God's reassurance, 79
God speaks to, 74–77, 79
as Hebrew, 73
humility of, 71, 84
Israelites, rescue from Egypt by, 74,
    81–82
Jesus, appearing to, 242
and Joshua, 189–190
leadership qualities of, 75, 82, 89
marriage of, 73
Midian, escape to, 73, 89
miracles of, 79–80, 89
and Miriam, 86
mother of, 71–72, 89
perseverance of, 87
and Pharaoh, 77–78
Pharaoh's daughter adopting, 71–72,
    89
prayers of, 78, 83
Red Sea, crossing, 82
as prince, 71–74
saved from early death, 71, 89
sermons of, 88
as shepherd, 73–74, 89
Ten Commandments, receiving, 83, 89
trials of, 71
trust in God of, 80
and Zipporah, 73, 76, 77, 86
Mote, **154**
Mount Horeb, 74, 137
    illustration of, 132
Mount Moriah, 26
Mount Sinai, 83
Murder, God forbidding, 112

N
Nabal, 96
Nagging, 129
    of Job's wife, 114
    by Samson's women, 128
Nahor, 25
Nakedness, 7, 8
Nathan, 99–100, 104
Nazirite,
    rules for, 122
    Samson as, 121
Nebuchadnezzar, King, 218–219
Nehemiah, 149, 169, 172, 173–184
    opposition to, 176–179
    prayers of, 174–175, 183
Nephilim (giants), 185–186

New International Version (NIV), xvii
New Testament, **xvii**, xviii
Nile River, 71, 80
Ninevah, 220–221
Noah, 107–112, 120
    Age, advanced, of, 107
    altar, building, 111, 120
    Ark (*see* Noah's Ark)
    blessing, God's after flood, 111
    corruption in time of, 110
    covenant, God's with, 111
    faithfulness of, 107–108, 110
    as father of human race, second, 111
    loneliness of, 108
    obedience of, 109
    rainbow, meaning of, 111, 112
    ridiculed, 109
Noah's Ark, illustration, 109
    animals on, 110
    boarding, 110
    description of, 108–109
    flood, chronology of, 111
    God's request for, 108
    leaving, after flood, 111
    120 years building, 107, 110
    rainbow, meaning of, 111, 112

O
Ockenga, Harold, on theophany, 15
Old age (*see* Age)
Old Testament, **xvii**, xviii
    Scripture as, xxi
Ogilvie, Lloyd John:
    on Barnabas, 256
    on the Holy Spirit, 247
Ortlund, Raymond C., Jr., on
    Creation, 6, 7

P
Packer, James I., on Christianity, 157
Palau, Luis, on Paul, 205
Panoramic, 150
Pariah, **257**
Passover, **81**
Patience:
    of David, 98
    God's, 23
    with God's plan, need for, 74
Patriarch, **13**
Patriarchal blessing, **42**
Paul, 227–236
    in Acts, book of, 227
    author, as, 233–234
    and Barnabas, 227–236
    Bible, books of written by, 233–234
    as Christian missionary, first (with
        Barnabas), 229
    death of, 234–235
    Jesus, meeting, 228
    journeys, significant events on, 230
    and Luke, 254
    and Mark, 254–255

as Pharisee, 227, 233
    qualities of, 233
    as Saul, 227–228
    writings of, xxi, 233–234
Peace, 51
Penn-Lewis, Jessie, on Job, 117
Pentecost, **248**
Persecution, 57
Perseverance:
    of Job, 119
    of Moses, 87
Persian Empire, 166–167
    illustration of, 167
    Nehemiah in, 173
Pessimism, of Thomas, 260–261
Peter, 237–244
    angel freeing from prison, 248
    change of, 247
    death of, 249
    Gentiles, vision of preaching to, 231
    Jesus and, 237–247, 249
    Jesus, resurrected, and, 245–247
    leadership activities of, 248
    life events, illustration of, 239
    miracles of, 248
    on Paul, writings of, xxi
    qualities of, 237–238
    sermon, first Christian, 248
    Simon becoming, 240
    walking on water, 238–240
Pharaoh, 72
    Abram and Sarai lying to, 16–17
    a God, perceived as, 80
    illustration of, 72
    Joseph and, 61–62, 67, 68
    male babies, killing of Israelite, 72
    Moses and, 77–78
Pharisee, Paul as, 227
Philistines, 93–94, 97, 122, 204
    giants among, 103 (*See also* Goliath)
    Gods worshipped by, 123
    Samson and, 121–129
    Samson's wife as, 122–126
    (*See also* Israel: battling Philistines)
Plague(s):
    of Egypt, 16–17, 80
    in Israel, 103–104
Plan, God's (*see* God's plan)
Planning, 19
Pollock, John, on Paul and other
    disciples, 232, 234
Polygamy:
    of David, 98–100
    of Solomon, 162
Potiphar, 57–59
Potiphar's wife, 59, 69
Power:
    of Elijah, 130–140, 148
    of Elisha, 140–148
    of God, 168
    men of, 121–148
    of Samson, 121–129, 148

on hope, 111
on Luke, 254
Scribe, **169**
Scripture(s), xvi
    as referring to Old Testament, xvi
    (*See also* Bible)
Semitic, **17**
Seraph, **211**
Sermons:
    of Moses, 88
    Peter giving first (Christian), 248
    of Solomon, 162
Serpent, 7
    illustration of, 8
Servanthood, 189, 263
Shame, 7, 8
Shecaniah, 171
Shechem, 48
Shedding, **81**
Shekels, 58
Shekinah, **216**
Shepherds, 67
    David as 91
    Moses as, 73–74, 89
Shimei, 156
Sickness, of Job, 114
Silas, 232
Silver, 57–58
Simeon, 64
    (*See also* Joseph's brothers)
Sin, **5**, 9, 10, 11, 17
    Christian response to, 110, 171
    consequences of, 101, 129
    constant battle against, 172
    first, results of, 11, 12
    God's forgiveness for, 66
    Noah, in time of, 110
    of others, 155
    persistence conquering, 188
Slain, **134**
Slave, Joseph as, 69
Slighted, **34**
Sling(shot), illustration of, 94
Sodom:
    Abram's prayer for, 16
    Lot in, 18–19
Solidified, **19**
Solomon, 146, 155–166, 184
    accomplishments of, 160
    and Adonijah, 155–157
    Bathsheba as mother of, 99, 104
    birth of, 99
    concubines of, 165
    David's advice for, 104–105
    David as father of, 99, 104
    decline of, spiritual, 164–165
    and Joab, 104, 155–156
    king, succeeding David as, 104–105
    lust of, 163
    marriage of, 157
    mercy of, 155–155
    peace and prosperity of, 158–160

prayer of, 162
polygamy of, 162
Proverbs, as author of, 160, 162–163
reign of, 158–160
sermon of, 162
Temple of, 99, 160–162, 167,
    illustration of, 161
trade routes, illustration of, 159
wisdom of, 143, 157–158
wives of, 162, 165
Soul, 8
Sovereignty, **77**
Spies, spying:
    Joseph accuses brothers of, 63
    sent by Moses, 87
Spiritual birth, **30**
Spiritual strength, 190
Spiritual tenor, **11**
Sproul, R. C., on Jesus, 258
Stedman, Ray, on enjoyment, 165
Stephen, 228
    faith of, 69
Stillness, 93
Strength:
    from failures, 67
    from trials, 80
    source of, 94
    spiritual, 190
Struggles:
    value of, 80
Subjugate, **207**
Success, pitfall of, 136–137
Supernatural, **74**
Suffering:
    God during, 119
    of Job, 112–120
    purpose of, 117
Supplants, **40**
Supplication, **174**
Swindoll, Charles R.:
    on Absalom, 102
    on Abraham, 14, 19
    on Caleb, 188
    on David as Robin Hood, 95
    on faith, 27
    on freedom, God-given, 5
    on God vs. Egyptian gods, 80
    on God's help and guidance, 191
    on the home, 30
    on idols, 49
    on the Jerusalem Wall, 179
    on Jonah, 222
    on leadership, 35
    on lust, 59
    on Paul, 228
    on Samson, 126

T
Tamar, 101
Tarshish, 220
Temple (of Solomon), 99, 160–162
    illustration of, 161

Temptation, **5**, 59
Ten Commandments, 83, 89
Terah, 17
Teraphim, illustration of, 49
Theophany, **15**
Thomas, 260–261, 266
Threshing, **195**
Timnah, 122
Tradition, **234**
Transcendent, **112**
Transformation, 263
Tree of the Knowledge of Good and Evil,
    3, **5**
Trials, value of, 80
Trinity, **xviii**
Trumpet, Gideon's, 198
Trust in God, 118, 186, 208
    by Caleb, 186
Truth:
    speaking, 116
    struggles with, 34
Tutankamen, illustration of, 72
Twenty-fifth of Elul, **179**

U
Unbelievers, Christians and, 124
Unger, Merrill F., on using a seal
    (as stamp, signature), 62
Uriah, 99–100
Usery, **177**
Uz, 112

V
Venison, **35**
Vilified, **230**
Vision, **231**
Vulnerability, **134**

W
Water Gate, 181
Webb, Barry G., on Isaiah, 212
Well and water jug (Rebekah's),
    illustration of, 32
Whirlwind, 144
Wickedness:
    Noah, in time of, 110
Wiersbe, Warren:
    on conflict, 255
    on Paul, 229, 232
    on Jesus, 246
    on Thomas, 261
Wigglesworth, Smith:
    on faith, 20
    on Jacob, 47
Wilcock, Michael:
    on Gideon, 195, 198
    on Nazirites, 122
    on Samson, 127
Wilkinson, Bruce H. and Larry Libby:
    on Elisha, 140, 146
    on Jacob, 44, 48
    on Jonathan, 204

Books by Starburst Publishers®
(Partial listing—full list available on request)

God's Word for the Biblically-Inept™ Series:

☞ **The Bible** by Larry Richards

☞ **Daniel** by Daymond R. Duck

☞ **Genesis** by Joyce L. Gibson

☞ **Health & Nutrition** by Kathleen O'Bannon Baldinger

☞ **Men of the Bible** by D. Larry Miller

☞ **Revelation** by Daymond R. Duck

☞ **Women of the Bible** by Kathy Collard Miller

Announcing Our New Series:
What's in the Bible for . . .™?

What's in the Bible for . . .™ Women
Georgia Curtis Ling

What does the Bible have to say to women? Women of all ages will find biblical insight on topics that are meaningful to them in four sections: Wisdom for the Journey; Family Ties; Bread, Breadwinners, and Bread Makers; and Fellowship and Community Involvement. This book uses illustrations, bullet points, chapter summaries, and icons to make understanding God's Word easier than ever!
(trade paper) ISBN 1892016109 $16.95

What's in the Bible for . . .™ Mothers
Judy Bodmer

Is home schooling a good idea? Is it okay to work? At what age should I start treating my children like responsible adults? What is the most important thing I can teach my children? If you are asking these questions and need help answering them, *What's in the Bible for . . . Mothers* is especially for you! Simple and user-friendly, this motherhood manual offers hope and instruction for today's mothers by jumping into the lives of mothers in the Bible (e.g., Naomi, Elizabeth, and Mary) and by exploring biblical principles that are essential to being a nurturing mother.
(trade paper) ISBN 1892016265 $16.95

What's in the Bible for . . .™ Teens
Mark and Jeanette Littleton

This is a book that teens will love! *What's in the Bible for . . . Teens* contains topical Bible themes that parallel the challenges and pressures of today's adolescents. Learn about Bible Prophecy, God's plan for relationships, and Peer Pressure in a conversational and fun tone. Helpful and eye-catching "WWJD?" icons, illustrations and sidebars included.
(trade paper) ISBN 1892016052 $16.95

The **God's Vitamin "C" for the Spirit™** series has already sold over 250,000 copies! Jam-packed with stories from well-known Christian writers that will lighten your spirit and enrich your life!

God's Vitamin "C" for the Spirit™
by Kathy Collard Miller & D. Larry Miller
(trade paper) ISBN 0914984837 $12.95

God's Vitamin "C" for the Spirit™ of Women
by Kathy Collard Miller
(trade paper) ISBN 0914984934 $12.95

God's Chewable Vitamin "C" for the Spirit™ of Moms
(trade paper) ISBN 0914984942 $6.95

God's Vitamin "C" for the Hurting Spirit™
by Kathy Collard Miller & D. Larry Miller
(trade paper) ISBN 0914984691 $12.95

God's Chewable Vitamin "C" for the Spirit
(trade paper) ISBN 0914984845 $6.95

God's Vitamin "C" for the Spirit of Men
by D. Larry Miller
(trade paper) ISBN 0914984810 $12.95

God's Chewable Vitamin "C" for the Spirit of Dads
(trade paper) ISBN 0914984829 $6.95

God's Vitamin "C" for the Christmas Spirit
by Kathy Collard Miller & D. Larry Miller
(cloth)   ISBN 0914984853 $14.95

The Weekly Feeder: A Revolutionary Shopping, Cooking, and Meal-Planning System
Cori Kirkpatrick

A revolutionary meal-planning system, here is a way to make preparing home-cooked dinners more convenient than ever. At the beginning of each week, simply choose one of the eight preplanned menus, tear out the corresponding grocery list, do your shopping, and whip up each fantastic meal in less than 45 minutes! The author's household management tips, equipment checklists, and nutrition information make this system a must for any busy family. Included with every recipe is a personal anecdote from the author emphasizing the importance of good food, a healthy family, and a well-balanced life.

(trade paper)   ISBN 1892016095 $16.95

God Stories: They're So Amazing, Only God Could Make Them Happen
Donna I. Douglas

Famous individuals share their personal, true-life experiences with God in this beautiful new book! Find out how God has touched the lives of top recording artists, professional athletes, and other newsmakers like Jessi Colter, Deana Carter, Ben Vereen, Stephanie Zimbalist, Cindy Morgan, Sheila E., Joe Jacoby, Cheryl Landon, Brett Butler, Clifton Taulbert, Babbie Mason, Michael Medved, Sandi Patty, Charlie Daniels, and more! Their stories are intimate, poignant, and sure to inspire and motivate you as you listen for God's message in your own life!

(cloth)   ISBN 1892016117 $18.95

Since Life Isn't a Game, These Are God's Rules: Finding Joy & Fulfillment in God's Ten Commandments
Kathy Collard Miller

Life is often referred to as a game, but God didn't create us because he was short on game pieces. To succeed in life, you'll need to know God's rules. In this book, Kathy Collard Miller explains the meaning of each of the Ten Commandments with fresh application for today. Each chapter includes scripture and quotes from some of our most beloved Christian authors including Billy Graham, Patsy Clairmont, Liz Curtis Higgs, and more! Sure to renew your understanding of God's rules.

(cloth)   ISBN 189201615X $16.95

God's Little Rule Book: Simple Rules to Bring Joy & Happiness to Your Life
Starburst Publishers

Let this little book of God's rules be your personal guide to a more joyful life. Brimming with easily applicable rules, this book is sure to inspire and motivate you! Each rule includes corresponding scripture and a practical tip that will help to incorporate God's rules into everyday life. Simple enough to fit into a busy schedule, yet powerful enough to be life changing!

(trade paper)   ISBN 1892016168 $6.95

Life's Little Rule Book: Simple Rules to Bring Joy & Happiness to Your Life
Starburst Publishers

Let this little book inspire you to live a happier life! The pages are filled with timeless rules such as, "Learn to cook, you'll always be in demand!" and "Help something grow." Each rule is combined with a reflective quote and a simple suggestion to help the reader incorporate the rule into everyday life.

(trade paper)   ISBN 1892016176 $6.95

God's Abundance
Edited by Kathy Collard Miller

Over 100,000 sold! This day-by-day inspirational is a collection of thoughts by leading Christian writers such as Patsy Clairmont, Jill Briscoe, Liz Curtis Higgs, and Naomi Rhode. *God's Abundance* is based on God's Word for a simpler, yet more abundant life. Learn to make all aspects of your life—personal, business, financial, relationships, even housework a "spiritual abundance of simplicity."

(cloth)   ISBN 0914984977 $19.95

Promises of God's Abundance
Edited by Kathy Collard Miller

Subtitled: *For a More Meaningful Life.* The Bible is filled with God's promises for an abundant life. *Promises of God's Abundance* is written in the same way as the best-selling *God's Abundance.* It will help you discover these promises and show you how simple obedience is the key to an abundant life. Scripture, questions for growth, and a simple thought for the day will guide you to a more meaningful life.

(trade paper)   ISBN 0914984-098 $9.95

Stories of God's Abundance for a More Joyful Life
Compiled by Kathy Collard Miller

Like its successful predecessor, *God's Abundance* (100,000 sold), this book is filled with beautiful, inspirational, real life stories. Those telling their stories of God share scriptures and insights that readers can apply to their daily lives. Renew your faith in life's small miracles and challenge yourself to allow God to lead the way as you find the source of abundant living for all your relationships.

(trade paper)   ISBN 1892016060 $12.95

More God's Abundance: Joyful Devotions for Every Season
Compiled by Kathy Collard Miller

Editor Kathy Collard Miller responds to the tremendous success of *God's Abundance* with a fresh collection of stories based on God's Word for a simpler life. Includes stories from our most beloved Christian writers such as: Liz Curtis Higgs and Patsy Clairmont that are combined ideas, tips, quotes, and scripture.

(cloth)   ISBN 1892016133 $19.95

God's Abundance for Women: Devotions for a More Meaningful Life
Compiled by Kathy Collard Miller

Following the success of *God's Abundance,* this book will touch women of all ages as they seek a more meaningful life. Essays from our most beloved Christian authors exemplify how to gain the abundant life that Jesus promised through trusting Him to fulfill our every need. Each story is enhanced with Scripture, quotes, and practical tips providing brief, yet deeply spiritual reading.

(cloth)   ISBN 1892016141 $19.95

Purchasing Information
www.starburstpublishers.com

Books are available from your favorite bookstore, either from current stock or special order. To assist bookstores in locating your selection, be sure to give title, author, and ISBN. If unable to purchase from a bookstore, you may order direct from STARBURST PUBLISHERS. When ordering please enclose full payment plus shipping and handling as follows:

Post Office (4th class)
$3.00 with a purchase of up to $20.00
$4.00 ($20.01–$50.00)
8% of purchase price for purchases of $50.01 and up

United Parcel Service (UPS)
$4.50 (up to $20.00)
$6.00 ($20.01–$50.00)
12% ($50.01 and up)

Canada
$5.00 (up to $35.00)
%15 ($35.01 and up)

Overseas
$5.00 (up to $25.00)
20% ($25.01 and up)

Payment in U.S. funds only. Please allow two to three weeks minimum (longer overseas) for delivery. Make checks payable to and mail to:

Starburst Publishers®   •   P.O. Box 4123   •   Lancaster, PA 17604

Credit card orders may be placed by calling 1-800-441-1456, Mon–Fri, 8:30 A.M. to 5:30 P.M. Eastern Standard Time. Prices are subject to change without notice. Catalogs are available for a 9 x 12 self-addressed envelope with four first-class stamps.

NOTES

NOTES

NOTES

NOTES

NOTES

NOTES

NOTES